O. P. McMAINS
and the
MAXWELL
LAND GRANT
CONFLICT

Oscar P. McMains, Agent for the Settlers.

O. P. McMAINS
and the
MAXWELL
LAND GRANT
CONFLICT

Morris F. Taylor

THE UNIVERSITY OF ARIZONA PRESS
Tucson, Arizona

Aʙᴏᴜᴛ ᴛʜᴇ Aᴜᴛʜᴏʀ . . .

MORRIS F. TAYLOR, professor of history at Trinidad State Junior College (Trinidad, Colorado) until his death in 1979, was well known for his long interest in the history of Colorado and New Mexico. The author of numerous scholarly articles, Taylor won two certificates of commendation for his historical writings from the American Association for State and Local History as well as the Hafen Award for the best article appearing in *The Colorado Magazine* in 1974. He held office in such professional organizations as the Colorado History Group, the State Historical Society of Colorado and the Western History Association. In addition to the present work, Morris Taylor had three other volumes to his credit: *Pioneers of the Pickwire* (1964), *Trinidad, Colorado Territory* (1966), and *First Mail West: Stage Lines on the Santa Fe Trail* (1971). He held a master's degree from Cornell University and was awarded an honorary doctorate of humane letters from the University of Colorado in 1969.

THE UNIVERSITY OF ARIZONA PRESS

Copyright © 1979
The Arizona Board of Regents
All Rights Reserved
Manufactured in the U.S.A.

Library of Congress Cataloging in Publication Data

Taylor, Morris F.
    O. P. McMains and the Maxwell land grant conflict.

    Bibliography: p.
    Includes index.
    1. McMains, O. P.   2. Maxwell Land Grant —
Biography.   3. Land settlement — New Mexico — History.
4. Land settlement — Colorado — History.   5. New
Mexico — History.   6. Colorado — History — To 1876.
I. Title.
F802.M38M327   333.1'6 [B]   78-14227
ISBN 0-8165-0652-3
ISBN 0-8165-0575-6 pbk.

In memory of
my parents
MARY MORRIS and FENTON J. TAYLOR
and
my parents-in-law
BESSIE SHERMAN and JOSEPH C. BELL

Contents

Illustrations

PHOTOGRAPHS

MAPS

Foreword

The Territory of New Mexico was a region of population explosion, rapid expansion and complex contradictions in the years following the Civil War. Freed from attack by the confinement of hostile Indian tribes to reservations, the livestock industry spread into the outlying valleys and plains. The discovery of rich mineral deposits brought miners and mine developers. Immigrants from other parts of the country and recent arrivals from foreign countries, attracted by the opening of large areas of the public domain, flocked in to take up homestead and preemption claims. A virtual commercial revolution took place as merchants and merchant capitalists were drawn by economic opportunities of all kinds. By 1880 the need for better and faster transportation brought the railroads. But not all of the newcomers came solely for economic reasons. Attorneys, surveyors, doctors and others of education and training were also quick to sense the advantages for professional and political careers in a territory whose governmental policies were largely determined by authorities in Washington. Federally appointed governors, judges and other officials sometimes combined business interests with regular duties.

Meanwhile, the native New Mexicans, only recently citizens of Mexico, although often bewildered and sometimes alarmed, refused to be completely overwhelmed, and by and large steadfastly attempted to cling to their familiar patterns of social behavior and ways of making a living and stubbornly strove to keep control of local politics.

In the resulting interaction of all these forces, interests and rivalries, political and economic turmoil was inevitable as opposing individuals and factions fought for supremacy. This was especially true in the rich Maxwell Land Grant area comprising much of Colfax County which was in a virtual state of war during the 1870s.

Permeating the political-economic struggle and manipulation for control, the rapid exploitation of rich economic resources and the social changes and tensions arising out of the impact of other cultures, legal systems and values on the older relatively uncomplicated Hispanic-oriented society, lay the age-old question of land tenure and title. One of the tragic facts of history in the expansion of the American frontier, both Spanish and Anglo, has always been the disruption of the way of life and dispossessing, in greater or less degree, of native peoples from their lands. In the Anglo-American West of the nineteenth century the process was pragmatic — military defeat and relocation of Indian tribes. But in the Southwest, especially in New Mexico reached by Spanish colonial expansion in the last years of the sixteenth century, occupation had taken a different course with respect to the original inhabitants. By that time the Crown had already promulgated comprehensive laws to protect the land rights of those Indian groups who lived in settled communities and accepted conversion. Both conditions were met by the New Mexico pueblo groups. Laws to the contrary notwithstanding, early colonists encroached upon the fields of the agricultural pueblos in the narrow valleys of the upper Rio Grande and its tributaries, since these were the most fertile areas. The hard lesson learned from the Great Pueblo Revolt of 1680, which drove the Spaniards into exile in the El Paso region for thirteen years, resulted, however, in a generally conscientious attempt by governors throughout the rest of the Spanish period, and during the brief years of Mexican national sovereignty, to enforce laws concerning pueblo prior land right. Campaigns were frequent against the nomadic Apaches and Navajos, and later the Comanches and Utes, who swept into New Mexico from the east and north and raided both pueblo and Hispanic villages. But military action against these groups was primarily in response to depredations, and little attempt was made to settle the area which these tribes considered as their homelands.

Land tenure policy for the Spanish settlers of New Mexico had, for two and a half centuries, also followed a far different pattern than that developed for the Anglo-American frontier. Governors were authorized to make grants to both individuals and to groups of landless householders, usually composed of neighboring families often interrelated by blood or marriage. As the population increased and tillable land in the settled areas became scarce, more community grants were made, especially since the small outlying settlements were effective barriers against hostile Indians. Individual grantees were given title only to their small agricultural tracts. In accordance with the long established Spanish policy of *usufructo*, the non-agricultural acreage, often mountainous in character, was stipulated for the common uses of grazing, wood gathering and hunting, and no property rights in the commons were vested in either the grantees or in the community itself.

To complicate matters several "colonization" grants of dubious legality had been hastily made by Governor Manuel Armijo to partnerships of Anglo-Hispano speculators in the years immediately preceding occupation, allegedly to promote settlement of outlying regions. Among them were the

Charles Beaubien-Guadalupe Miranda grant, which later came into the hands of Beaubien's son-in-law, Lucien Maxwell; the Sangre de Cristo, purportedly given to Beaubien's thirteen-year-old son and Stephen Louis Lee; and the Gervacio Nolán. The recipients were, however, not to treat the grants as their private property but were to allot agricultural tracts to those who agreed to settle and to designate areas for common uses.

Private ownership, not common use of large areas by a village community, was the tenure pattern brought into New Mexico with U.S. sovereignty in 1846. A far different administration of the public domain for the expanding Anglo-American frontier had developed as a result of the adoption of the public survey system in 1805 by which newly occupied areas were precisely surveyed in the standard gridiron township-range-section fashion. The 1848 Treaty of Guadalupe Hidalgo had stipulated that property rights held under Mexican law were recognized by the United States as valid, and Mexican property right, basically Spanish in nature, derived from individual and community grant. Unfortunately, Congress did not create the machinery for determining what constituted Mexican property right until 1854 when the Office of Surveyor General for New Mexico was created and the public survey system introduced for the administration of the public domain. Under the provisions of the act, claimants of the original grantees, or their legitimate successors, could submit their granting documents to the surveyor general who, after investigation, would recommend the grant for confirmation or disallow it. If the commissioner of the General Land Office approved the decision, the outer boundaries were then surveyed, and upon acceptance by the commissioner the grant was submitted to Congress. If confirmed, patent was delivered to the claimants.

The problems and tensions arising out of the situation were overwhelming. Proceedings before the surveyor general often would never have passed a legal test for court procedure.

Little attempt was made to verify the authenticity of documents or to properly cross examine witnesses. Claims were
often magnified all out of proportion. Many claimants, while
the proceedings were in progress, had conveyed their interests, including a "share" in the commons to the newly arrived
speculators. The so-called "colony" grants, such as the Sangre
de Cristo in 1856 and the Maxwell in 1857, were quickly
approved as private claims and rushed through congressional
confirmation. Surveys, all too often based largely on self-serv-
ing statements by claimants as to boundaries, were made even
though in the meantime much of the area had been treated as
public domain and open to settlement. Nor did the Utes and
Apaches in the Mt. Baldy-Moreno valley area of the Maxwell
willingly accept intrusion into their traditional hunting lands.

The conflict and litigation over the Maxwell Land Grant
which kept much of northern New Mexico in turmoil for some
twenty years reached its climax with the fateful April 18, 1887,
U.S. Supreme Court decree. As William A. Keleher has sum-
marized it: "The Indians, early Mexican and Spanish-Ameri-
can settlers, early American pioneers, the latter seeking homesteads and settling on what they believed to be free land, each
in turn, discovered in the end, that they had no rights superior
to 'grant' rights."

Aspects of the Maxwell Land Grant have not been neglected by New Mexico chroniclers. Attorney-historian Keleher's *Maxwell Land Grant, a New Mexico Item*, published
over thirty-five years ago, gave a provocative overview of its
history. Jim Berry Pearson meticulously traced the involved
story of successive British and Dutch control. The roles of
some leading early protagonists within the grant company
factions, such as William R. Morley and Thomas B. Catron,
have been discussed, from somewhat different points of view,
by Norman Cleaveland, Victor Westphall and others. Morris
Taylor's account, however, details the long, drawn-out litigation within the context of the whole chaotic land develop-
ment-exploitation situation, as oriented around the life of the

articulate and tireless agent for the "anti-granters," the Rev. Oscar P. McMains.

Victims of social injustice, and the dispossessed, have often had articulate champions, even on the American frontier. The lives of those whose crusades have succeeded have usually become a part of the literature of the period. Those who failed, or apparently failed, have too often been largely forgotten, or ignored, although some have lived on as local folk heroes. Until now, this has been the case with McMains. Most writers concerning events in northern New Mexico and southern Colorado during the late 1880s have referred to him only briefly — sometimes sympathetically, often disparagingly. This study is the life story of the Protestant preacher who first set out only to bring the murderers of a fellow clergyman to justice. As a result of the tragic circumstances resulting from that effort he emerged as the appointed, and sometimes self-appointed, agent for the Maxwell Grant settlers who for twenty years, before presidents, congresses, courts and territorial legislatures, pleaded the cause of those who struggled to keep the land they had occupied in good faith against the impossible odds of political power and corporate wealth.

MYRA ELLEN JENKINS
State Records Center and Archives
Santa Fe, New Mexico

O. P. McMains –
His Place in History

There are many facets of land grant history in the American Southwest — some have been thoroughly examined;
others have been superficially treated; many await the historian's consideration. The present work had its first impulse
years ago in a quest for a dissertation topic, an unfulfilled
destiny. During extended research I became especially interested in the concerns of everyday people with the big Maxwell
Land Grant and its claimants, a fresh approach influenced
by living and teaching in an area where the Maxwell and other
grants are an important part of local history. Interviews with
men and women whose experiences encompassed events that
attracted me have provided an important foundation for this
study.

A growing awareness of one man as the central figure in
the long, arduous, and unsuccessful struggle against the Maxwell Grant gave the research a strong biographical overtone.
I soon suspected that most brief evaluations of O. P. McMains
in secondary sources — as a demagogue, a radical, a crank —
were unfair, uncritical stereotypes based on attacks by his
opponents, particularly hostile newspaper editors.*

---

*See F. Stanley, "O. P. McMains, Champion of a Lost Cause," *New
Mexico Historical Review* 24 (January 1949): 1–11.

Unfortunately, there is no aggregation of material that can be called the McMains papers. The closest to it is a now destroyed collection of his pamphlets and broadsides, of which I made copies. I found a few of his letters in both private and public sources, supplemented by one or two of his wife's. Recollections of contemporaries, a large amount of newspaper copy, and extensive public records provide much of the information about him. An invaluable source are the records of the Maxwell Land Grant Company, which were in the company office at Raton, New Mexico, when I obtained permission to consult them.

McMains' remarkable persistence for years against the Maxwell Grant, supported by a sequence of competent public officials from county sheriffs to cabinet officers, as well as by firm friends from many walks of life, resulted in an accumulation of evidence that even today raises serious questions about the federal courts' acceptance of the alleged size of the grant — 1,714,764.94 acres. His basic contention — upheld by three secretaries of the interior and a commissioner of the General Land Office — that the grant under Mexican law did not exceed ca. 96,000 acres was never directly refuted but rather largely ignored by the judges, by presidents and by other executive officials. Similarly obscured was his argument that the Maxwell patent conveyed no title because the United States had no title to pass. McMains and others held that title came from the Mexican government to the grantees, and that the American government was obligated under the Treaty of Guadalupe Hidalgo (1848) to determine only the validity of the grant under Mexican law. The federal courts asserted that Congress, in its sovereign power, had actually created its own grant (a grant *de novo*, or new grant), an opinion that made the Maxwell patent virtually unassailable if not indubitably correct.

McMains, who signed himself as Agent for the Settlers, never abandoned his key points against the Maxwell Grant, but when they were officially discounted his exasperation and frustration pushed him to other positions of attack that were less sound and often to emotional tirades against people who defended the Maxwell patent. His tactics over the years varied to suit circumstances, but restriction of the grant to about 96,000 acres was always his goal.

The dedication of this Methodist clergyman to a secular cause was maintained at considerable personal cost: he was eased out of his ministry; several friendships were either broken or sorely strained; and constant demands on his time and energy gravely weakened his never robust health. His singleness of purpose never overcame the promoters and developers of that day, but his notably individualistic leadership may have been a serious drawback.

The Maxwell Grant was the chief object of McMains' attacks for several reasons, the least important being the fact that he lived there. It was the largest of the confirmed Mexican grants (more than 1,700,000 acres), and to have secured its reduction to about 96,000 acres (allowed to an individual under Mexican law as a personal estate) would have had an influence far beyond its local impact.

In many ways the Maxwell was the most thoroughly managed and exploited of the several Mexican land grants of the region, especially after Dutch investors took direct control in 1885. Cattle raising, the primary activity on some of the grants, was secondary to the company's plans to sell mining claims, timber tracts, irrigated agricultural land, and grazing acreages. The more people bought parcels of the grant, the more people had a stake in defending the Maxwell patent against McMains and his followers.

Of the Mexican grants on either side of the Colorado-New Mexico boundary, the Maxwell was the one directly in the path of the wave of immigration that was settling the central and southern plains through the medium of the railroads built across them. Raton, New Mexico, was a railroad town developed by the Atchison, Topeka and Santa Fe on land acquired from the grant company, and the two corporations worked together to attract settlers onto the grant. And an abundance of coal for railroads and industry was another strong fillip for those exploiting the property. Some grants, especially those west of the Sangre de Cristo Mountains, have not been significantly touched by comparable developments to this day.

During his years of anti-grant leadership, McMains was pitted against an array of lawyers and businessmen whose competences, as well as their motives and methods, were alien to his experience. Frustration in trying to cope with such opponents caused McMains occasionally to resort to demagogic attacks that were almost pathetic in their failure. Broadly speaking, however, he was defeated by an exuberant, ruthless, and increasingly corporate capitalism that was expanding over the plains and foothills of the last frontier. The entrepreneur types who gained control of land grants were akin to those who extended their livestock operations over millions of acres of the public domain and to those who dominated large areas by means of the near-monopoly of railroad companies. McMains understood that, but he was never able to assemble a countervailing influence great enough to break the legalistic grip that the grant claimants maintained through some very questionable court decisions.

Chronology

꩜

1840   Oscar P. McMains born, date uncertain.

1858   Joined Methodist Episcopal Church.

1859   Appointed minister on trial, Beverly, Illinois.

1860   Same appointment at Payson, Illinois.

1861   Transferred to Jacksonville (Illinois) Circuit.

1862   At Virginia and Griggs Chapel, Illinois, as ordained deacon.

1863   At Mattoon, Illinois.

1864   To Denver, Colorado Territory, in October, and appointed to Blackhawk, Colorado.

1865   Formally transferred from Illinois Conference and assigned to Burlington Circuit.

1866   Organized First Methodist Episcopal Church, Loveland, Colorado. First poem published in *Daily Rocky Mountain News* (Denver).

1867   Appointed to Central City and Nevadaville, Colorado Territory. Visited brother in San Francisco, California.

1868   Appointed to Platte River Valley. Transferred to Colorado City and Pueblo.

1869   Assigned to Pueblo, Colorado Territory. Began construction Methodist Episcopal Church.

1870 In charge of Colorado Conference arrangements at Pueblo.

1871 Secretary of Conference in Denver. Rode circuit south of the Arkansas River.

1872 Terminated connection with Methodism; became Congregational minister. First used nom de plume of A. Bach, in writing for *Colorado Chieftain* (Pueblo).

1873 Moved to Rocky Ford, Colorado Territory.

1874 Moved to West Las Animas, then to Cucharas and Saguache, Colorado Territory.

1875 To Cimarron, New Mexico Territory. Assistant to Methodist Rev. F. J. Tolby and printer for Cimarron *News and Press.* Tolby murdered in September.

1876 Indicted for murder of Cruz Vega. Suspended from work with New Mexico Missions.

1877 Found guilty in "fifth degree." New trial set.

1878 Case dismissed. Appointed to Cimarron-Elizabethtown Circuit.

1879 Married Mary B. Messner. Became active in Colfax County Anti-Grant Association.

1881 Moved near Raton, New Mexico Territory. Started *Raton Comet.* First and second trips to Washington.

1882 Third trip to Washington. Eviction confrontation at ranch.

1883 Elected by Anti-Grant Party to territorial legislature. Fourth trip to Washington.

1884 Member New Mexico Legislative Assembly. Seized Crow Creek Ranch. Fifth trip to Washington.

1885 Sixth and seventh trips to Washington. Testimonial dinner. First use of title, Agent for the Settlers.

1886 Eighth trip to Washington. Ninth trip to Washington. Interview with President Cleveland.

1887 Tenth and eleventh trips to Washington.

1888 Arrest in Washington. Stonewall War (August 25). Indicted for manslaughter.

1889   Acquitted of manslaughter. Arrested and indicted on charge of conspiracy.

1890   Twelfth trip to Washington. Convicted of conspiracy.

1891   Imprisoned for six months. Thirteenth trip to Washington.

1894   Defeated as Populist to Colorado General Assembly.

1896   Fourteenth trip to Washington.

1899   Died on April 15.

Chapter 1

Accepting the Call

DENVER CITY. COLORADO TERRITORY. October 1864. A slight, neatly dressed young man with dark eyes, curly hair and beard was taking in the sights. The little town was in transition. Log and frame structures were giving way to brick and stone. The Methodist Episcopal Church and its Colorado Seminary* had opened its doors to students that fall.[1] Miners in flannel and buckskin and men armed with revolvers walked the streets, passing men and women who could have stepped from the pages of *Godey's Lady's Book*. Although the Civil War was not a prime concern in the territory,† Colorado supported the North, and Union blue seemed almost as common to the young man as it had in the Illinois towns he had left.

---

* Later to become the University of Denver.

† That the Civil War in 1864 was not a prime concern was due to the smashing of Confederate hopes by the Colorado Volunteers in New Mexico in 1862, an achievement of great pride. Prominent in the campaign had been Major, now Colonel, John M. Chivington. See William Clarke Whitford, *Colorado Volunteers in the Civil War: The New Mexico Campaign in* 1862 (Denver: The State Historical and Natural History Society, 1906), pp. 50–51; Stan Hoig, *The Sand Creek Massacre*, (Norman: University of Oklahoma Press, 1961), pp. 19–20.

A commercial center supplying gold camps in the Rockies to the west, Denver was a haven for those who reached it from the East. Plains Indians, taking advantage of the white man's pre-occupation with his own war and protesting infringements of treaty rights, raided isolated ranches and stage stations and attacked wagon trains. To provide protection against them, a regiment of "Hundred Days Men" was recruited with Colonel John M. Chivington, a former presiding elder of Colorado Methodism, in command.[2]

But the young man had arrived safely, and in a few days would travel to the renowned gold camp of Central City, there to take his place among new colleagues at the Second Annual Colorado Conference. He had entered the ministry at nineteen and had already held five appointments in Illinois. Oscar P. McMains was now twenty-four years old and eager to begin work in the West.

The second child of a young merchant and his wife, Oscar was born in the small town of Milford, Ohio. Milford, in the 1840s and 50s, hummed with life along the banks of the Little Miami River: grain waved in the fields, livestock grazed leisurely on the hills, and orchards reputedly planted by Johnny Appleseed produced copiously. Millers turned the grain into flour, and distillery owners got good prices for whiskey made from local corn. Although now well-to-do farmers who had replaced their log cabins with respectable homes, older settlers could very well remember the days when Milford was scarcely more than a mill site, for settlement on the Little Miami and its East Fork had begun only in the last decade of the eighteenth century.[3] Among the many who had come into that bounteous land was a young Pennsylvanian named William McMains, who secured his future by his marriage, in February 1810, to Mary Fairchild, the daughter of a prosperous farmer on the East Fork. Since her father had died the previous autumn, his properties needed a sure hand, and William McMains kept the holdings intact.[4]

To William and Mary a son, christened Robert, was born the following year. The babe arrived when chances of a second war with Great Britain threatened the Old Northwest, so when war finally came in June 1812 Captain William McMains recruited a company of volunteers.[5] After his safe return in 1815, he became an ardent Methodist in a land where Methodism was mighty and under the strong leadership of the Reverend Philip Gatch.[6]

Upon reaching his majority in the 1830s, their son, Robert F. McMains, married and made his home in Milford. His bride, Nancy, was of the Perry family and related to Oliver Hazard Perry, hero of the Battle of Lake Erie. Robert became a well-respected general merchant in the town and took an active role in civic affairs. His election to the board of trustees in 1838, followed by his election to the office of mayor in 1850, reflected the trust and confidence placed in him by the citizens of Milford.[7]

Five children were born to young Robert and his wife: Mary Louise, 1837; Oscar, 1840;* Robert A., 1842; William, 1850; and Nancy, 1852.[8] Shortly after the latter's birth their mother died suddenly. Although her sister, Aunt Debbie Mount, did what she could for the stricken group, the household of Robert McMains never recovered. After some months of trying to reconstruct the shattered pattern, Robert gave up and arranged for the adoption of Nancy. Hoping for a new start, he then left for California via Panama with his second son, Bob.[9]

Mary Louise, Oscar, and Billy adjusted to the new conditions in Milford. Mary Louise was courted by William Pinkney Fishback, a young attorney from the nearby village of Batavia. On St. Valentine's Day 1855 they were married,

---

* The day and month of Oscar's birth are not known. The 1850 census simply puts his age at ten, and only one obituary gives his natal year, 1840. And the census lists him as Oskar, a common misspelling. His personal correspondence is signed Oscar, while his business papers and publications carry O. P. McMains. One may speculate that his middle initial stood for Perry, a family name. Two minor sources give his middle name as Patrick, which probably was guesswork.

Robert and Nancy McMains' children, ca. 1854. Left to right: William, Mary, Robert, Oscar.

and not long thereafter they took young Billy into their home.[10]

Oscar, now fifteen, followed an independent course. He learned the printer's trade, and his later facile use of language showed that he learned a great deal more than the Three Rs — probably through the counsel of a friend and benefactor, perhaps a Methodist minister. There is no evidence of his having gone to college, but the strength of religion greatly influenced the boy, whose qualities of mind were ready and eager to absorb it. At eighteen he joined the Methodist Episcopal Church; at nineteen he was preaching.[11]

The twenty-sixth Illinois Annual Conference of the Methodist Episcopal Church convened at Danville on September 21, 1859. The conference greatly needed help, so it was thrilling for Oscar to be appointed to the little town of Beverly, Illinois, in the Griggsville District, many miles from his home. In 1860 the conference kept him on trial (not unusual in those days) and appointed him to Payson in the same district. Still on trial in 1861, Oscar was transferred to the Jacksonville Circuit, and the following year he was at Virginia, Illinois, and Griggsville as an ordained deacon. Mattoon in east central Illinois was his charge in 1863–64.[12]

Although little is known of his activities in those years, Oscar P. McMains proved his worth: the conference of 1864 at Danville made him an elder and reappointed him to Mattoon. But he had other ideas. Perhaps he was inspired by traditions of the Reverend Philip Gatch in early-day Milford; men on the frontier needed the Word of God; the West lured him; the new Colorado Conference desperately needed young and willing assistants. Whatever voice called him, the Reverend Oscar P. McMains responded, and in a few days headed in that direction.[13]

Central City was in the heart of the gold diggings of Gilpin County, Colorado Territory. But after only five years the gold was giving out. New discoveries in far-off Montana and Idaho pulled the restless and dissatisfied, although in 1864 recovery by silver had set in.[14]

The opening session of the 1864 conference was on October 20.[15] The young elder from Illinois might be called to bring the Gospel to people among the placers and stamp mills, or he could find himself riding circuit on the plains, where homesteaders settled along fertile bottom lands. His suspense ended on the third day, when "Father" John L. Dyer, famous as the "Snow Shoe Itinerant," announced the appointments. The fortunes of Methodism in nearby Black-hawk were entrusted to the conference's newest member.[16]

The buildings of Blackhawk clustered along the curve of a gulch near the famous Gregory Lode — and so close by were Central City and Nevadaville that the three towns seemed almost as one. Methodist Hall was a large room in a brick building, and there the local flock gathered to hear their new pastor at morning service on Sunday, October 30. In fact, he was an assistant to the Reverend B. T. Vincent, of Central City, who came to Blackhawk for evening service.[17]

Cultural life in mining camps was modest enough in the days of McMains' pastorate, but it seemed fairly extensive compared to the crudities which followed the rush of 1859. Lawyers, school teachers, merchants, ministers, and especially their womenfolk now gave a different cast to the towns. Furtherance of the new influences was expected from a man of the cloth, and the Reverend Oscar P. McMains needed no encouragement. Soon he was in demand as a speaker by such groups as the St. Paul's Library Association, and within a few weeks he satisfied his superiors that he could handle the Blackhawk church by himself.[18]

The telegraph brought the shocking message of the shooting of President Lincoln in Ford's Theater, Washington. He died the next morning, Saturday, April 15, 1865. On Sunday churches across the land filled with mourning throngs. Methodist Hall in Blackhawk was packed, and when the Rev. Mr. McMains denounced traitors, disregarding those from below

McMains' Ministries in Colorado
1864–1874

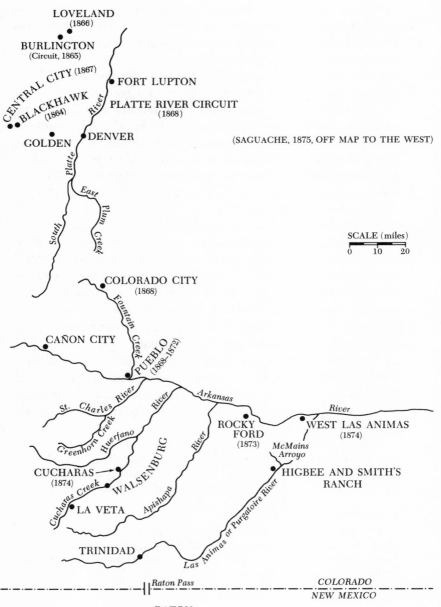

LOVELAND
(1866)

BURLINGTON
(Circuit, 1865)

CENTRAL CITY (1867)

BLACKHAWK
(1864)

FORT LUPTON

PLATTE RIVER CIRCUIT
(1868)

GOLDEN   DENVER

(SAGUACHE, 1875, OFF MAP TO THE WEST)

Platte River

South Platte

East Plum Creek

SCALE (miles)
0   10   20

COLORADO CITY
(1868)

CAÑON CITY

Fountain Creek

PUEBLO (1868–1872)

St. Charles River

Greenhorn Creek

Huerfano River

Arkansas River

ROCKY
FORD
(1873)

McMains
Arroyo

WEST LAS ANIMAS
(1874)

River

CUCHARAS
(1874)

WALSENBURG

Cucharas Creek

Apishapa River

HIGBEE AND SMITH'S
RANCH

LA VETA

Las Animas or Purgatoire River

TRINIDAD

Raton Pass

COLORADO
NEW MEXICO

RATON

the Mason and Dixon Line who might not view Lincoln's death as a national disaster, several of his congregation headed for the door. Before they could leave McMains asserted that their departure disturbed him not in the least and continued with his sermon.[19]

At the Third Annual Conference in Denver (1865), Bishop Calvin Kingsley announced the formal transfer of O. P. McMains from the Illinois Conference and his assignment to the Burlington Circuit in Colorado. The contrast could hardly have been greater between the mountain mining camp and the scattered villages and ranches of the valleys and plains north of Denver. The little settlement of Burlington on the south bank of St. Vrain Creek (near the present Longmont) was his base.[20]

The next year McMains was reappointed to the Burlington Circuit. His most enduring achievement was the First Methodist Church in Loveland, organized in February 1866.[21] Occasionally he made use of revival meetings (although he was not addicted to that mode of religious expression), conducting one in a dirt-roofed, log schoolhouse on the north bank of Left Hand Creek,[22] which aroused memories of camp meetings in the wooded groves of his native Ohio.

Although not a hell-fire and brimstone preacher, McMains did set limits, of course, for his congregation. But his leniency was remarkable for his day and work. His descriptive article published in Denver's *Daily Rocky Mountain News* is revealing:

> On last Thanksgiving night [1866], the St. Vrain Creekers (and I might say Sand Creekers, for nearly every man of them was in that fight*) assembled at the hotel of

---

*A reference to the hundred-day recruits of Colorado Volunteer Cavalry, commanded by Colonel John M. Chivington, former Methodist presiding elder, who annihilated Cheyenne and Arapaho Indians in the Sand Creek Massacre, November 29, 1864 (Hoig, pp. 145–62).

Mrs. Allen, in Burlington, to enjoy the festivity of the occasion. A committee of ladies, who for business tact and good taste cannot be beaten west of the Alleghanies [*sic*], had made all the necessary arrangements for a big supper and a fine time. Social chat, instrumental and vocal music to delight the soul, and a delicious supper to tickle the palate — this was all, but this was *some*. As for the conversation, if it was not a "feast of reason," it was truly a "flow of soul." I hope they will not have to give an account for all they said; they were "only in fun;" but they said "heaps of things." That the music was excellent may be inferred from the fact that every "bach" and maiden were enchained, and when their ears were full of the melody, their mouths flew wide open to catch the balance. As for the supper, there was not only plenty, "such as it was," but a great plenty of the best there is. The table was five times filled, and yet a large proportion of cakes, pies, &c., remained untouched. Mr. Editor, it was then I perceived that it was not "good for a man to be alone," he loses by it; those good things would have fallen to my wife if a wife had ever fallen to me. However, I pocketed a hundred dollars as my share of the festival, and retired, hoping they felt no worse in parting with their money than I did in receiving it. Heaven bless the Burlingtonians; they respect the gospel of Christ, are determined to build a church, and I hope a great many more will join it.[23]

Clearly McMains could not abide the austere demeanor which some felt more becoming to his calling. His temperament put him closer to people who were practical and optimistic, many of them confining their worries about salvation and the powers of darkness to the Sabbath. Some came to services only because the Methodist system of circuit riders brought religion to them.

Although sometimes isolated and lonely due to the rigors of circuit riding, McMains took pains to keep informed of events in the outside world. The vanguard of urban, industrial America was on the horizon, and he thrilled to the prospect. Current excitement about the rapid extension of the Union

Pacific Railroad caught him up, and he expressed his response in "The Iron Horse Is Coming," a long poem published by the *Daily Rocky Mountain News* on December 20, 1866.* Many people felt that such quick progress required statehood for Colorado, and the young preacher on the Burlington Circuit agreed in their opposition to Governor Alexander Cummings, who was vehemently against it. Poetic license allowed McMains to say that the coming of the railroad would clear the way:

> All hail! for with thy coming we shall be
> From Territorial reign forever free!
> The death-knell of our present ruling "king,"
> Is sweetly sounded in thy merry ring! [24]

In June 1867 eleven ministers journeyed to Colorado City for the annual conference. The stage road south from Denver led through hostile Indian country. Arms and ammunition had been furnished them on order from A. Cameron Hunt, the new territorial governor. Nine of the party were on horseback, while McMains drove an open buggy in which rode Bishop E. R. Ames.[25] The little cavalcade arrived without trouble at the cluster of cabins called Colorado City, dating from 1859 and serving as the first territorial capital.[26] Conference appointments placed McMains at Central City and Nevadaville, adjoining his first charge at Blackhawk.

His reception at these towns was hardly cordial due to the members' disappointment over the transfer of B. T. Vincent, a popular preacher who had been McMains' superior in Blackhawk.[27] McMains tried to cope with the sullenness, but he was unable to improve relations with his flock. (His countermeasures are not a matter of record, but it is possible that he contributed to the difficulty.) By midsummer mutual

---

*On January 23, 1867 that paper published his "Apostrophe to the Train," a tribute to wagon trains in the building of the West.

dissatisfactions had piled up to such an extent that he decided to have no more of it. But what should he do? He was in no mood to accept another assignment if one had been available.

Out of the past came recollections of childhood and memories of his brother Bob. Nearly fifteen years before, Bob and their father had set out for California. The despondent parent had died not long after reaching there, but Bob had been adopted by a family named Fisher, whose name he took. He was then living in San Francisco with his wife of less than a year, and at the moment recovering from a serious leg injury. Nostalgia and his present miserable conditions convinced Oscar that here was a chance to see his younger brother. He obtained a leave of absence and temporary status as an elder without definite assignment,[28] and by stagecoach he headed for the Golden Gate in late summer 1867.

Bob Fisher and his wife had a large circle of young friends, and Oscar insisted that they not be told he was a minister. After a few relaxing weeks in San Francisco, his visit had served its purpose. The change had reduced his difficulty to proper scale, and he was ready to return to the Colorado Conference before winter set in and blocked the mountain passes.

Denver's slump of the mid-sixties had passed, and the territorial legislature was on the verge of designating the town as the capital. There was no vacancy in the conference, so the bishop gave McMains a location north of Denver near Fort Lupton, where for three years farmers and ranchers had called for a minister. So gratifying was their response that by early 1868 the Reverend O. P. McMains had built a circuit of which he could be proud, and an admirer informed the *Daily Rocky Mountain News* that:

> Brother McMains . . . after a vigorous effort aroused the people to the fact that they were 'born to die, and after death the judgment!' Bro. Mc has succeeded in drawing out very respectful houses at several appointments along the Platte. . . . I deem it only justice that Brother Mc has

Oscar P. McMains and his brother, Robert (McMains) Fisher — taken in San Francisco in 1867.

the hearty support in the cause in which he is enlisted, and trust that his work may end in a rich and bountiful harvest for the Lord's larder.[29]

Only six preachers responded to roll call at the June conference in Golden City, where retrenchment and increase of pastors' burdens were necessary. In the shuffle McMains was asked to double up on Colorado City and Pueblo, roughly a hundred miles south of Denver and about forty miles apart.[30] Before departing he was pleased to accept an invitation from old friends along the Burlington Circuit to deliver a Fourth of July oration. It was a gala time, and for him Independence Day allowed an indulgence of his flair for patriotic speeches. His listeners noisily applauded "a very appropriate and eloquent production"[31] — a fitting farewell to northern Colorado.

Chapter 2

Unorthodox Pastor

McMAINS HAD SEEN COLORADO CITY* during the previous
year's conference, but of Pueblo to the south he knew nothing.
The locale was a drier one, with yucca and cactus, juniper
and piñon, changing the landscape by the time one reached
Pueblo on the Arkansas River. "Pueblo" hinted of Taos and
Santa Fe, and the influence of another culture was certainly
felt in the presence of the Spanish language and the Roman
Catholic Church — both alien to McMains' experience. From
1819 to 1848 the Arkansas River had been the boundary
between the United States and the lands of the Spanish crown
and the Republic of Mexico, a fact which was the source not
only of the Spanish influence but also of the land grant problems which were to consume much of McMains' life.

Yet McMains quickly adjusted to conditions in the two
places and set to work diligently among the scattered farms
and ranches in the vicinity, especially those along Fountain
Creek (Fontaine Qui Bouille). The people of Pueblo read

---

*The forerunner of Colorado Springs; not to be confused with the
present Colorado City, south of Pueblo.

this comment in their new paper, the *Colorado Chieftain*[*]: "He is recommended as a young man of culture and talent, who will take his place among us as a preacher of the gospel, and not for the purpose of perverting his sacred calling to a political mission, as has too often been the case with others of the same profession."[1]

Indian troubles were also a fact of life in 1868, with the Denver-Santa Fe stage running only once a week in September because raiding parties had run off so many of the company's horses[2] and farmers and ranchers nervously watching for painted warriors. The Rev. O. P. McMains got through the year without notable incident, however, and went to Central City in June for the 1869 conference where Pueblo was assigned to him under the supervision of George Murray, pastor at Colorado City and presiding elder of the new Arkansas District.[3]

Upon returning to Pueblo, McMains immediately set to work on plans for building a church. The congregation responded enthusiastically: during the Christmas season a large benefit festival for the church was held in Conley's Hall, and by mid-January 1870 the cupola was underway and the interior nearly ready for plastering.[4]

Never content with the narrow role of a Methodist minister, McMains revived his secular hobby of writing, with the editor of the *Colorado Chieftain* agreeing to publish his work under the nom de plume of "A. Bach." Over the next couple of years a series of varied articles came from McMains' pen.

Discontent with bachelorhood kept McMains from fully enjoying the respected position he had attained in the community. But that reason for unhappiness seemed about to

---

[*] The *Colorado Chieftain* was also a newcomer to the town, having been in publication only a month. See Barron B. Beshoar, "No Windy Promises," *The 1961 Brand Book of the Denver Posse of the Westerners*, ed. Don L. Griswold (Boulder, Colo.: Johnson Publishing Company, 1962), pp. 84–88.

disappear when he fell in love with the attractive and popular Luna Jordan.* When she suddenly gave her attentions to another, McMains, feeling despondent and humiliated, felt that he had to get out of Pueblo. He tried to obtain a transfer — the farther away the better. But he would not learn whether or not he was successful until the next conference.

In the meantime, his church-building activities kept him busy, and, since the up-coming conference was to be in Pueblo and he would be in charge of arrangements, he hastened to get as much of the church finished as possible.

When the members arrived for the opening session on June 23, the roof was on, the floor was down, and the windows set in. Thirteen clergymen sat on chairs and improvised benches in the unplastered auditorium. With conference prospects brighter than at any time since its organization, twenty men worked under Bishop Ames's direction. Ministers came from distant gold camps and from faraway missions in New Mexico Territory.[5]

As conference secretary, McMains recorded proceedings and, of course, worried about his appointment for next year. But Bishop Ames first introduced newcomers: Thomas Harwood, from the West Wisconsin Conference, was assigned to the New Mexico missions, and Kansan E. J. Rice to Trinidad in the extreme south of Colorado.[6] At last the old members' assignments were announced, and McMains heard his name linked with Pueblo again. Springing to his feet, he cried out to the bishop that he would not stand such tyranny. In fact, he would not return.[7]

---

* In 1876 Luna Jordan married Mahlon D. Thatcher, who was prominent in the business and social life of Pueblo and southern Colorado. Mrs. Lucy Reed Wills told the writer that she believed her own resemblance to Mrs. Thatcher was the reason that McMains was so kind to her (Interview with Mrs. Wills, September 14, 1948; R. M. Stevenson, "History of Pueblo County," in *History of the Arkansas Valley, Colorado* [Chicago: O. L. Baskin and Company, 1881] p. 818).

Whatever the amazement of others, Ames turned to McMains with sang-froid and said, "'Don't be hasty, Brother McMains. Come and see me, and we will talk the matter over.'" Distraught and disappointed, McMains strode from the church, followed by Brothers Brooks and Swift. Outside, he grasped both friends by the arm: "'Boys, I tell you that old Bishop Ames is a tyrant.'"[8]

Nevertheless, McMains later took tea with the bishop, and toward the end of evening service came into the church. He appeared to be in repose. After the closing prayer he said to Brooks and Swift: "'Why, boys, did you know that Bishop Ames is an angel. Why, he just talked to me so kindly, and prayed with me and promised to help. I am going on with my work.'"[9]

Details of the bishop's means of persuasion are lacking; perhaps he convinced McMains that a degree of Christian asceticism would bring him peace of mind. In any event, the Methodist church was finished by mid-November, 1870,* and McMains returned to a regular schedule of preaching every Sabbath morning and prayer meeting every Wednesday evening.[10]

Suppressing his personal feelings in the demands of community and professional work did not really improve matters for McMains. Peace of mind was difficult to come by. Gossip may have been right that he was losing his struggle to forget the young lady, but other factors had bearing as well. By spring it was evident that a rift with the church was near. Criticism of McMains' acceptance of dancing had arisen, and in defending his liberalism he attacked other inhibitions

---

* The summer of 1870 was uneventful for McMains, except that he was featured speaker at a big Fourth of July celebration in Wildeboor's Grove.

placed on ministers. Unhappy and vexed, he had struck hard, thereby exposing beliefs he had previously kept hidden. Had he been willing to admit them earlier he might not have gone into the ministry; now, however, he could do little more than justify his feelings, which, of course, played into the hands of his critics. Reports of his utterances went to the bishop in Denver, and official remonstrance seemed likely soon. Meanwhile McMains spent more time out of town with friends in his favorite valley of the Greenhorn.[11]

The 1871 conference convened at Denver in mid-July with McMains again acting as secretary. He was nominated to the committee on temperance, which suggested that dismissal was not imminent. In the appointments he was granted a new location at his request. The conference minutes state no reason for such a transfer. A new location at one's own request was a technical device of varying interpretation, signifying either a voluntary request because of age, health, or other reasons; or a forced change with permission to ask for a new location in order to avoid humiliation. The latter carried an inference that a man had ceased to be an effective preacher.[12] Probably McMains fell in that category. In any case, the bishop now wanted him out of Pueblo, and McMains was satisfied with the designation of traveling elder and the opportunity to continue his work in the countryside. The Pueblo pulpit was given to the Reverend J. H. Merrit, whose first major task was the dedication of the church edifice.[13]

A circuit rider was welcome south of the Arkansas, and calls for McMains came from the three large counties of Pueblo, Huerfano, and Bent. Every now and then he rode into Pueblo to perform a clerical duty or simply to visit old friends, occasionally appearing at a meeting, as in February 1872 when he read an essay on Hebrew poetry before the Pueblo County Ministerial and Lay Association.[14]

The strict elements in the conference would not abandon their attacks on McMains' liberal attitudes. McMains had often expressed himself: he did not disapprove if the dance were private and properly chaperoned. But Merrit forced a confrontation to make McMains recant or get out. First some prominent laymen called on McMains, but he reiterated his position. Then Merrit made a direct approach. He was told the same thing, that McMains had no objection to "parlor dancing." Merrit insisted that dancing in any form was sinful, and the conversation took on a sharper edge. Each stood firm, with Merrit announcing that he would preach on the subject of dancing next Sabbath evening. McMains accepted the challenge. The ensuing debate, studded with biblical citations, clearly showed the deadlock.[15]

In the absence of official support McMains knew that the next move was up to him; therefore, on April 19, 1872, he terminated his connection with Methodism. As a condition of withdrawal he asked if he might keep the parchments that certified his ministerial status. Merrit assented, remarking, however, that they would not do him any good.[16]

After nearly thirteen years in the ministry the break was not easy, but abandonment of the Lord's work was not his intention. So many people supported him that he made arrangements to use the schoolhouse in Pueblo for morning and evening Sabbath services.[17] A personal following was gratifying, yet much could be said for denominational ties in the long run. This McMains knew. So early in May he took a northbound stage to Denver to keep a preaching engagement in the Congregational church. His Denver weekend made the break with Methodism complete. Noting his resignation, the *Daily Chieftain* reported that McMains would have charge of a Congregational church in Pueblo, and before long he was again an influence in religious and civic life.[18]

During the remainder of 1872 McMains vigorously pursued his clerical duties, polished his rhetoric and writing skills, and developed a new interest in the Arkansas River valley east of Pueblo, which was to culminate with his move to

Rocky Ford the next spring. In July he shared a podium with
Mrs. Sarah Lippincott to celebrate the arrival in Pueblo of
the narrow-gauge Denver and Rio Grande Railway.* (Mrs.
Lippincott, wife of the publisher and a nationally popular
writer under the pen name of Grace Greenwood, had recently
published the praises of the new town of Colorado Springs,
having been hired to do so by the Colorado Springs Company.[19]) And in August and September he explored the
Arkansas valley on horseback, setting down his impressions
for the *Chieftain.*

In a semi-serious piece for the paper, McMains claimed
one trip was an electioneering one against Republicans George
Chilcott and Jerome Chaffee. (Most of his readers knew he
was an admirer of Horace Greeley, who was running for
president on the Liberal Republican-Democratic coalition
ticket.[20]) On another trip he reached the Higbee and Smith
ranch on the Nine Mile Bottom of the Purgatoire during the
throes of an Indian scare and then went southwestward to
Trinidad.[21] In the spring, traveling east of Las Animas,
McMains was angered by the sight of buffalo carcasses scattered as far as he could see, and the appearance of a woman
firing away with indifference was simply incredible.[22] And,
reporting on a roundup in May, the preacher praised the
ingenuity of the cook, who had worked over fire and Dutch
oven to produce "fried ham and potatoes in one skillet, stewed
fruit in another, light white shortcake in another, with golden
drip to 'sop' it in, and the 'powerfulest' cup of coffee I have
drank in an age."[23]

In spite of these activities, McMains had hardly forgotten
his breach with Methodism. In fact, he worked for some time

---

*A special train on July 2 had brought distinguished visitors, includ-
ing Edward McCook, governor of the territory.

on a theological treatise, "The Second Adam," in which he provided a rationale for his unorthodox beliefs. The *Chieftain* commented that:

> The inception, style of treatment and conclusions reached are purely original with Mr. McMains, and will not fail to command attention, from the broad and liberal views expressed of christianity, and the evident care taken to expose the heresies and illogical tendencies of the old school of theology. Mr. McMains is well known throughout the territory as a brilliant thinker, and in the present work he has combined the observations, reading and experience of several years of pulpit work. The book will soon be ready for press and we bespeak in advance a rapid sale.[24]

That McMains still held his credentials as a Methodist minister irked many people. The feeling was expressed openly in the minutes of a district conference: "*Resolved*, That the said O. P. McMains is not authorized by these parchments, which he improperly holds, to perform any of the functions of a minister of the M. E. Church, and this fact is hereby certified."[25] In response McMains sent a long statement to the *Chieftain*, pointing out that Merrit had allowed him to keep the parchments albeit admitting that Elder Murray later had asked that they be turned in. Not to have complied was "criminal neglect," and he would have the credentials sent to Merrit at once. Following a detailed review of the old controversy over "parlor dancing," he concluded:

> And for this, I had to *withdraw* from the M. E. Church like a criminal — my pastor would not give me a letter; I lost my parchments, but I still hold to Solomon and not J. H. Merrit, on the subject of dancing, and I am licensed to preach by a Congregational Church; and I love to preach and will continue to preach just the same as if you had never "whereased" and "resolved."[26]

At least one paper came to his defense. The Denver *Daily Rocky Mountain News* thought that "Brother McMains held to the very sensible proposition that it was the abuse of dancing that was wrong, not dancing itself; and that there was no harm in a 'parlor dance' as he terms it. We advise him to stick to it. He can beat the fogies on that ground every Sunday in the year."[27]

Visiting Las Animas in June, McMains called at the office of the local newspaper, the *Las Animas, Col., Leader*. Editor Charles W. Bowman wrote that he was "requested to do so frequently."[28] Undoubtedly Bowman knew of A. Bach through the Pueblo *Chieftain* and was pleased to publish his pieces in the *Leader*.

Although not a resident, McMains soon learned, through his work on the paper, that Las Animas was having its difficulties: titles to town lots were not clear. The Las Animas Town Company held the townsite as a derivative claim from the immense Vigil and St. Vrain Grant. William Craig, known to McMains in Huerfano County, had laid out the town in 1869 and was president of the company. Yet many settlers treated the site as public land. Consequently, community leaders were seeking a workable agreement with company officials.[29] A. Bach observed that "what Thomas Benton called a 'compro-mise' is virtually effected by which the *derivative claim* will be immediately withdrawn, the town site legally entered, and town lots with perfect titles can be had cheap for cash, and will go off like hot — I mean will sell very rapidly."[30]

Another problem for Las Animas involved the railroad. It seemed inevitable that the Kansas Pacific would build directly into the town. So unthinkable was the contrary that A. Bach wrote: "A man that thinks Las Animas is not going to be a railroad point is so stupid that if my fighting weight were equal to that of Mr. John Warner, of Pueblo, I would not hesitate for a moment to call him an idiot."[31] But the incredible happened nonetheless. A new town received the tracks across the plains from the north, and by mid-November West

Las Animas (present Las Animas) boasted a population of 500. Fifty houses were complete and a hundred more under construction. It was claimed that two-thirds of the buildings at Kit Carson had been reerected at the new place, and Las Animas itself was on the move. Old Town and New Town became familiar terms.[32] From that evolved a major scandal, called the Moffat Patents, after David Moffat, a railroad speculator and territorial official.

McMains had a peripheral role in the scandal for he had moved, in June 1874, from Rocky Ford to West Las Animas to preach in the new Baptist church.[33] Charles Bowman had been called away for a couple of weeks and had asked McMains to take over the editorship with the June 19 issue of the *Leader*. Trying his wings in the storm over the Moffat Patents, Editor McMains published a report of the U.S. grand jury on the alleged land grab — with strong critical comments of his own.[34]

The editorial pencil was a fascinating implement, and his time at the helm of the *Leader* was too short. He had maintained a regular preaching schedule in town, but when he left the paper he resumed his circuit riding in the country.

At age thirty-four, apparently unsatisfied with life in Bent County, the Reverend O. P. McMains quietly terminated his work there — leaving a water hole and side canyon near the Nine Mile Bottom of the Purgatoire River named for him* — and went west to Cucharas, a new town northeast of Walsenburg, Colorado. The *Las Animas Leader* simply

---

* The present Kim-La Junta road goes through McMains Canyon on the north side of the Arkansas River. A well-known natural feature, the Great Bear Rock, at the north end of Nine Mile Bottom was the subject of a long article and poem by A. Bach in the *Daily Chieftain*, April 13, 1873.

informed its readers that he had departed, carrying with him
the best wishes of the people.[35] No romantic frustrations or
church troubles were hinted. Perhaps restlessness, a recurrent
symptom of inability to come to terms with himself, had overwhelmed him again. He had no wife, and evidently no close
friend, with whose help he could have reduced churning
thoughts to some communicable order.

Just when and under what circumstances McMains
returned to the Methodist Episcopal Church as a traveling
elder are not known. Of course, he had never been unfrocked
in the usual sense of the term; his return probably was based
on a mutual agreement with a presiding elder or the bishop,
although nothing suggests what sort of compromise, if any,
was reached on his doctrinal intransigence. Methodism was
in his blood, and the Colorado Conference still needed all the
help it could get.[36]

McMains was at Cucharas but a short time before he went
back to Las Animas for a Methodist meeting in October 1874.
He was transferred to Saguache, beyond the front range of
the mountains and on the far side of the flat, intermontane
San Luís Valley.[37] But again his tenure lasted only a few
months before he headed south into New Mexico — a move
which was to have a profound effect on the course of his life
thereafter.

Chapter 3

Three Murders

CIMARRON — a wild, unruly animal. The town had an appropriate name. No longer simply an adobe village dominated by Lucien B. Maxwell's rambling, verandahed house and his three-story, stone gristmill, the New Mexico town showed frame structures with false fronts among the "dobes," and English rivaled Spanish for communication.

Several aspects of the frontier were there when O. P. McMains arrived from Colorado in June 1875.[1] Indians — Mohuache Utes and Jicarilla Apaches — periodically received their government rations and annuities at Maxwell's mill. Fort Union was not far to the south, and men from that post patronized Cimarron's places of entertainment. Goldseekers from the mountains to the west around Baldy and the mining camp of Elizabethtown represented the mining world. Cattlemen and cowhands rode in for supplies and amusement, while the growing number of families crossing the plains in their wagons foretold disappearance of the open range. About all that was lacking in Cimarron's frontier cosmopolitanism were railroad workers.

The influence of Mexico was unmistakable, and the Roman Catholic Church held only slightly disputed sway. But

Methodism was there in the charge of the Reverend Franklin J. Tolby, who had come from Indiana on January 1, 1874, to serve the circuit between Cimarron and Elizabethtown — also known as Elizabeth City and very commonly as E-Town.* His parishioners were "Americans" and not very religious, according to the Reverend Thomas Harwood, from the West Wisconsin Conference, who attended the 1870 Colorado Conference at McMains' church in Pueblo and was now head of Methodist missions in New Mexico.[2]

As Tolby's assistant, McMains needed additional means of support; a printer by trade, he soon was hired to help get out the *Cimarron News and Press*, that was owned by Frank Springer and William R. Morley, with Will Dawson as publisher-printer. The *News and Press* was a recent creation, resulting from a joining of the defunct *Cimarron News* and an Elizabethtown paper† in December 1874.[3]

The newspaper office was a place of call for prominent and ordinary citizens alike, and before long the new hand had acquaintance with many people in Colfax County. Someone found that he was a poet of sorts and had experience on programs celebrating the national holiday, so McMains was chosen to read an original patriotic poem in Cimarron's observance of the Fourth of July.[4]

Merging easily into community life, McMains became aware of the regional importance of the Maxwell (Beaubien and Miranda) Land Grant, which Congress confirmed in the same act of June 21, 1860, that had dealt with the Vigil and

----

*The mining camp was named for Elizabeth Moore, daughter of an early settler and sister of George W. Moore, whom the writer interviewed in preparing this work.

† William A. Keleher, *Maxwell Land Grant* (Santa Fe, N. M.: Rydal Press, 1942), p. 68, says the full name was the *Cimarron News and Elizabeth City Railway Press and Telegraph*. See also Ritch Notebook, vol. 2, p. 56, in the William G. Ritch Collection, Henry E. Huntington Library, San Marino, California.

St. Vrain Grant.[5] He already knew Puebloans George M. Chilcott and Jerome B. Chaffee, who had had an interest in it, and he heard about organized resistance of "squatters" to the Maxwell Land Grant and Railway Company.[6]

McMains was less than ten years older than his employers. William Raymond Morley was born in Massachusetts in 1846 but was raised on an Iowa farm. A Union veteran of Sherman's march through Georgia, Morley enrolled at Iowa State University in 1869, and during his college years his closest friend and classmate was Frank Springer. Although he did not complete work on an engineering degree, Morley followed that profession, eventually going to Colorado as a surveyor for the Kansas Pacific Railroad, construction of which was in charge of General William Jackson Palmer, who in 1870 was president of the Maxwell Land Grant and Railway Company.[7]

General Palmer was favorably impressed, and through his influence young Morley was hired to take charge of certain engineering and surveying matters in developments planned by the Maxwell Land Grant and Railway Company. On July 2, 1872, the directors of the company appointed William R. Morley as vice-president and executive officer* with duties including the editorship of the *Cimarron News*, the house organ of the Maxwell Land Grant and Railway Company. Company president was an Englishman, John Langham Reed; General Palmer had resigned from official connection with the company.[8]

When his new responsibilities prompted Morley to seek legal counsel, no one came more naturally to mind than his old friend Frank Springer, who was practicing law back in Iowa. Accepting the job offer, Springer arrived in Cimarron in February 1873 and plunged into the work, which included

---

*Morley was sponsored by Henry M. Porter, one of the company directors.

his handling numerous lawsuits against squatters as well as assuming the associate editorship of the *Cimarron News*.[9]

In 1872–73 Stephen Benton Elkins was president of the Maxwell Land Grant and Railway Company and in the latter year was elected delegate to Congress from the Territory of New Mexico. And the prominent Santa Fe lawyer, Thomas Benton Catron, was legal counsel for the company. It appears that growing mistrust by Morley of Elkins and Catron, because they were closely identified with a political machine known as the Santa Fe Ring, may have been the reason why he sought Springer's services.[10]

In any event, by the time the *News and Press* succeeded the *News*, just before McMains arrived in Cimarron, Morley and Springer were becoming more and more estranged from Elkins and Catron although editorial policy continued to be pro-grant. Working for the paper soon made McMains aware of the growing political and economic tensions in Colfax County, augmented by the problems of the Indian Agency at Cimarron and the not-so-faint aura of lawlessness in the area.

Franklin J. Tolby, McMains' ministerial colleague, was concerned about much more than the spiritual welfare of his flock. For him the well-being of the Indians had high priority; Mohuache Utes and Jicarilla Apaches feared closure of the Cimarron Agency and removal from the Maxwell Grant. In empathy Tolby acquired a large tract in the mountains on both sides of the Vermejo River for a reservation; he and William D. Lee, another Indianan and Vermejo resident, gave promissory notes aggregating $12,000 to rancher Taylor F. Maulding, whose title derived from Lucien B. Maxwell.[11] This transaction suggests that Tolby was not ardently anti-grant, a conclusion supported by his close association with William R. Morley and Frank Springer, both grant company employees. His antipathy was aimed at members of the Santa Fe Ring who dominated the grant company and exerted a strong political grip on Colfax County.

The summer of 1875 saw a very hard-fought political campaign in Cimarron. An idea of its permeation was given by the Cimarron paper when it said that one Sunday the Reverend O. P. McMains preached "to a very fair audience in these times of political excitement."[12] Melvin W. Mills and Dr. Robert H. Longwill were reelected to the legislature and the probate judgeship respectively, which caused much anger and disappointment because they were regarded as Ring men with close ties to Elkins and Catron. Mills and Longwill* allegedly had used their influence to prevent an indictment of Francisco (Pancho) Griego, who, while dealing a monte game at the St. James Hotel that summer, had killed two soldiers. That apparent display of Ring power had stimulated Tolby and Morley to prepare a series of articles denunciatory of the political climate of Colfax County and appearing anonymously in the *New York Sun†* during the summer. Many people believed that his role as *Sun* correspondent was a cause of Tolby's assassination.[13]

Amid those intricacies McMains continued to set type and preach, only casually interested in local matters since he might not stay long. In fact, the mission at Silver City was vacant, and in the late summer he received the appointment.[14] As he prepared to leave, a shocking and mysterious tragedy kept him in Cimarron and pushed him into a series of bizarre events which violently split Colfax County, bringing him to the fore as a dramatic, partisan leader.

---

* Longwill was a stockholder in the Maxwell Land Grant and Railway Company and was active in its management. See Minutes, Maxwell Land Grant and Railway Company Stockholders Meeting, January 27, 1874, and Directors Meeting, January 29, 1875, MLG.

† There can be little doubt of the Tolby-*Sun* connection, but later one Simeon Harrison Newman, former publisher of the *Las Vegas Weekly Mail*, claimed to have written one of the letters attributed to Tolby and Morley (Simeon Harrison Newman III, "The Santa Fe Ring," *Arizona and the West* 12 [Autumn 1970]: 269–288).

❧

The Reverend Franklin J. Tolby, returning from Eliza-bethtown on September 14, 1875, rode into the head of Cimarron Cañon, which led down between craggy cliffs and timbered slopes to Cimarron some twenty miles away. Someone shot him twice in the back. His body was found two days later in a thicket about two miles below Pascoe, where the bridge crossed the creek. Nothing was stolen, his horse was tethered to a tree about 600 yards away, and his saddle was found about 900 yards distant in another direction.[15]

Tolby's funeral at Cimarron on September 18 featured Masonic honors, he having been the senior deacon of the Cimarron Lodge. His wife, Mary, and two little daughters were left to mourn.[16] A stunned community watched the last rites, but one person present, in particular, among them responded with more than passive horror or vague promises of vengeance. Because of a sense of personal loss and an impelling desire for justice, Oscar McMains set out to solve the murder.

When an appointment to "supply" on the Cimarron-Elizabethtown circuit went to McMains, he achieved a double purpose: he could preach, and, while riding circuit, he could investigate the murder of his friend.[17] But that combination gradually subordinated the work of the church to the search for an assassin.

The Reverend Thomas Harwood, missions superintendent, was upset by a report that a man in Taos said, before general news of the crime had reached there, that "a Protestant heretic had been killed." Harwood failed to track the man down, which convinced him that nothing could be gained by chasing every rumor and report. McMains disagreed and argued that undivided attention should be given to the manhunt, while his colleague felt that mission work should go on normally on the theory that murder will out. McMains seems not so much to have prevailed as to have ignored Harwood's advice, causing the superintendent to observe that McMains "was too strong to be led."[18] McMains talked about it with everyone he could.[19] A chance remark here; a suspicion there; bits of evidence however circumstantial; answers to leading questions — all were examined and put together.

Excitement, fear, and speculation seized Colfax County. Indeed, there was such a swirl of supposed explanations that to pick the correct one now would be impossible. Ethnic bitterness, religious bigotry, elimination of a witness to a shooting affray, and political motivation — each explanation had its proponents.[20] In the latter category, when people recalled that Tolby had been actively opposed to the appointment of Samuel B. Axtell (governor of Utah Territory) as governor of New Mexico Territory, who was the Santa Fe Ring's choice, it was easy to suspect the Ring.[21]

For several weeks McMains and those helping him sorted out bits of evidence that, when put together, pointed to one man — Cruz Vega, a resident of Cimarron who had been hired for one day — the one on which Tolby was killed — to carry the mail from Elizabethtown to Cimarron. Vega was so employed by Florencio Donaghue, the mail contractor and alleged tool of the Ring. McMains, favoring the political explanation, became certain that Vega knew something and should be questioned. How to arrange a meeting was a problem; Vega probably knew he was watched, so he was wary about walking into a trap.[22]

As a first move McMains went to see a man named William Low, stating frankly that he wanted Low to act as a decoy. The man spoke Spanish, and the rewards offered for Tolby's murderer — $500 by Governor Samuel B. Axtell and various sums by other parties — attracted him. McMains explained, "If you can get him out, I don't want the man hurt in any manner whatever. All I want is to get him to confess what he knows." As for Low's fear of personal risk, McMains had a safeguard: "I will take the responsibility on myself. They won't trouble you. I will see that you are all right."[23]

Low agreed to try and outlined a plan he thought would work. He had a cornfield in Poñil Cañon, where he might hire Vega to guard the corn at night against wild game. The field was secluded enough to be suitable for such an interview. Vega accepted the job for the nights of October 29, 30, and 31 (Friday, Saturday, and Sunday).

On the second night Low went to the field with Vega, and they built a small fire near the corn. Low fell asleep. Guided by the fire, a number of horsemen closed in. Most of them waited up the road in the timber, but five or six rode on to the fire. Low and Vega heard them coming, when one disguised rider called out, and, going up to Vega, put a lariat around his neck, telling him and Low to come along.

Terrified and sensing they were Tolby's friends, Vega insisted that he did not kill the minister but that one Manuel Cárdenas did. Low had more than he bargained for. Could McMains, a man of God, have anything to do with a lynching? He was there all right, disguised, but he revealed his identity when Low asked for him. Others told Low to clear out, but he stayed nearby in the darkness and watched with fascination. In the uncertain glow of the campfire a short distance off, McMains directed questions to Vega, who, thoroughly alarmed, gave answers that were unsatisfactory to some of the riders. It was clear to Low that McMains had more than he could handle when one of the men, grasping the end of the rope around Vega's neck, climbed a telegraph pole and dropped the rope over the wire. Others helped to hoist the struggling captive, then, after a few tense seconds, lowered him to the ground. It was useless.

Next Low heard McMains say, "I think we have all we want here." With that feeble attempt to call a halt, he left Vega with his captors and walked back to the horsemen among the trees. Perhaps he hoped that his withdrawal would quickly bring the incident to a harmless end. If so, he was mistaken.

After a few words with the other riders, McMains and a few horsemen headed down the road towards Cimarron. Low followed them, afoot, until they crossed the Poñil bridge, where he waded the stream and went to his house. Somewhere along the way McMains turned back alone and rode up the cañon. He had serious misgivings but hoped that Vega had been released and gone to Low's place. Suddenly several shots cracked and echoed higher in the cañon. McMains reined up, fearing the worst, and then turned his horse, crossed the stream, and went to Low's house. Neither said much; the shots were not mentioned. They tried to sleep and got up at sunrise. McMains, agitated and remorseful, was weeping.

"What is up now?" asked Low.

"Did you hear that shooting last night?"

"I did; I don't suppose they killed the man."

"I don't know," replied McMains, "I came away last night, . . . I found that I had no control over the men [sic], so I left."

"Well," Low said, "I'll go over and see; if the man is killed he is certainly there somewhere."[24]

But Low changed his mind, deciding to go to town and tell what happened.[25] Either he knew that Vega was dead or he made a good guess.

News of the killing of Cruz Vega swept over Cimarron and Colfax County. The excitement and tension caused by the Tolby murder had hardly begun to subside when this new shock struck. Talk was heard of vigilantes riding in the hills, and Vega's death took on the ugly aspect of a clash between Spanish-speaking people and those of Anglo background — greasers and gringos. Armed groups of the former, threatening vengeance, gathered in Cimarron.[26]

Against whom, specifically, to be vengeful was not clear. There was great reluctance to reveal the identities of the riders on the Poñil that night. McMains could hardly have avoided suspicion, and it was rumored that R. C. (Clay) Allison, a Vermejo rancher with a growing reputation as a gunslinger, was a leader in the Vega incident, although it was thought unwise to say so publicly. What evidence there is points to Tolby's murder as the reason Allison terminated his support of the Ring politicians, whom he had backed in the recent election. The abrupt shift bespoke a strong personal regard for Tolby, and, of course, there may have been other reasons long since lost.

On the following Monday night, November 1, 1875, shots were heard in the barroom of Henry Lambert's St. James Hotel. The lights went out, and patrons rushed into the street. In the darkened room lay the body of Pancho Griego, shot by Clay Allison for a reason that added immeasurably to the tautness of the townspeople.*

Apparently Allison and Griego had met in front of the hotel. Griego had been saying around town that Allison was a leader of the vigilantes who killed Cruz Vega (who may have been a relative of Griego). The two men entered the hotel, and, in company with friends, started drinking. Later Allison and Griego withdrew to a corner of the room, where the latter persisted in his accusation. The next thing anyone remembered was a burst of gunfire — three quick shots — and Griego slumping, killed instantly.[27]

---

* There are several versions of this celebrated encounter that vary in details (just as Allison's killing of "Chunk" Colbert at Clifton House may be found in differing narratives). An unpublished version says that Allison walked up to the bar and ordered a brandy. Spotting Pancho in a corner of the saloon, Allison stirred his drink and kept his eye on him. When Pancho started to draw his six-shooter, Allison whirled and shot him between the eyes. There was only one shot. This account is found in an undated manuscript by Olliver [sic] (Ollie) Reed and annotated by his sister, Mrs. Lucy Reed Wills. See also Norman Cleaveland, *The Morleys: Young Upstarts on the Southwest Frontier,* pp. 101–3, and Dale T. Schoenberger, *The Gunfighters* (Caldwell, Idaho: Caxton Printers, 1971), pp. 7–8.

"*Clay Allison a fine looking man. Black eyes and hair, well developed . . ." (Reed-Wills Manuscript). Shown here with Attie and Joseph Matthews, probably in the period 1867–70. Allison was said to have shot himself accidentally in the foot, hence the crutches. (A picture of Allison alone, taken at the same time, is in the collection of Barney Hubbs, Pecos, Texas. The picture used here was obtained from the son of Joseph Matthews.)*

Then the harassed town felt a reaction of the Anglo group. Allison and about forty of his friends rode into Cimarron, liquored up, and made frightening threats.[28] Apprehensive, the townspeople wondered who the next victim might be. Some elements of the dime novel were present, and it was not long before the next chapter was ready. As in other aspects of the case, contemporary sources are not unbiased, but their general agreement on many of the basic facts makes possible a reasonable reconstruction.

Manuel Cárdenas, the man accused by Vega before his death, was arrested in Elizabethtown on Saturday, November 6. He said that Vega was the one who shot Tolby but admitted that he and Vega had been hired to do the job by three prominent citizens of Cimarron, a statement that had strong political implications. McMains was active in publicizing the Cárdenas confession, which angered many people. Although the sheriff of Colfax County said he could maintain order, the Santa Fe *Daily New Mexican* rushed to the defense of the accused trio in an article with the hysterical headline: "Anarchy at Cimarron." Two of the men named by Cárdenas — Melvin W. Mills and Florencio Donaghue — were placed in protective custody, and the third, Dr. Longwill,* managed to escape to Santa Fe, unsuccessfully pursued by a posse led by Clay Allison and his brother, John, who was a deputy sheriff. On Monday, November 8, a cavalry detachment from Fort Union arrived in Cimarron, an act which many people regarded both as unnecessary and as another example of the dangerous influence of the Santa Fe Ring.[29]

On the same day Cárdenas, having been brought down from Elizabethtown, retracted his accusations. Mills and Donaghue were given a hearing before a magistrate anyway, and Cárdenas was further examined. The investigation was orderly

---

*Frank Springer said that both Vega and Cárdenas implicated Francisco (Pancho) Griego as one of the instigators of Tolby's death (Springer Affidavit).

and not a mob court, as was said, although some questioning by McMains may not have been strictly in accord with the rules of evidence.[30]

Further interrogation, however, was clearly up to a grand jury. The general excitement had calmed somewhat when, without warning, yet another murder occurred. Cárdenas, under escort, was shot in the head and killed almost at the door of the county jail.* Because the assassination was bound to bring strong official reaction, a citizens' committee was hastily formed, with O. P. McMains as chairman and Frank Springer as secretary. The new organization was supposed to defend the investigations thus far and plan for their continuation; it took advantage of the initiative by quickly passing a resolution placing responsibility for the Vega and Cárdenas killings on members of the Santa Fe Ring.[31]

Some people feared McMains' tactics. The local stage-line agent said passengers were afraid to pass through Cimarron, and he asked the Reverend Thomas Harwood to curb McMains' "foolish efforts to ferret out the murderers." That proposal was akin to Harwood's own opinion that "the unwise efforts of Mr. McMains served to cover up the tracks of evidence and they have never been found."[32]

Another article appeared in the *New York Sun*, approving the local investigation of the Tolby murder and reminding readers of the animosity between Tolby and territorial Chief Justice Joseph G. Palen, who was also judge of the first district that included Colfax County. Palen had publicly berated Tolby in Cimarron, the article maintained, for remarks critical of the district court, and Tolby had replied that he would have something to say about the judge in a paper with 200,000 readers.[33]

---

* It is not clear whether Cárdenas' assassin acted alone or with accomplices. No one was ever identified as the assassin, so no charges were brought.

Among Palen's close friends were Stephen Benton Elkins and Thomas Benton Catron, which was enough to damn the jurist in the eyes of anti-Ring residents of Colfax County. Judge Palen died in office on December 21, 1875, and editor Dawson published a very laudatory obituary in the *Cimarron News and Press*. And on December 31 Dawson strongly criticized the recent *Sun* article. That editorial brought on widespread resentment and a letter signed by more than 125 citizens, defending the Tolby murder investigations and demanding that Dawson publish the *Sun* article in the Cimarron paper. Among the signers, in addition to McMains, Morley, and Springer,* were: R. C. [Clay] Allison, H. M. Porter, Harry Whigham, Manley M. Chase, William Terhune, John B. Dawson, and George W. Cook.[34] In time the relations of these men with McMains would become sharply altered, in some instances to the point of personal enmity.

How close were Allison and McMains in their search for Tolby's assassin? There is no certain answer, but Allison as self-constituted judge and executioner and McMains as self-appointed detective were complementary factors, whatever McMains' intention in the apprehension of Cruz Vega. Despite Allison's later denials of their association, there is strong evidence that they collaborated actively.

A Tennesseean about McMains' age, Clay Allison served in the Confederate army. He may have come to New Mexico and Colorado as early as 1866 as a trail hand with Oliver Loving (Charles Goodnight's partner, who directed a cattle drive northward over Raton Pass to the Denver area), but by the early 1870s he had his own place on the Vermejo in the

---

* It is by no means clear why Morley and Springer allowed Dawson to editorialize in a manner so at variance with their own views. It may have been a contractual reason, while they continued in ownership of the paper's physical plant (Norman Cleaveland, *The Morleys*, p. 109).

vicinity of Tolby's Indian reservation project, where he and his brother, John, ran cattle and ignored the grant company's claim to the land.[35]

Allison was an idiosyncratic character, but that he suffered "from manic-depressive psychosis,"[36] as is claimed by some, is much less certain. His shooting affrays seem to have commenced in New Mexico, where his reputation as a gunman was firmly established in early 1874 after he killed "Chunk" Colbert at the Clifton House,* the well-known stage station of the Barlow and Sanderson Company not far south of Raton Pass.[37]

The killing of Colbert and Griego both fit the popular view of Allison's ruthlessness — that, when drunk, he felt called upon to rid the world of unsavory characters, an explanation that probably is too simplistic. He evidently had respect for religion and men of the cloth, a feeling enhanced by liquor. One story has him summoning a minister to a Cimarron saloon on Christmas Eve to conduct services, while he exacted the proper reverence from the patrons.[38] Perhaps Tolby or McMains was the object of such attention, regarding him as a friend and minimizing his exotic features. Another attraction may have been Allison's good manners and politeness, noted by contemporaries.†

---

* There is also evidence of an earlier killing in an Elizabethtown saloon. Mr. Alvin Stockton, whose family built the Clifton House, told the writer that Colbert was not killed in the main Clifton House but in a small adjacent building that was run by a Mexican woman as an eating place.

† Reed-Wills.

Chapter 4

Trial

THE GRIMMEST TRAGEDY usually has some comedy relief, and the high drama at Cimarron was no exception. But the fact that Clay Allison played the role of comedian removed it from the realm of slapstick, and few in Cimarron were detached enough to appreciate the amusement. He was contemptuous of the paper as the creature of the Santa Fe Ring, and was angered by Dawson's attitude towards the *New York Sun* article and the Tolby murder inquiries.[1]

On a mid-January night in 1876, Allison and friends broke into the darkened office of the *News and Press* on the Cimarron plaza. Nobody tried to stop them. One side of the week's edition had been printed, but soon the other side was inscribed in letters of red: CLAY ALLISON'S EDITION. Then they wrecked the press and threw it into the Cimarron River. And the story has come down that, next morning, Allison hawked his edition on the street at twenty-five cents per copy.[2]

The vandalism of Allison and his cronies was aimed at Dawson and the Ring rather than at Morley and Springer, which would explain Allison's gallantry next morning when he gave an angry Mrs. Morley a sum of money — perhaps the proceeds from his special edition — with the comment: "I don't fight women. Go buy yourself another press."[3]

The immediate cause of Allison's ire was a recently passed act of the territorial legislature joining Colfax County to Taos County for judicial purposes, which popular resentment in Colfax County saw as a miserable political move by the Santa Fe Ring. Ironically, even editor Dawson urged caution and advised Governor Samuel B. Axtell not to sign the bill. Either Allison did not know that, or it counted for little with him. Morley and others pressed the governor to prevent the measure from becoming law, but he declined in a manner that said the lawlessness and violence in Colfax County amply justified it. As a result the grand jury investigating the Tolby, Vega, and Cárdenas murders was composed of Taos County people and held its sessions in Taos, and when it was empaneled during the April term a company of troops was brought in to forestall trouble.[4]

The town was crowded. About fifty men had been summoned to testify, and it was said that the foreman of the grand jury was a Ringite. A wrong word or a false move in a Taos saloon could easily induce gunplay and riot. The chief justice of the Territorial Supreme Court, Henry Waldo (who had close professional relations with Elkins and Catron and was regarded as one of the Ring),[5] recognized the delicate situation in his charge to the grand jury: "Your jurisdiction is extended over a district of country to whose inhabitants no doubt such annexation was and is somewhat obnoxious, and who may be disposed to resent such legislation, as a reproach to them as a community." In the same statement he explained that the districts had been combined because Cimarron's reputation was notorious and the three killings were only the more spectacular examples of the lawlessness. Instructing the jurors to try to identify and indict the killers, he also directed them, in the Tolby case, to return indictments for libel if certain men had been maliciously and falsely implicated.[6]

McMains, regarded as a star witness, gave little help from the witness stand. Thomas Harwood said McMains was called because of his "constant declaration . . . that he knew who the murderers were."[7] But McMains did not talk — perhaps because he knew he had no direct proof. The Tolby case foundered: "From the evidence placed before the grand jury it appears that the only persons who it is reasonable to suppose had any knowledge of the assassination, were themselves murdered in the custody of persons ostensibly engaged in an investigation to discover the facts about Mr. Tolby's murder."[8]

McMains returned to Colfax County before deliberations were complete. But word eventually reached him that the grand jury had indicted him, along with fourteen others, for the murder of Cruz Vega. He rode into Cimarron and was arrested, being lodged in the adobe jail without bail. William Terhune and Jimmy Thorp were detained on the same count. Friends immediately set about raising money for McMains' defense. M. M. Chase and others raised $1,300 and hired Frank Springer, who filed for a writ of habeas corpus; Judge Waldo set a hearing in Santa Fe on May 25, but the best that could be achieved was bail set at $20,000. That figure put McMains right back in the Cimarron jail.[9]

In Colorado the editors of the Pueblo *Colorado Chieftain* and the *Las Animas, Col., Leader*, old friends of McMains, denounced the indictment, the *Chieftain* flatly alleging that McMains (who was Cimarron correspondent for that paper) had become the scapegoat of the Santa Fe Ring.[10]

The indictment was awkward for the Reverend Thomas Harwood; consequently he decided that McMains should be suspended from his missionary work. Harwood reasoned that otherwise he himself would be in contempt of court, an explanation that was indignantly rejected in pro-McMains circles.[11]

A jail cell was a dull place. Friends did much to cheer McMains and relieve the monotony. William R. Morley brought his six-year-old daughter, Agnes, to receive a little bow and arrow that McMains had made for her. Occasionally Clay Allison stopped by. And McMains was always delighted to see Olliver Lee (Ollie) and Lucinda (Lucy) Reed, and

Mr. and Mrs. Mortimer Columbus (Comp*) Reed, who came down from their mountaiñ ranch on the Vermejo River. The Reeds were personal friends, church members, and believers in his innocence, and they brought him a basket packed with home-baked goods. Among the first to settle among the pine-clad hills of Vermejo Park in July 1873, they had gone there as part of a larger emigration. Comp Reed was a Kentuckian, and his wife was from a Culpepper, Virginia, family.[12]

Incarceration was not strict, however, McMains often being let out to have a meal or socialize with friends. Dinner at the Morleys was always a pleasant experience, and Mrs. Morley's mother, Mrs. Mary McPherson, actively tried to secure support for McMains from the upper hierarchy of the Methodist Episcopal Church.† Talk at those gatherings naturally turned to the problems of his defense, although what could be achieved by contacts with high-level clergymen and influential laymen remained rather nebulous, except perhaps the raising of money to defray court expenses.

Part of the fear for McMains' well-being grew out of the hated judicial attachment of Colfax County to Taos County.

---

*There is evidence that the nickname was Cump, but since Comp was used in contemporary newspapers and letters, it is the version used herein. Reed also acquired a place on Red River called the 200 Ranch, northeast of his home on the Vermejo.

†Mrs. McPherson had fully approved of the Reverend Franklin J. Tolby's secular actions against the Santa Fe Ring and had written to Washington officials blasting Ring members. Her daughter, Mrs. Morley, feeling that her mother had gone too far, retrieved the letter from the receiving box at the postoffice, which earned her an indictment for mail theft, but Mrs. McPherson continued her crusade. Those matters were part of the complicated, bitter animosities in Colfax County that inevitably had some bearing on McMains' situation (Norman Cleaveland, *The Morleys: Young Upstarts on the Southwestern Frontier* [Albuquerque, N. M.: Calvin Horn Publisher, 1971], pp. 91–94; McPherson Pamphlet and letter from Emma Hunt to Mrs. McPherson, February 28, 1877, Nos. 2185 and 1699, William G. Ritch Collection, Henry E. Huntington Library, San Marino, California).

McMains felt that his friend, Colorado Senator Henry M. Teller (a strong Methodist), might help to break that combination, but he refused to write to Teller personally. McMains doubted the efficacy of all the string-pulling, and he was embarrassed by Mrs. McPherson's expenditure of her personal funds in his behalf. Nor was he sanguine that Methodist bishops would rush to his defense — he was too controversial and unmanageable. Events bore out the soundness of that judgment.[13]

However, McMains did tell his friends of his influential brother-in-law, William Fishback, in Indianapolis — an eminent Republican, a former law partner of future President Benjamin Harrison, ex-associate editor of the *St. Louis Democrat*, and one-time editor-in-chief of the *Indianapolis Journal*.* Mrs. McPherson, on a trip east mainly to see Methodist bishops, went to Indianapolis to confer with Fishback, but he was out of town. In October of 1876 Frank Springer, on his honeymoon trip,† called on the Indianapolis lawyer.

Whatever McMains' ambivalence towards the pretrial maneuvers undertaken for him, they produced results as the April term of court drew close: William P. Fishback moved swiftly to his support. It happened that in March 1877 Secretary of the Navy R. W. Thompson was in Indianapolis, and through him Fishback made arrangements to see President Hayes. The two men hastened to the White House to explain McMains' predicament. The president referred Fishback to Attorney General Charles Devens, who acted quickly.[14]

---

* Fishback bought a large interest in the *St. Louis Democrat* in 1872 (*Colorado Chieftain*, June 13, 1872).

† Springer married Miss Josephine Bishop in Cimarron on October 10 (Cleaveland, *The Morleys*, p. 125).

By telegram Devens ordered the attorney general of New Mexico to suspend action against McMains. The order had a stunning effect, even though it was not made public in Santa Fe immediately "because of the singularity and informality of the proceeding."[15] The matter was leaked, however, and a sharp editorial duel ensued.

The *Colorado Chieftain* defended McMains and referred to Justice Department opinion that Colfax County defendants could not be tried in a Taos County court. In reply the Santa Fe *Daily New Mexican* asserted that in no way was the case a federal one and that Devens had been meddling outside his jurisdiction.* To have the trial was "the most admirable way of getting themselves out of an unpleasant dilemma which overzealousness on their part for a dead ministerial friend got McMains and others into, and prompted him and them to take the law into their own hands."[16] Attorney General Devens then telegraphed Governor Samuel B. Axtell to suspend the proceedings, but the governor refused.†

The trial was an anti-climax. By a *nolle prosequi* the prosecution indicated it would proceed no further in that

---

*Victor Westphall, *Thomas Benton Catron and His Era* (Tucson: University of Arizona Press, 1973), p. 125, says that Catron, as U.S. attorney, advised Devens that only the territorial attorney general could call for a suspension.

† By then Governor Axtell's antipathy for Colfax County and many people in it was reaching its peak. In the spring of 1878 an alleged death plot, generated by the governor and aimed at Frank Springer, William R. Morley, Clay Allison, and Henry M. Porter, was revealed. As a result, special agent Frank Warner Angel came out, made his investigation and devastating report, and President Hayes removed Axtell in September, replacing him with Lew Wallace, the novelist. Those dramatic developments did not touch McMains' career directly, but they were part of what is sometimes called the Colfax County War (including the Tolby murder and its aftermath), which in time was overshadowed by the better-known Lincoln County War (Cleaveland, *The Morleys*, pp. 149–52, 157).

action against McMains and Terhune, but another grand jury
brought in a new presentment against McMains for the Vega
murder. Springer and his colleague secured a change of venue
to Mora County in the August term. Bail was raised, and
McMains once more sought calm in writing by doing a serial
story for the *Colorado Chieftain* and writing for the *Cimarron
News and Press* under his old pen name, A. Bach.[17]

In June McMains was permitted to resume his ministry,
and the people on his circuit gave him a warm welcome. Also
the Reverend Thomas Harwood came to Cimarron with
Bishop Thomas Bowman. Their official tour of the New
Mexico missions was timed by a letter to the bishop from William P. Fishback, requesting that he have a direct look at the
McMains case. Bowman "found him in good spirits, and quite
confident of his ultimate triumph,"[18] but there is no evidence
that the bishop did anything special in the matter.

Lawyers, litigants, witnesses, and onlookers headed
southward for Judge Waldo's court at Mora where the case
of the *Territory* v. *O. P. McMains* was tried on August 22 and
23, 1877. William Breeden, New Mexico attorney general and
alleged Ring member, aimed for conviction of first degree
murder. Defense counsel Springer and Lee admitted that
McMains planned the capture of Cruz Vega and was present
when he was seized, but they contended that some of the
masked riders were drunk and beyond control. McMains was
not present when Vega was killed. Testimony by William
Low, the principal witness, was in accord. On Thursday evening the jury retired, and the following afternoon the twelve
men brought in a unanimous verdict that McMains was guilty
in the fifth degree and should be fined $300.[19]

Guilt "in the fifth degree" aroused astonishment, and
spectators wondered that the verdict was not an acquittal.
McMains refused to accept the decision and pay the fine
because that would have been an admission of complicity.
Next morning, Springer and Lee asked for a new trial, arguing
that the verdict was contrary to the evidence and the court's

instructions. Judge Waldo denied the motion. Whereupon they asked for a new trial because of a technicality in the verdict — it did not state of what McMains was guilty. The judge concurred.[20]

The conviction and fine were widely discussed. The *Colorado Chieftain* derisively asked: "By the way, what sort of crime is murder in the 'fifth degree?' That is a dilution a little beyond anything we have ever heard before. But, we presume, it is like the justice dealt out to McMains, an article indigenous to the soil of New Mexico, and unknown to the ignorant outside barbarians."[21]

The new trial at Taos in the spring of 1878 collapsed, and the case was thrown out for lack of evidence.[22] After two and a half years at the center of a sensational series of episodes, the Reverend O. P. McMains, now thirty-eight, planned a return to the work of the Cimarron-Elizabethtown circuit. The mystery of F. J. Tolby's death was not solved, nor has it been to this day. McMains' efforts were admired by many people, but that appreciation was not echoed by some of his clerical colleagues.

Matthew Simpson, the eminent Methodist bishop who had given Abraham Lincoln's funeral eulogy at Springfield and who had been interviewed about McMains by Mrs. McPherson in Washington, had come out for the Annual Conference of the New Mexico Missions at Santa Fe in October. He was not enthusiastic about returning McMains to the circuit in Colfax County, and it may be doubted that the Reverend Thomas Harwood was delighted at the prospect. (McMains had described Harwood as a weakling with no backbone.) But Simpson and Harwood squelched their misgivings, the bishop saying, " 'I don't like to appoint Bro. McMains to Cimarron and Elizabethtown, but I wish you would.' "[23] Harwood complied because of the softly worded order and because he knew that a strong petition in favor of McMains had been sent from Colfax County to the Missionary Society.[24]

෧๚ඉ

McMains' resumption of his ministry came under the influence of two new circumstances. He acquired a small ranch near Cimarron, which demanded time and energy, and bachelorhood ended for him early in 1879, when he wedded Mary Messner,* a milliner in Cimarron. His marriage plans came as a surprise, even to close friends. One day he rode to the Reeds' Vermejo ranch. Without preliminaries he said to Comp's wife, Julia, "I guess I am to be married!" Astonished but approving, the family wanted to know all about her. Julia Reed knew, however, that he had never forgotten his jilt in Pueblo.[25]

Oscar and Mary went to the mission at La Junta (now Watrous), where they were married on January 20, 1879, by Thomas Harwood, whose relations with McMains had improved by that time. Mary was thirty-two and Oscar about forty, an age when most men had established themselves and expected to pass the remainder of their days in the comfort and security of familiar ways.[26]

Mary B. McMains must remain rather enigmatic because the data about her is slight. One source described her as small in stature,[27] while another said she was stout, which she may have been, especially in later years. Apparently she was a person of few words, and there is a clear impression that she and the Reeds were not friendly, which must have been embarrassing for McMains.[28] There is no indication that they were not a devoted couple, but she seems to have grown understandably tired of the almost incessant tension that resulted from her husband's increasing activity against the Maxwell Land Grant.

---

* In his Church Record, Harwood wrote the surname as Messner. Mrs. Wills spelled it Missner. The former is presumed to be correct.

Chapter 5

The Maxwell Land Grant

CONTROVERSY OVER THE MAXWELL GRANT was marginal while
the turbulence of the Tolby murder and its aftermath beset
Colfax County. There was some acceptance of a claim of
ca. 2,000,000 acres at the Department of Justice, but at the
Department of the Interior, which had rejected a survey of
close to that figure, support remained strong for a severe
limitation on its size as specified by Mexican law. Opposition
to Elkins, Catron, Longwill, and others was based more on
their associations with the Santa Fe Ring than on their con-
nections with the Maxwell Land Grant Company. And
McMains' intimacy with the Morleys and Frank Springer
showed that he had no real misgivings then about the grant.

In 1877, however, changing circumstances revealed that
the grant people had been quietly active. They had secured
an official survey for ca. 1,800,000 acres, and its acceptance
at the Department of the Interior made the issuance of a U.S.
patent for that amount practically a certainty. Their success
at the Interior Department was related to the new administration in Washington, especially to the personnel change at the
General Land Office, approved by President Hayes. Now
McMains, with his ranch, had a direct stake in those events,
and as he rode circuit he heard expressions of concern and

alarm from hundreds of settlers, many of whom had recently settled within the survey boundaries, either in defiance of the grant company or in the belief that their claims were on the public domain. In those circumstances McMains' own anti-grantism was born and nurtured.

The grant claimants, in other words, argued that Carlos Beaubien and Guadalupe Miranda had asked for an *empresario* grant, embracing all the land within certain outboundaries. That may have been true, but the survey lines were believed by many people to be in gross error, including an amount of land far in excess of what the petitioners asked for. And some of the wording in the official documents convinced others that Beaubien and Miranda had asked for personal estates, limited by Mexican law to ca. 48,000 acres per grantee, to be selected within the outboundaries.

Beaubien and Miranda petitioned for their grant in 1841. Governor Manuel Armijo approved with a brevity that defies any clear understanding of his thoughts on the matter, and two years later juridical possession was given by Cornelio Vigil, a justice of the peace at Taos, for an indeterminate amount of land. After the Mexican Cession to the United States in 1848, Congress provided guidelines in 1854 for examining and judging Mexican and Spanish land grants in New Mexico. Under those rules the surveyor general of New Mexico recommended congressional confirmation of the Beaubien and Miranda (No. 15), which was given (along with others) in the vaguely worded Act of June 21, 1860. That legislation made no mention of size, except that it restricted the Vigil and St. Vrain Grant (No. 17) to twenty-two square leagues, or ca. 96,000 acres to the grantees jointly,[1] apparently reducing it to the same limitations tacitly imposed on the Beaubien and Miranda and others.

During the years 1858 to 1867 Lucien B. Maxwell, Beaubien's son-in-law, brought the unsurveyed estate under his

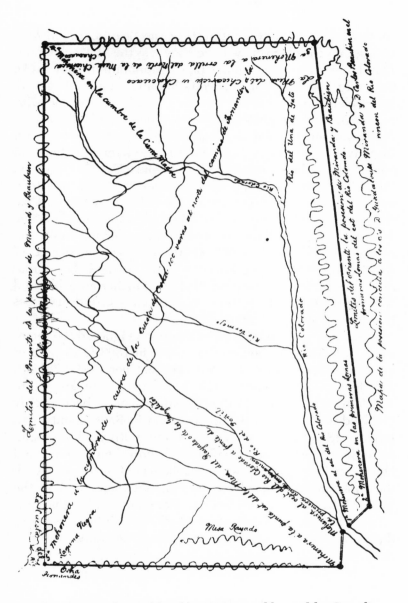

This Mexican diseño *(sketch) was presumably used by Cornelio Vigil in giving possession to Beaubien and Miranda in 1843.*

control by acquiring the interests of the Beaubiens and Mirandas; thus the claim came to be known as the Maxwell Grant. The discovery of gold around Baldy Mountain in 1867 broke the pastoral serenity of Maxwell's holdings, and he began to assert claim to ca. 2,000,000 acres — wildly out of line with the maximum of eighteen square leagues (ca. 79,884 acres) that Beaubien claimed in 1844, and greatly at variance with that given by important witnesses in the later litigation. An official survey being conducted by Deputy U.S. Surveyor W. W. Griffin was suspended on December 31, 1869, by a telegraphic order from Secretary of the Interior Jacob D. Cox, who required that the Maxwell be held down to the same acreage as the Vigil and St. Vrain, basing his interpretation of the Act of June 21, 1860, on the colonization decree of August 18, 1824, by the Mexican Congress, and the regulations thereunder of November 21, 1828. Furthermore, he cited two Supreme Court decisions in analogous California cases that upheld such a limitation.[2]

Maxwell and his wife (Luz Beaubien) ignored the secretary's order, having bound themselves in 1869 to dispose of most of their claim to Charles F. Holly, George M. Chilcott, and Jerome B. Chaffee. (The latter two were known to McMains from Colorado days, Chaffee having been deeply involved in the Moffat patents business in Bent County.) In January 1870 Chaffee signed a contract with Griffin to complete the survey, which Chaffee filed with the General Land Office. In May the Maxwells reached final agreement with the three promoters, who then assigned their bond to the Maxwell Land Grant and Railway Company, and to that new corporation the Maxwells deeded all their rights except for their home ranch* near Cimarron and other minor reservations.[3]

---

* It was later sold to John Collinson.

Secretary Cox's decision and resentment of alien owner-ship* aroused defiance of the Maxwell Land Grant and Railway Company in 1870, mainly by miners, directed at the control exerted by John Collinson, a London promoter and president of the company. There were charges of violent repression by hired guns, including resort to murder. Resistance was neither widespread nor well organized, and by 1873 it took the form of refusal to pay rents, followed by court actions and frequent verdicts by local juries in favor of the grant company, which weakened the squatters' clubs at E-Town and Cimarron.[4]

To secure acceptance of an interpretation of the Act of 1860 — that Congress intended to confirm the Maxwell for all the land within the vaguely defined outboundaries, the grant company in 1871 published supporting opinions by several eminent lawyers in a pamphlet, *The Maxwell Grant: Opinions as to Title*. It contained the first expressions of a tremendously significant construction placed on the Act of June 21, 1860, to the effect that Congress, in its sovereign power, had really created a new grant, which made the laws of Mexico irrelevant.

Although the new Interior secretary, Columbus Delano, believed his predecessor was wrong in limiting the Maxwell Grant, he refused to reverse Cox's ruling because a decision by a department head was "final and binding upon his successor." Congress could make the change. Attorney General G. H. Williams believed the Cox decision should be thrown out, but Delano's action gave it an air of permanence that in time made it a central feature of anti-grant doctrine. Fresh

---

* To forestall criticism of alien ownership the incorporators were Americans: William A. Pile (governor of New Mexico), Thomas R. Spencer (surveyor general of New Mexico), and John S. Watts (chief justice of the New Mexico Supreme Court). See *Transcript of Title*, pp. 66–67.

encouragement was given to settlers by a General Land Office directive of January 28, 1874, ordering the surveyor-general of New Mexico to treat the Maxwell claim as public domain by extending the public surveys over it, which Secretary Cox had ordered in 1869. The 96,000 acres allowed to the grantees within the outboundaries had not been selected (and never were), but it was expected that the tract would be on the Cimarron River and Rayado Creek, thus including the home ranch that Maxwell reserved from his sale of the claim in 1870.[5]

In 1877 the Supreme Court, in the rather obscure case of *John G. Tameling* v. *The United States Freehold Land and Emigration Company,** ruled that congressional confirmation of a land grant for which no specific amount of land within the outboundaries was mentioned by the surveyor general included, therefore, all the land within those boundaries. In other words, without that specific limitation such claims were assumed to be *empresario* grants. John G. Tameling, a settler, contended that the 1,000,000-acre Sangre de Cristo (Lee and Beaubien) Grant was void because, under Mexican law, it should have been limited to 96,000 acres. To that, the company's lawyers replied cryptically that "the grant was not void, but at the most was simply voidable." And their central argument was that even if the grant was absolutely void, the act of a sovereign power (i.e., Congress) made valid a void conveyance; Congress had created a grant *de novo* (a new grant), which eradicated any defects in the title prior to that confirmation. Mr. Justice David Davis upheld that reasoning

---

* This action was originally brought in a Colorado district court by the company to evict Tameling from 160 acres that he claimed to be public domain. Losing there and in the Colorado Supreme Court, Tameling appealed to the United States Supreme Court. See *Tameling* v. *United States Freehold Land and Emigration Company*, 2 Colorado Reports 411 (1874).

in his opinion sustaining the state courts' decisions against Tameling.[6]

Similarities between the Maxwell and Sangre de Cristo Grants made it natural that eventually someone would suggest the applicability of the Tameling decision to the Maxwell controversy.* Documentation of the connection commences with an unexplained letter of March 10, 1877 (the Tameling decision was handed down on March 1), from Land Office Commissioner J. A. Williamson to the secretary of the Interior, pointing out the discrepancy between Secretary Cox's ruling and the Tameling case opinion. Williamson asked the secretary for instructions in similar cases in the *future*, and Secretary Carl Schurz told Williamson to be guided by the court's ruling in similar cases *hereafter* (italics mine). Instead, for no certain reason, Williamson applied it to the Maxwell Grant, thus reopening the case and ordering a new survey.[7]

The ramifications of the "new grant" concept were greater than was at first realized. It provided a convenient rule of thumb that made it unnecessary for a judge to be knowledgeable of Mexican or Spanish land laws in determining the validity of any grant that Congress had confirmed without mention of a particular amount of land. In that circumstance, the Mexican law limiting a certain type of grant to 48,000 acres per grantee was, in effect, repealed. The Tameling decision was the impregnable bastion from which assaults against the Maxwell Grant could be and were repulsed; it was the immovable obstacle which McMains and the anti-granters could neither eliminate nor circumvent.

A few years later, another land office commissioner, William J. Sparks, directly questioned the authority and validity

---

* It may have been A. T. Britton, one of the attorneys for the United States Freehold Land and Emigration Company. He was a member of the Washington law firm of Britton and Gray (specialists in land cases), later retained by the Maxwell Land Grant Company.

of Williamson's decision, commenting that Williamson acted "of his own volition." His summary of it is worth noting:

> The Secretary [Schurz] ... instructs the Commissioner what shall be done *"hereafter"* "in similar cases," not that anything shall be done in cases already settled [Secretary Cox's order having disposed of the Maxwell case]. He is not instructed to reopen any case that had been decided. The Commissioner asked for no instructions in respect to the Maxwell Grant, and received none. This grant was not before him for a review of the decision of the Secretary of 1869; he had no duty to perform in regard to it; but he proceeded upon his own motion, apparently, to order a new survey, and he directed it to be made "in strict accordance with the juridical possession;" not according to the grant, which must have been determined by the law [an act of the Mexican Congress of August 18, 1824]; not according to the confirmation, ... but precisely according to those exaggerated boundaries [expansion of the grant from 150 square miles to 2,700 square miles].[8]

Those "exaggerated boundaries" referred to the Elkins and Marmon survey,* which was undertaken to provide the basis of an imminent U.S. patent because the private Griffin survey had not been accepted as official. In addition to Sparks' statement, another strong argument against the patent held that the U.S. government could quitclaim only a tract already valid under Mexican law, which limited the grant as Secretary Cox had ruled; the government could not convey what it had never owned. However, that contention could be demolished by the Tameling decision, which said that the sovereign power of Congress had created a new grant — regardless of Mexican law or a treaty.[9]

---

* The surveyor general of New Mexico signed a contract with John T. Elkins (brother of Stephen Benton Elkins, former president of the grant company) and Robert T. Marmon to run an official survey of the Maxwell in the summer and fall of 1877.

The Surveys

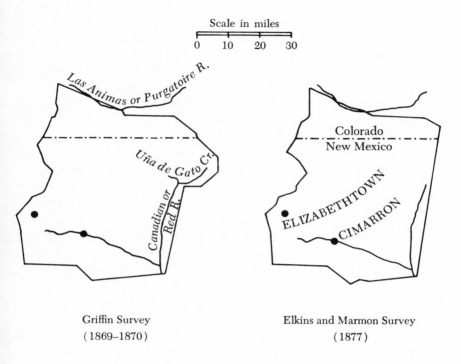

Griffin Survey
(1869–1870)

Elkins and Marmon Survey
(1877)

Compiled from maps in Federal Archives and Records Center, Denver.

The William W. Griffin survey *of the Maxwell Land Grant (1869–1870), for 1,817,767.65 acres was not complete when the Secretary of the Interior, on December 31, 1869, ordered that the grant be limited to twenty-two square leagues. In 1870 it was finished as a private survey for the Maxwell Land Grant and Railway Company. The survey was distinguished by the eastward bulge around Uña de Gato Creek on the northeast corner of the claim.*

The Elkins and Marmon survey *of the Maxwell Land Grant (1877) for 1,714,764.94 acres became the basis of the U.S. patent issued in 1879. In this survey the eastern boundary was made as a straight line, in accord with the original Mexican sketch map (diseño), and disallowing the large bulge in the Griffin survey around Uña de Gato Creek.*

Anti-grant tactics in the long run would have to secure either a clear interpretation that the Tameling decision was not applicable to the Maxwell or a reversal of the Supreme Court's opinion in the Tameling case. Such possible legal solutions were rather nebulous in those pre-patent days.

The immediate course of attack on the new survey was set on December 20, 1877, when twenty-five men in the Stonewall country of Colorado petitioned Secretary of the Interior Carl Schurz, protesting the Elkins and Marmon survey that included land for which some of them already had their government papers. And a new organization, the Colfax County (New Mexico) Anti-Grant Association, aimed at overturning the survey plat. O. P. McMains was one of the men selected to guide its efforts. The goal of the two groups was not to eliminate the Maxwell Grant but to reduce it to something less than 100,000 acres. Doubtless McMains knew of the Tameling decision and regarded it as inapplicable to the Maxwell, confining his criticisms to the survey. He could hardly have done otherwise.

Direct contacts in Washington seemed the best approach, and McMains was picked as emissary. Someone suggested that the government should foot the bill for the journey, since, after all, the government had paid the cost of the survey. He proposed that in a letter to Secretary Schurz dated April 9, 1879, and he rather mildly noted that errors in the survey had caused lawsuits to be brought against innocent settlers. A reply said there was no money to pay his expenses and no opinion could be expressed against the survey since no examination of it had been made.[10]

In a second letter to the secretary on May 5, McMains was more trenchant and explicit in his animadversions directed towards the survey. He declared that some Mexican documents pertaining to the grant were fraudulent. He found grave discrepancies in placenames and geographic features relative to the boundaries — especially the location of the Chicorica Mesa, on which the crucial northeast corner of the

Maxwell supposedly was placed. (He could not have known that Land Office Commissioner Williamson had pointed out errors by Elkins and Marmon in a letter to the surveyor general of New Mexico, which Williamson did not send because, for obscure reasons, he switched to support of a patent.) So it was that McMains undertook to contest the Maxwell Grant, a commitment that would dominate the rest of his life. On May 19, President Hayes signed a quitclaim (or relinquishment of claim) by the United States to Charles Beaubien and Guadalupe Miranda, their heirs and assigns.[11]

Now hundreds of settlers faced an eventual choice of coming to terms with the grant company, getting out, or stepping up their resistance. Those who chose the latter course accepted McMains as their spokesman.

The Reverend O. P. McMains was not reappointed to the Cimarron-Elizabethtown circuit, so he spent much of his time at the little settlement of Otero, some miles to the northeast on the Santa Fe Railroad.* He was again a traveling elder, which suggests that his Methodist superiors were not pleased with him but did not know what to do with him. McMains was popular with the people. To have dismissed him probably would have prejudiced Methodism's interests, and, besides,

---

* By early March 1879 the Atchison, Topeka and Santa Fe Railroad had reached a waterhole in Colfax County about five miles south of Raton Pass, where a division point and a new town were established. Named after Miguel A. Otero, head of the commission house of Otero, Sellars and Company and a member of the first board of directors of the Maxwell Land Grant and Railway Company, the town enjoyed prosperity during the winter of 1879–80, but there were signs of a short life span. In 1879, Miguel Otero's nephew, Mariano, was New Mexico's delegate to Congress and had introduced a bill to settle all private land claims in the Mexican Cession (L. L. Waters, *Steel Trails to Santa Fe* [Lawrence: University of Kansas Press, 1950], pp. 55, 97–100; Jay T. Conway, *A Brief Community History of Raton, New Mexico, 1880–1930, Commemorating Her Fiftieth Birthday* [Raton: Gazette Printing, 1930], p. 8; *Transcript of Title of the Maxwell Land Grant Situated in New Mexico and Colorado* [Chicago: Rand McNally and Company, 1881], p. 67; Las Vegas *Daily Optic*, December 22, 1879).

the town of Otero needed help. That his oratory had not lost any of its impact is attested to by an anecdote of a summer evening's lecture in 1880:

> Mr. Warnkly, of the art gallery, is a Latter Day Saint, and yesterday preached in the schoolhouse. We all expected to be converted and have two or three wives, but we were sadly mistaken when he told us he was not a poly-gamist. . . . When he had convinced all there was no hell, oh, what a happy, contented smile could be seen on all, especially the ladies. Among his attentive listeners was Rev. McMains of the M. E. Church. When the Latter Day Saint closed his ser-[mon] he invited Rev. McMains to speak, who in a few words brought the congregation back to a sense of duty by convincing them there was a hell and to flee from it. Then you could see that sad, sick-ening smile creeping over the face of the boys again.[12]

As traveling elder, McMains rode from Otero into the hinterland to preach, marry, and bury. Some of his trips took him to the disputed Maxwell east line and beyond. Along streams like the Chicorica and the Chico, in that fascinating country of dormant volcanoes and mesas with lava-flow rim-rocks, he heard strongly voiced opinions rejecting the Max-well survey's northeast corner as fraudulent, as well as much talk about the strange Uña de Gato Grant that probably was a forgery, although it was surveyed by Elkins and Marmon under the same contract as the Maxwell.[13] Exposure to vehe-ment criticisms of Mexican land grants helped to shape his attitude towards them.

With the rapid decline of Otero,* the Reverend and Mrs. O. P. McMains responded to the new railroad community of Raton. But instead of settling in town, they took over a small

---

*An adequate water supply for pusher-engines was found at the foot of Raton Pass. Much of Otero was moved there, and soon nothing was left but the graveyard.

property on Red River, a short distance to the south. Like his other place near Cimarron, the ranch was within the Elkins and Marmon survey of the Maxwell, and the grant company, of course, expected him to buy it.[14] His refusal to comply put him squarely on the side of the anti-grant settlers. It may be presumed that Mary McMains supported her husband's leadership of the anti-grant cause, but there is little data on her activities.

Letters of protest from members of the Colfax County Anti-Grant Association made scarcely an impression at the Department of the Interior.[15] Anti-grant arguments needed wide publicity, popular understanding and sympathy in order to force a reexamination of the Elkins and Marmon survey. If enough people were convinced that American citizens were being cheated and despoiled by an enormous fraud connived at by Washington officials, they might generate a roar of disapproval that could not easily be ignored. The problem was how to accomplish that quickly.

A vociferous newspaper with strident editorials against the grant would help. When discussion veered in that direction, it led right to McMains. He knew the printer's trade, had written for papers, and had editorial experience. He was game to try, and soon a small press was purchased and set up at his ranch. Early in 1881 a weekly sheet, the *Raton Comet*, started after the Maxwell Grant and its claimants. Nor was it gentle with suspected public officials: in one of his first editorials McMains accused Henry M. Atkinson, surveyor general of New Mexico, of defrauding the United States by accepting false surveys. And the *Comet's* fulminations were supplemented by serious anti-grant consultations, which Maxwell people slurringly referred to as "squatters' meetings."[16]

When McMains assumed direction of the anti-grant *Comet*, his friendships with pro-granters and company officials, of course, quickly terminated. William R. Morley expressed the bitterness of those people in a letter to Mrs. Morley, recalling all that Manley M. Chase, Frank Springer,

Harry Whigham, and John B. Dawson had done for McMains at the time of the Tolby and Cruz Vega murder trials. That McMains did not believe the northeast corner of the survey was fraudulent, and that he started the whole ruckus simply for notoriety, Morley was convinced.[17] It was an understandable misreading of the circumstances and of McMains' character.*

Grant people had enough trouble without having to cope with the surge of anti-grantism. The Maxwell Land Grant and Railway Company had foundered on financial difficulties. In March of 1880 Frank Remington Sherwin and Judge Lucien Birdseye, of New York, purchased the grant at a court-ordered sale of the mortgaged property, and in May they conveyed it to the new Maxwell Land Grant Company, incorporated in the Kingdom of The Netherlands. Sherwin was president, and headquarters were retained at Cimarron. Dutch investors lacked confidence in the new management, so Captain J. T. Niewenhuisen appeared in Cimarron that fall, representing Dutch stockholders and directors. He soon was at variance with Sherwin, who resented his presence. Denunciations of company management were frequent that winter, and the captain's cables to The Netherlands depressed Maxwell securities on European exchanges. Niewenhuisen once was thrown out of the office, but the cynical looked on all that internal strife as camouflage of a deal between Sherwin and Niewen-

---

* When he wrote this appraisal of McMains, Morley was no longer with the Maxwell Company. In fact, he had left it in 1876, several years before the reorganization. After a short stint with the Denver and Rio Grande he worked as a civil engineer with the Santa Fe Railroad. Morley was killed in January 1883 in a shooting accident on a train about 200 miles south of Chihuahua, while serving as chief engineer for the Mexican Central Railroad (Norman Cleaveland, *The Morleys, Young Upstarts on the Southwest Frontier* [Albuquerque, N. M.: Calvin Horn, 1971], pp. 159, 212).

huisen to cause Maxwell securities to sag for reasons best known to the company.[18]

The rift appeared genuine to McMains. It was something anti-granters should not miss. He and Niewenhuisen spent much time together, the latter sending copies of the *Comet* to Holland. But it turned out that the intracompany clash was a tempest in a teacup: Niewenhuisen was recalled, and McMains' hopes were dispelled.[19]

Even getting out a newspaper on a ranch several miles from its town circulation was an unstable venture. The first *Comet* went out of business, but not without promises that it would "come out of its retirement, and shine hereafter from Raton, where the office is now being moved. Mr. McMains is about to make some decided improvements, and establish a job office in Raton."[20] By that time, however, anti-granters knew that an active paper could not get official attention by itself. Not a sign in their behalf had come out of Washington recently.

Direct action was the key, so they thought, and they arranged to send McMains to the Department of Justice and the Department of the Interior with a petition asking for a lawsuit to vacate the Maxwell patent. But first McMains went to the Stonewall country in Colorado,* where nine settlers in that beautiful mountain region — namely, Richard D. Russell, Abisha Stowell, Alfred F. Tremaine, Frank B. Chaplin, José Benito Martínez, Jesús María Córdova, George A. Storz, Santiago Martínez, and Miguel Antoniò Treviño — had made their final homestead entries and been in possession of their

---

* The Stonewall Valley was first known as St. John's Valley (Valle de San Juan) after Juan Gutierrez, early settler. Richard D. Russell later called it Stonewall (Mrs. Hal Russell, "Memoirs of Marion Russell," *The Colorado Magazine* 21 [March 1944]: 72–73).

Stonewall country — looking westward along the Middle Fork of the Las Animas or Purgatoire River. In the distance is the "Stonewall" and behind it the Sangre de Cristo Mountains, allegedly the west boundary of the Maxwell Grant. Culebra Peak (14,069 ft.) is left center; its name is sometimes given to this segment of the Sangre de Cristos.

ranches for some time. They believed that the north line of the Maxwell was an intentional fraud to include the choice Stonewall area — a central point in McMains' arguments before the attorney general.

In dramatic coincidence while McMains was there, stunning news came from Washington that the nine homestead entries had been suspended. However, the letter from Commissioner Williamson had also stated that "the exterior boundary lines have not been established by the public surveys closing upon the grant as patented by metes and bounds."[21] Hopefully, then, the north line of the Maxwell was undetermined, and if they worked fast they could prove in time that it should be in New Mexico rather than Colorado.

McMains canceled a trip north to La Veta, where he would have met with men resisting a Vigil and St. Vrain Grant claim. Hurrying down from Stonewall, he disposed of the *Comet* to Captain Lenfestey of the *Trinidad Daily Times*, sacrificing his anti-grant paper to his trip east. Waiting for new survey reports from along the alleged north line of the grant caused delay, but McMains also took time to go down to Elizabethtown, New Mexico, to perform the marriage of Joseph Lowry and Elizabeth Moore (for whom the mining camp had been named), the bridegroom being a prominent anti-granter who had extensive mining interests in the area. On June 23 McMains was on his way to Washington at last, his expense money provided by settlers from all over the Maxwell Grant.[22]

Chapter 6

First Trip to Washington

A SANTA FE TRAIN took McMains across the Vigil and St. Vrain claim in southern Colorado, where he first had seen the features of a land grant controversy — the case of the Moffat Patents. Now, seven years later, he was on his way to Washington with a brief against the Maxwell Grant, of a scale beside which the Moffat Patents were trivial.

About the time that McMains arrived in the capital, his former friend, Harry Whigham, secretary of the grant company, released a letter from the acting commissioner of the General Land Office, announcing that suspended homestead entries within the exterior boundaries of the Maxwell Grant would be canceled to the extent that they were in conflict.[1]

The Washington trip also coincided with the assassination of President James A. Garfield, who was shot on July 2, 1881, but lingered through the summer. The resulting uncertainties slowed action on the petition to bring suit against the Maxwell patent, which was filed by McMains on July 15. A month later Secretary of the Interior Samuel J. Kirkwood recommended that suit be brought, and he transmitted the papers to Wayne MacVeagh, the attorney general.[2] In view of the positions taken by former Secretary Schurz and Com-

[74]

missioner Williamson,* the favorable reception at the Interior
Department was very encouraging.

Secretary Kirkwood's recommendation was based on
McMains' application for assistance; the petition charged
gross error, fraud, and perjury relating to the Maxwell boundaries. From it, and probably talks with McMains also, the
secretary was persuaded "that great reasons exist for assuming
that the patent was improvidently issued," and he viewed
testimony by claimants' witnesses as "in the highest degree
loose and contradictory, besides being meager and unsup-
ported." He agreed with the settlers' rejection of a sketch map
(in English) showing the grant extending into the drainage
of the Las Animas or Purgatoire River in Colorado.† The
original diseño or sketch map (in Spanish) showed only
streams that flowed south to the Red River in New Mexico.

McMains also pointed out that the public surveyors
failed to find any markers or monuments on the alleged Maxwell north line. From that, Kirkwood was convinced that no
survey of the north line had been made and that placenames
and geographical points had been "deliberately changed from
those already officially reported by the township surveys and
plats." But he also thought that matters had gone too far for
his department to correct; remedy lay with the Justice Department.[3]

No wonder McMains wrote confidently to the *Trinidad
Daily Times* of his prima facie case of fraud against the Maxwell patent and of the suit that probably would be docketed

*Commissioner Williamson had resigned from the General Land
Office to take a position with the Santa Fe Railroad (*Trinidad Daily
Times*, May 28, 1881).

† Later the *Raton Guard*, quoting the *Omaha Bee*, stated that Williamson said one thing and the sketch (presumably the map in English)
another; for example, Williamson's instructions said not to take in the
Las Animas valley in Colorado, while the map included it (*Raton Guard*,
January 20, 1882).

in Colorado. There would be some delay, however, because
Frank Springer, the Maxwell Company attorney, had asked
to be heard at the Department of Justice, and Attorney General MacVeagh had granted the request.[4]

How far the paths of Oscar McMains and Frank Springer
had diverged. Their association on the *Cimarron News and
Press* and their client-counsel relationship during the Vega
murder trial were now matters of memory, and there would
be no pleasant reminiscences together in the future: they
were at opposite poles. In the years ahead they would face
each other often as ardent spokesmen for contending causes.

In addition to Springer, Maxwell company president
Frank Remington Sherwin* also tried to influence the attorney
general, through a mutual friend. His letter to a Washington
business associate is revealing of the tactics employed by,
and the personal animosity of, some pro-granters:

> I think you once mentioned to me that you had a
> friendly acquaintance with Mr MacVeagh. . . . you may
> perhaps render him a service by saving him the annoy-
> ance he will most assuredly experience if he persists in
> his present course against the Maxwell Land Grant. He
> has been listening to the representations of one O. P.
> McMains, preacher, scurrilous Editor, blackmailer, and
> lacking only the element of courage to make him a des-
> perado. In the year 1876 he was indicted in this County
> for murder in the first degree and was only saved from a
> long term of imprisonment by the strenuous exertions
> of Hon: Frank Springer, counsel of this Company, whom

---

*Sherwin was a speculator-promoter of uncertain probity, whose
administration of company affairs was a near disaster that followed
serious neglect of the grant during the receivership of William T. Thornton (Thomas Benton Catron's law partner) and E. Platt Stratton (Jim
Berry Pearson, *The Maxwell Land Grant* [Norman: University of Oklahoma Press, 1961], pp. 78, 94–95; Victor Westphall, *Thomas Benton
Catron and His Era* [Tucson: University of Arizona Press, 1973], p.
112).

Frank Springer, Maxwell attorney, 1881.

he now assails at Washington as he has recently done in
the columns of his scurrilous Squatters Newspaper now
extinct. . . . He has been guilty of many other offenses
against law, morality and decency in this and neighboring communities, among others the crime of bigamy.*. . .⁵

Sherwin's epistolary maneuver did not secure a dismissal
of the hearing, however, and Springer was given more time
to prepare the Maxwell Company's next move. Postponement
enabled McMains to return to the grant, where he was joy-
ously received by anti-granters and their families. During the

---

*Nowhere else in the sources is bigamy even hinted at. The charge is
an indication of Sherwin's unscrupulousness, which is quite evident
throughout his letters in the Maxwell Company records.

interval President Garfield died, and Attorney General Mac-
Veagh handed in his resignation.[6]

On the night of October 24, O. P. McMains boarded a
Santa Fe train at Trinidad on his way back to Washington.[7]
The Maxwell hearing was in early November before A. R.
Dutton, of the attorney general's office. Under attack was the
northeast corner of the Elkins and Marmon survey, which,
if erroneous, would invalidate the entire north boundary. The
petition contended that the survey map's Chicorica Mesa, on
which the northeast corner turned, was a falsification; that
the real Maxwell north line was south of the Red (or Canadian) River in New Mexico. In rebuttal Springer submitted
affidavits from the well-known scout, trapper, and Indian
trader, Richens Lacy ("Uncle Dick") Wootton, and Jesús
Silva, a former employee and personal friend of Lucien B.
Maxwell. Both men testified that the Chicorica Mesa* of the
Elkins and Marmon survey was the correct one; they said
they had been with Cornelio Vigil when he built the boundary
mound on the mesa in 1843 and had pointed it out to Elkins
and Marmon in 1877.[8] A careful reading of their affidavits,
however, reveals serious errors in relation to distances and
directions which impugn their credibility and shows that
Wootton may not have been with Vigil and party at all.

A. R. Dutton could not evaluate from personal knowledge, of course, but he evidently was impressed by Frank
Springer's presentation. In his report Dutton said: "Upon the
whole matter my conclusion is, that a suit brought by the
United States to set aside the patent, would in all probability
fail."[9]

Although repulsed in the first skirmish, McMains did not
retreat in disorder. He moved to appeal to Dutton's superior,

---

*Apparently the settlers' petition held that Eagle Tail Mountain was
the real Chicorica Mesa, a contention that later was abandoned, but not
in favor of the Wootton-Silva version.

Acting Attorney General S. F. Philips. For his second venture into the civil law and its technicalities he retained two attorneys. Simultaneously he published in Washington on December 7 a pamphlet very critical of former Commissioner Williamson and his dealings with Maxwell officials. In his debut as a pamphleteer McMains clinched his points by citing the letter from Secretary Kirkwood recommending that suit be brought, in itself a criticism of Williamson, and claimed that the hearing had slighted the settlers' petition.

In late December the acting attorney general released his opinion upholding Dutton. But this second failure did not draw an admission of defeat from McMains either. He stayed in Washington, and his letters home expressed encouragement and confidence. Garfield's successor, President Chester A. Arthur, selected Benjamin Harrison Brewster for attorney general, and, after calling upon him, McMains came away, buoyant and hopeful.[10]

Meanwhile in Trinidad and Raton everyone awaited the arrival of mail-trains and telegrams for the latest advices. With every issue newspaper editors hoped for word before going to press. An editorial battle reached extremes between the *Raton Guard*, heir to the anti-grant policies of the *Comet*, and the *News and Press* of Raton, successor to the old *Cimarron News and Press*.[11]

The Dutton and Philips opinions left the advantage with the Maxwell Land Grant Company. Harry Whigham, secretary, warned some settlers on the north edge of Raton that they would be ejected if they did not pay the company. The threat was aimed at W. W. Boggs, who lived on the historic Willow Springs place;* that part of north Raton claimed by

---

* The source of the railroad's water supply, the place also had been the site of a stage station and a government forage station.

him was known as Boggstown. Boggs posted notices that he
was the rightful owner — anyone who bought from the company did so at his own risk and would be subject to a lawsuit.[12]
Some people thought Boggs was bluffing, but with the following result:

> Old man Boggs tried the effect of a little "higher law"
> at Raton the other day towards some parties who were
> proposing to lay off some ground which he claims and
> which is also claimed by the Maxwell Grant Company.
> After the parties had a square look into the Winchester
> carried by Boggs they said they were satisfied he was
> right about it.[13]

In Colorado, Olney Newell was sharply critical of
McMains in the *Trinidad Daily News*, shortly after the turn
of the year. Charging him with "blind insinuations" in his
pamphlet, the editorial went on:

> McMains is a "crank." He is as rattled on land titles as
> Guiteau [Garfield's assassin] is on theology.... Senator
> Teller of Colorado can do more for the people in a
> minute than this fellow McMains could in a lifetime; and
> he will not pass around his hat to raise a subscription
> either.... No doubt if one was sliding on the downward
> road that leads to perdition the Reverend McMains could
> snatch him from the wrath to come ... much better than
> attorney Yeaman [a Trinidad lawyer] could, but Yeaman
> would draw a brief that would put to shame this reverend
> "crank." That is all there is of it.[14]

Messrs. Lanstrum and Donaghe, editors of the *Raton
Guard*, severely upbraided Newell for his harsh tone, but they
were smitten by some of the same doubt, expressing their
misgivings more gently. Their comments were "... not
intended to reflect upon Mr. McMains, a gentleman, who has
without compensation, or without desiring it, done more
against the Maxwell Land Grant in the interest of the people,

than all others combined. . . . In our opinion, if he is guilty of any fault, it has been an error of the head — not of the heart."[15] In short, they wondered if the anti-granters should not obtain the guidance of first-class legal talent.[16]

The sounds of discontent reached McMains in Washington. Unannounced, he arrived in Raton in mid-February and tried to allay fears and pacify impatience. He asserted that the settlers' cause was far from lost; within a few days the government would move against the company. And he had a personal matter of concern: The Maxwell Land Grant Company had filed an ejectment action against him in the district court.[17]

Although he spent much time pleading for continued confidence, McMains found it good to be home. Mary was happy. In November she had visited for a while in the town of Springer, and in late December she had welcomed Oscar's brother-in-law, William P. Fishback, from Indianapolis, who had accompanied his son, Robert, who wanted to set up in the cattle business in New Mexico. Robert purchased some cattle with E. C. Griffith and planned to pass the winter at a ranch on the Nolán Grant near Springer. McMains was pleased to have his nephew try it as a rancher but was disappointed to have missed his brother-in-law. Perhaps his encouragement had prompted the Fishbacks to invest in cattle there in the first place.[18]

On Saturday, February 25, 1882, O. P. McMains received support for his reassurances of success in Washington. A telegram from Attorney General Brewster asked him to return at once for the final hearing in the Maxwell matter, set for the following Wednesday.* The settlers' representative caught the evening train out of Raton, expecting to be back in a couple of weeks or so as the bearer of good tidings.[19]

---

*Perhaps unknown to McMains, a Pennsylvania attorney, Pierce Archer, who was interested in New Mexico and Colorado mining properties, helped secure the action (Harold H. Dunham, "Coloradans and the Maxwell Grant," *The Colorado Magazine* 32 [April 1955]: 135).

Chapter 7

❦

The Grant Company Defied

FOR ANTI-GRANTERS the intervening days were not idle ones. If the government brought suit, months, even years, might be consumed in litigation; so the settlers and the grant company persisted in their local struggles. A company agent tried to persuade anti-granters to buy their places or leave. W. W. Boggs, dubbed "Major General" by his admirers, still held the fort at Willow Springs, although the district court decided in the company's favor for possession. It was said that McMains himself soon would be evicted* from his ranch near Raton.[1]

For some time prominent opponents of the Maxwell Grant had talked of organizing an anti-grant party to provide unity and present its own ticket to the county voters. Recent developments had given the idea wide acceptance. A call went out for a meeting at Raton on March 22, and settlers on the Colorado portion of the grant were asked to attend.[2] Success might force the Maxwell people to seek a means of politi-

---

*The case had been taken on a change of venue to Santa Fe County (*William T. Thornton and E. Platt Stratton, Receivers,* v. *O. P. McMains, Ejectment,* No. 137, Record, Civil and Criminal, Colfax County, p. 167).

cal expression, thus transforming the issue from a private to a public one, thereby helping McMains' cause.

Settlers in Colorado had passed some "rattling" anti-grant resolutions which, among other things, gave strong support to McMains. Those were forwarded to the president, the attorney general, and the Colorado senators. Much to the gratification of the Stonewall people, Senator Henry M. Teller obtained passage of a resolution calling for investigation of the Maxwell boundaries.[3]

To McMains' delight, Attorney General Brewster decided to file suit against the Maxwell Land Grant Company.[4] McMains, exhausted, headed for Raton and a pleasant pastoral life, confident that the course of justice would be unimpeded. En route he stopped over in West Las Animas, where friends awaited an imminent Supreme Court decision on the Moffat Patents, which had been pending for nearly two years.[5]

A later train carried McMains through the night towards the Raton Mountains. The lights of Trinidad were left behind; after the long pull over Raton Pass, he arrived at Raton the next morning, Sunday, March 12. His was no heroic entry. A sick man met by a few friends, McMains went directly to his ranch and bed.[6]

Lack of confidence in McMains vanished when news spread that the suit to vacate the Maxwell patent would be tried in the United States Circuit Court, District of Colorado, because the vulnerable north boundary of the grant lay in that state. Most anti-granters believed that the Elkins and Marmon survey would be erased from the map.[7]

For a while happy excitement obscured the immense responsibility on the shoulders of the anti-granters. The case would require incontrovertible proof of error and fraud. Just what McMains promised the attorney general is not known.

But in the hint of victory it was exhilarating to think that Washington was waking up to the land scandals in the Southwest.

The anti-grant political meeting convened on the night of March 22 in Bayne and Frank's Hall, Raton. Not fully recovered, McMains came in for his first public appearance since his return, and a large crowd greeted him and other anti-grant leaders. Under the presidency of J. H. Hunt, the first item of business was a unanimously passed set of resolutions. The several "whereas" clauses denounced the grant company; paid tribute to McMains, who "with a lean purse, attacked and persistently fought to a successful issue"; and termed the lawsuit "one of the grandest victories of right against might on record."[8] Then it was resolved:

> That this convention, representing the settlers within the fraudulent boundaries of the Maxwell Grant, pledges itself to make any reasonable sacrifice of time and money to carry forward to a speedy decision the suit now ordered to set aside the Maxwell Grant for fraud.
>
> That the Maxwell Company officials, as it is only a few months before their patent will be tested in the United States Court of Colorado, be, and hereby are respectfully requested to desist from bull-dozing, as such proceeding, now that the settlers have a case, is likely to be resented and make trouble.[9]

McMains then spoke, his slight, carefully dressed figure dominating an audience in which there were some who had doubted and others who still were skeptical. But now he could tell everybody firsthand in a message of faith, service, and ultimate victory. Personalities were not, probably could not have been, left out: he condemned the tactics of Frank Springer and scornfully referred to several local pro-granters. A. R. Dutton he dismissed as an insignificant underling, while lauding Attorney General Brewster. Noisy applause interrupted him frequently and praised him when he sat down. Other speakers followed, and then the hall resounded to three lusty cheers in McMains' honor. As a final recognition, the meeting authorized him to take charge of organizing anti-grant clubs in all the voting precincts.[10]

The Raton *News and Press* defended the Maxwell Company and sarcastically told its readers that the "crank" McMains would run as an independent for delegate to Congress in the fall election. Maxwell officials ignored the resolutions, feeling that Brewster had said merely that suit would be brought; it still had to be filed and official notification given.[11] They could see no reason to knuckle under. They, too, had cleared serious obstacles in the past, finally obtaining a patent to the grant.

Any doubt about the Maxwell Company's response was dispelled when writs of ejectment were served on W. W. Boggs and O. P. McMains. When Sheriff A. C. Wallace went out to McMains' ranch he took five deputies with him. McMains was not there, but his wife was. She defied them to put her out, and they contented themselves with driving off the horse herd to a Raton livery stable.[12]

Thus was the gauntlet thrown down before McMains and the anti-granters. And the challenge was accepted. The *Raton Guard* ridiculed the size of the posse, berated Wallace for going in McMains' absence, and ignored the fact that the sheriff was carrying out the orders of the court. Some of McMains' friends started collecting money to pay the judgment ($300 damages and $40.15 court costs) against him, but he publicly declined to accept:

> I wish no subscription to pay the judgment against me. I will give my friends a lien on my herd of horses for the amount due, and I will soon make up this sum by having the Nolan Grant thrown open for settlement as public domain.
>
> O. P. MCMAINS[13]

Announcement in such an off-hand way that he would also take on the 575,000-acre Nolán Claim No. 39 was a major development; there was a hint of his being hired to do it. Given to Gervacio Nolán by Governor Manuel Armijo in 1845, No. 39 was on the plains south of the Maxwell and east of the Mora Grants. Nolán also held another grant, No. 48 on the south bank of the Arkansas River in Colorado that was known to McMains when he rode circuit out of Pueblo. Robert M. Fishback, McMains' nephew, ran cattle on the Nolán No. 39.[14]

Riding down to Cimarron, the Colfax County seat, McMains was on hand for the next move against him. The authorities announced a sale of his horses on April 19. He responded by calling a meeting at which he would discuss conditions on the Maxwell Grant. Many people would have come to hear him even if he were a poor speaker, but his mastery of the spoken word was a great incentive.

About 8 P.M. on April 4 a crowd filled a room in the county clerk's building. McMains first told them that some anti-granters had wired the attorney general, asking if he could stop the ejectments. Brewster replied that he could not until the Maxwell case was in court, but he added: " 'I consider the proceedings of ejectment against the settlers, as suit has been ordered . . . to vacate the patent on account of fraud, to be *unjust* and *impolitic*.' "[15]

But the main issue was the horse sale. Warming up, McMains castigated the sheriff for having moved with "indecent haste," and bypassed the fact that the law officer had no choice. He thought the sheriff should serve no writs until the Maxwell case had been tried. About the sale, he was vague, inviting everyone to see for themselves if the company's "bulldozing" would be tolerated.[16]

In pro-grant quarters McMains was accused of being an "agitator" endeavoring to organize a mob. His defenders retorted that he was preparing for self-protection, a course which any man who was not a fool would follow.[17]

Two weeks later little groups gathered on street corners in Raton. Gradually more than 200 men converged on the place of assembly — presumably Bayne and Frank's Hall. It was the night before the horse sale, and both Anglo and Mexican settlers were there, along with McMains and the sheriff. After a call to order by J. H. Hunt, resolutions were unanimously passed describing the ejectments as persecutions and pledging funds for McMains. Hunt blasted accusation in the town that the men seated before him were a law-defying mob; they simply sought to protect themselves against injustice. Then he presented McMains to the appreciative crowd.

The anti-grant champion declared it to be the proudest day of his manhood: how heartening to know that men would defend their convictions, whatever the hazards. He called for calm, cool, intelligent consultation, but he promptly forgot his own advice. When he finished ripping into George Canis, editor of the *Raton News and Press*, he recalled that occasion in 1876 when Clay Allison and friends dumped the press and type of that paper's predecessor into the Cimarron River. However, the " 'old thing' " should not be destroyed again; if left alone it would really help the settlers and eventually would fall apart by itself.*

Throughout, McMains drew upon a broad range of oratorical technique, and applause interrupted him many times. As a climax he conjured up visions of the next day's horse sale and played skillfully on receptive emotions. When he asked if he were to be protected, the assurance — " 'You bet!' " — came from the crowd. Would he be avenged if harm came from the Maxwell people? The answer came in unqualified shouts: "We protect him who protects us. They harm you, they'll hang."[18]

---

*After the destruction incident, Springer and Morley had the following week's edition printed in Colorado. Meanwhile they found the old press of the extinct *Cimarron News* (its office burned in 1871) and restored it with a couple of new parts, so the *News and Press* was barely interrupted (Norman Cleaveland, *The Morleys: Young Upstarts on the Southwest Frontier* [Albuquerque, N. M.: Calvin Horn Publisher, 1971], p. 118.

McMains sat down amid the anger, excitement, and applause that filled the hall. In an apparently surprise move Hunt called Sheriff Wallace to the platform. Wallace's position was unenviable. He began by saying he agreed with his " 'friend' McMains," that the Maxwell Company was " 'false as hell.' " But he was worried that tomorrow's business would be an ugly collision; he had his bondsmen to consider and his duty to carry out the court's orders. Advising restraint, he read from the statute providing a year in prison or a $300 fine for obstructing the law. Someone shouted, "Damn cheap," and the crowd laughed.

The meeting was out of control; minds were made up that McMains would not be dispossessed. Wallace tried to go on in the face of strong heckling but finally gave up when the crowd called in unison: "Down with him! McMains! McMains!"[19]

During the uproar McMains returned to the rostrum and crystallized opposition to Wallace's plea for moderation. There had been no talk of violence, he said. So why was it said that troops would arrive from Santa Fe on the morning train? Some men in the audience had faced worse things and would again to protect their property. But McMains was careful to recognize that violence, unless forced on them, would hurt their cause.

There was a hint of concern that their ardor could be cooled, as their confidence had weakened while he was in Washington. He referred to " 'his mob' " — an inference that Hunt tried to avoid — and declared he would be their leader as long as they wanted him. Then he invited only anti-grant men to the "business meeting" at his ranch the next day.

Vigorous applause and cries of approbation accompanied him to his seat,* and the *Guard* reported that "the people

---

*After McMains spoke, Juan Francisco Córdova addressed the crowd in Spanish for about thirty minutes.

would have listened to him until the 'break of day.' "[20] The meeting was a personal triumph, but his oratory had more than a trace of demagoguery, which started the alienation of some influential supporters.

Wednesday, April 19, 1882, dawned brightly over the great mesas, and Eagle Tail Mountain was clear on the southern horizon. Around 9:30 people began to arrive at the McMains ranch. By noon the gabled, white frame house was surrounded by wagons, buggies, and tethered saddle horses. About 150 to 200 people awaited the sale and ejectment, which was called for 2 P.M.

Sheriff Wallace and his deputy, Mason (Mace) T. Bowman, rode in with the horse herd, and Wallace quickly announced the sale was open. A voice in the crowd called out, " 'Shall this stock be sold or not, gentlemen?' " In unison the people shouted, " 'No!' " The sheriff had to go through the motions, at least, so he read the documents of the court and asked for someone to bid on the mare " 'next to the fence.' " No one said a word. So ended the horse sale.

Next on the agenda was ejectment of McMains and his wife, who apparently stayed in the house during the sale. At that moment a committee of settlers came forward and informed the sheriff that he must go no further. They warned him that if McMains were molested again the anti-granters would pay their respects to Maxwell officials in Cimarron. The law officers acquiesced, and gradually the crowd departed.[21]

Probably violence was avoided because the law officers did not persist. McMains said he eschewed violence, but his words aroused dangerous sentiments nonetheless. (The flaws in that combination were seen on the Poñil the night Cruz Vega faced the masked riders.) The men who obstructed the sheriff that morning thought their reasons unassailable. To speak to them of the rights of the grant company would have been a waste of time. Court actions against Boggs and

McMains had been started before the attorney general agreed to file suit, and now the anti-granters demanded forbearance at a time when the company was in no mood to practice it. Years later a company officer said that "the settlers would have reinstated McMains and no doubt done great bodily injury to officials of the Company and great damage to its property. In fact, open threats of this were made."[22]

Following that dangerous incident, a lull continued into June. McMains purchased a fine brood mare, provoking the *Raton Guard* to remark: ". . . if the 'Agitator' keeps on buying horses the next land grant sale at his ranch will be large."[23]

Summer brought political straws on the wind. A county anti-grant convention was scheduled, and the opposition stamped the anti-grant party as also anti-railroad. The charge was denied, although there may have been some truth in the allegation since general talk against monopolies had linked the Santa Fe Railroad with the Maxwell Grant[24] (perhaps reflecting the growing movement that would culminate in railroad regulation under the Interstate Commerce Commission Act of 1887). But anti-railroad feeling in Colfax County was incidental to the test of strength between the settlers and the grant company.

Early in the political maneuvering an event occurred that helped the anti-grant movement. On the evening of June 17 Territorial Governor Lionel A. Sheldon came to Raton, where he urged recruitment of a militia company in Colfax County. For many anti-granters that meant but one thing — the use of military force against them. That opinion may have been strengthened by the fact that the governor's daughter-in-law was the sister of Frank Remington Sherwin, president of the Maxwell Land Grant Company.[25] In fairness, it should be noted that Sheldon's administration was plagued by lawless violence, Colfax County being only one of the trouble spots, and the governor responded across the territory with militia companies. Thirty of them were ready for action.[26] In any event, the *Raton Guard* sounded the tocsin with an extreme editorial by McMains:

> In Colfax county, especially, there must be a standing army or a fallen grant. In view of the suit to vacate the patent to the Maxwell Grant for fraud in the survey, the Attorney General of the United States is of the opinion that ejections of tenants by the Maxwell Company is [*sic*] unjust and impolitic; and it has always required the military power to compel a spirited people to submit to injustice; and, as the settlers of Colfax county are spirited, the die is cast, the Rubicon is crossed and the Colfax county *infant-ry* will soon be tearing Jordan loose! . . .
>
> Come on, then, with your Legalized Land Grant Mob, and, in the poetical language of the lamented Thomas Corwin,* we will "welcome you with bloody hands to hospitable graves."[27]

---

* The closing quotation (not an exact one) was from a speech by Senator Thomas Corwin, of Ohio, opposing the war with Mexico in February 1847: "If I were a Mexican, I would tell you, 'Have you not room in your own country to bury your dead men? If you come into mine, we will greet you with bloody hands, and welcome you to hospitable graves.' " Familiarity with Corwin's speeches may have come to McMains through his brother-in-law, William P. Fishback, whose father had been appointed by Corwin (while governor of Ohio), as a judge of the Court of Common Pleas in 1841. And, of course, McMains as a youth and Corwin may have been personally acquainted. See U.S., *Congressional Globe*, 29th Cong., 2nd sess., February 11, 1847, Appendix, p. 217; Joseph Thomas, ed., *Universal Pronouncing Dictionary of Biography and Mythology*, 5th ed. (Philadelphia: J. P. Lippincott and Company, 1930), p. 722; Willis Miller Kemper, *Genealogy of the Fishback Family in America* (New York: Thomas Madison Taylor, 1914), p. 132.

Chapter 8

❧

Editorials, Politics, and Lawsuits

A FEW DAYS AFTER the alarm cried against the militia, O. P. McMains became more deeply committed to the anti-grant movement. He acquired the *Raton Guard* and, with the plant and equipment, revived his *Raton Comet*. The first edition of the new *Comet* appeared on the streets on July 14, 1882, with the old motto, "Open Warfare Against Secret Fraud," at the masthead and a leading editorial entitled "Greeting to Our Friends, Defiance to Our Foes" developed in explicit terms:

> *The* fraud, by way of eminence, that we propose to fight — a towering, majestic, 2,000,000 acres fraud — is, of course, the Maxwell Land Grant. A more glaring, impudent, outrageous steal was never perpetrated. Instead of "fifteen to eighteen" leagues which the original grantees swore their grant did not exceed, here is a grant of about four hundred leagues. Manifestly the present size of the Maxwell Grant indicates unwholesome obesity and fatty degeneration of the heart. It has fed on fraud and fraud will kill it. Its demise, however, can be hastened by newspaper, as well as legal, treatment, and hence THE COMET will go for the diseased and unwieldy corporiety of the Maxwell Grant hot and heavy.[1]

The old enemy was not the only foe; the Nolán Claim No. 39 would be subjected to attack because it "is public

[92]

domain by final act of Congress."[2] In other words, when Gervacio Nolán accepted from Congress No. 48 in Colorado, he relinquished No. 39 in New Mexico. "Fraudulent entries on the public domain and the unlawful fencing of enormous tracts of the same" would be given rough treatment by the *Comet*, a reference to big cattle outfits with their claims on water holes that gave control of thousands of acres on the plains.[3]

The enlarged scope and impassioned tone of his editorials left no doubt that McMains had gone far beyond a question of land ownership. He saw the troubles on Mexican grants and the public domain as part of a nationwide battle against injustice, greed, and corruption, and he accepted local leadership against those evils.* His appraisal could be rationalized as wrestling with the devil in a different guise, but his matured social consciousness spoke in an idiom well known in post-Civil War America — the protest in behalf of the common man against grasping corporations. Not many years before he had lauded the arrival of railroads and urged industries to hasten westward. Now, disillusioned, he opposed the abuses of wealth and privilege by direct action and through the *Comet* in prose and poetry sometimes inspired, often banal, always lively, and occasionally alarming.

W. W. Boggs was still ensconced in his log house when the *Comet* carried a conversation with him about Boggstown, which concluded with the old point that Lucien Maxwell did not believe his grant extended north of Red River. It was not easy to prove, and the need to convince a United States district judge in Colorado was fast approaching.[4] But McMains

---

* The inclusive and integrated scope of the struggle as seen by McMains anticipated by several years a similar view that helped organize Farmers' Alliances in Colfax County. See Robert W. Larson, *New Mexico Populism: A Study of Radical Protest in a Western Territory* (Boulder: Colorado Associated University Press, 1974), pp. 21–34, for the Alliance movement there.

disapproved of another lawsuit in New Mexico, because it would be very difficult to show all the boundaries of the Maxwell as anti-granters saw them.[5] An original bill was filed August 22, 1882, in the United States Circuit Court, District of Colorado. Attorney General Brewster focused on the point that the north boundary of the Maxwell should not be in Colorado. If made to stick, another patent would be necessary and probably would be based on twenty-two square leagues.[6]

A visit from William P. Fishback in August provided a pleasant diversion for McMains, and the Indianapolis lawyer received a lot of gratuitous information about his brother-in-law. The two men went to a meeting in Raton on the night of August 19 at McAuliffe and Ferguson's Hall, where the visitor realized that McMains was the guiding spirit of a popular and potentially powerful movement. The resolutions submitted were his creation, and, following the usual practice, he addressed the crowd on the expected, familiar, and approved subject — the grant. Then the chairman called upon Fishback to say something; his remarks were "short and appropriate," without comment on local matters.[7]

A mass meeting of the Anti-Grant Party at Raton on September 15 produced a ticket of candidates. Few were surprised that O. P. McMains headed it as candidate for representative from Colfax County in the territorial legislature.* The Anti-Grant Party supplanted the Democratic Party in

---

*An interesting choice was that for sheriff — Mace Bowman, the deputy who assisted in the sale and ejectment fiasco at McMains' ranch. He was widely admired as a man fast on the draw, who had met the formidable Clay Allison on even terms. And he was an anti-granter, having squatted on a claim on the Nolán No. 39 within an enclosure fenced by the Red River Cattle Company. Those qualities prompted people to regard his part in the episode at McMains' place as simply in the line of duty — an explanation not accepted from Sheriff Wallace (*Las Vegas Daily Gazette*, September 24, 1882; *Raton Range*, July 22, 1887; *Raton Comet*, June 15, 1883).

Colfax County, making it awkward for an anti-granter to stay with the Republicans. Running against McMains for the legislative seat was Colonel J. W. Dwyer, an important cowman and staunch Republican.[8]

McMains campaigned vigorously, having with him the hopes of hundreds of small farmers and ranchers as he stumped Colfax County. In Colorado pro- and anti-granters watched and commented on politics across the line. In the *Trinidad Democrat* appeared this sample:

> "Hurrah for McMains!" said an Irishman, and enthusiastic admirer of "Little Mack" in Raton the other day. "What are you yelling for him for?" inquired a representative of the Raton News and Press, "you can't elect him." "Arrah, be jabers, we'll mack manes* to do so at all hazards."[9]

Little Mack was unable to hit the hustings continuously. A telegram called him to Washington about October 1, but he was back in the local fray before the month was out.[10]

During October two incidents intended to be politically embarrassing for McMains revived old problems. At a Methodist Episcopal Conference someone asked Bishop Bowman about the relationship of O. P. McMains to the New Mexico Missions; to which the bishop replied, " 'He is not a member of this mission, and so far as we can ascertain, he is not a member of the church† in this territory.' "[11] Although McMains had not had a specific appointment since 1878, his position as traveling elder had not been withdrawn. However, McMains had become the leader of a serious secular movement and now a candidate for the legislature. So far from the

---

* The surname frequently was misspelled MacManes or McManes.

† McMains evidently believed he was in good standing and fully authorized to perform ministerial functions. In July, for example, he had conducted a funeral service in Raton (*Raton Guard*, July 7, 1882).

clerical orbit had he moved that he had, in effect, abandoned
the ministry. Thus, Bishop Bowman may have been glad to
seize upon a fait accompli in issuing his statement of sever-
ance.

Late in the afternoon of October 30, 1882, newsboys
peddled a special edition of the *News and Press* on the streets
of Raton. Purchasers were handed a seven-page supplement,
and many were infuriated to read that editor George Canis
had resurrected the Cruz Vega murder accusations against
McMains. McMains, followed by angry anti-granters and
many of the curious, set out to find Canis. Someone spotted
him having supper at a nearby hotel, and McMains and his
friends entered the dining room just as he was leaving. When
asked whether he had files of the old Cimarron paper, with
editorials supporting McMains' innocence, Canis said no. That
produced such an uproar that everyone was asked to leave the
hotel in deference to some sick people in the rooms overhead.

The two editors and the crowd walked to the office of
the pro-grant paper, and as many as could wedged into the
place. Stepping inside the railing by his desk, Canis smoked
and faced McMains, who said they might just as well have a
mass meeting then and there, rather than later that night as
he had planned. Turning to the crowd, McMains pleaded for
his reputation, acknowledging he had lured Vega to the cornfield but declaring he was unable to control the other men.
When he demanded a retraction, Canis said he would make
one, sat down at his desk, and wrote. Finished, he stood up,
read the letter aloud, and then shook hands with McMains.
Mace Bowman, deputy sheriff and deputy United States
marshal, asked Canis if he made the retraction voluntarily.
Canis assured the deputy that he had — a questionable admission under the circumstances.[12]

McMains, however, was satisfied, and the encounter
quickly collapsed. Canis asked for protection back to his hotel.
A day or two later he and his printer left Raton for Las Vegas.[13]

Sheriff Wallace took the precaution of deputizing seventy-five men because of possible reprisal by anti-granters, but election day was not marred by major violence.[14] The returns added up to a clear victory for McMains and the Anti-Grant ticket. A banquet in Raton celebrated the triumph. McMains had the place of honor, and his oratory entertained the guests. Never had the future been more cloudless for the settlers. Headed for federal district court was the lawsuit to vacate the Maxwell patent, and, with their representative in the New Mexico Legislative Assembly, the cause might be advanced in that stronghold of large property interests — Santa Fe.

Being a representative-elect brought a minor, though customary, distinction. More and more frequently he was addressed as "the Hon." O. P. McMains, but never would that supersede the familiar "Rev."* Some people used the clerical title in sincere affection; others employed it from force of habit; his enemies found it useful to twist to their own purposes — opposition papers mentioned him now and then as the Rev. (?) O. P. McMains.[15]

The fledgling lawmaker did not have to assume his duties at once. The assembly met biennially, the next session not convening until early 1884. The lawsuit required his presence

---

*Opposition editors often ridiculed his clerical background, as, for example, in this piece that appeared in the *Trinidad Daily Reporter* on February 3, 1883: "The junior editor of the COLFAX COUNTY STOCKMAN, on his trip over the mountain the other night, went to sleep and had a dream. It was that [he] died, went to Heaven, and while there another new-comer was announced from Raton. The 'n.-c.' came up with a pompous air to where God Almighty and Jesus Christ were sitting on their thrones, and introduced himself as O. P. McMains. The Supreme Being gazed at him a moment, to make sure that he was not mistaken, and then turning to the younger member of the firm, remarked, 'Get down, my son, and let the gentleman have your seat.' It was but a dream."

in Denver, where A. W. Brazee, the United States attorney, formulated the government's charge of fraudulent extension of the Maxwell Grant into Colorado by alteration of maps, plats, and field notes.* So as to be unhampered, McMains gave up his beloved *Comet*, turning it over to his partner, C. B. Adams.[16]

As winter faded, settlers in the hill country planned for raising funds to assist in the lawsuit. Committees were appointed, and a man named McPherson (apparently not related to Mrs. Mary McPherson) was sent out from Raton as a liaison man. On March 10 he predicted fine success and was elated by the money already collected in Colorado.[17]

McMains was in Denver, returning the same weekend that McPherson made his report. On Monday evening an "uncommonly large crowd" in McAuliffe and Ferguson's Hall heard him summarize the latest lawsuit matters. Though generally optimistic, he did not hide his concern over the government's slowness, and he admitted some nervousness over its plan for special counsel. He favored a Washington attorney, James Coleman† (whom he probably had used in the capital), or some other lawyer who would have the people's confidence.[18]

A telegram cleared the air over government special counsel early in May: J. A. Bentley,‡ former commissioner of

---

* The Justice Department filed its bill of complaint on August 22, 1882, and the Maxwell attorneys answered on November 9. Brazee's affidavit was dated December 29, 1882.

† In August 1882, James Coleman and I. H. N. McPherson had been appointed special assistants (without compensation) to the U.S. District Attorney for Colorado (S. N. Phillips, Acting Attorney General to Coleman and McPherson, August 16, 1882, Transcript of Record). This may have been the McPherson who was soliciting funds on the grant.

‡ Bentley was a member of the Denver law firm of Bentley and Vail (Harold H. Dunham, "Coloradans and the Maxwell Grant," *The Colorado Magazine* 32 [April 1955]: 135).

patents, had been appointed. The *Comet* praised the choice, and McMains was satisfied, going to Denver at once for conferences.[19]

In a letter to his brother Robert, in the latter part of March, McMains wrote about the lawsuit and himself with revealing candor: "I cannot but smile when I think of my big lawsuit involving millions, that if successful, will set me up and your patent [?], that, successful, will set you up. It's a long lane that has no turn. . . ."[20] In his public utterances he was never quite so frank. Success would set him up in the sense that possession of his ranch could no longer be disputed by the Maxwell Company, but the pace of recent months was proving too much for McMains.

Never of strong physique, he was forced into inactivity for quite a few days. "Overwork has broken him down," was the way the *Comet* put it. Recuperation was not fast. On April 4 he spent a short time in Raton, but weakness prevented his staying long or doing much.[21]

With the lawsuit gaining momentum and the legislative session only six months off, McMains needed help and ardently hoped that brother Bob would become his partner on the ranch. More personal factors* had their appeal as well:

> One thing is certain: as we have no children my wife and I long to have you all within reach of us that life may not be so unlively around the home precinct. . . . My wife is so anxious to be near you all; she loves not many but loves her chosen few with strong affection and has set her heart upon my brother's wife and children. She & I send our love to you all.[22]

It was not to be. Bob could not make a quick change, and his wife did not want to leave California.[23]

---

*Word from brother Robert that their younger brother, Billy, had died, brought sorrow to McMains.

Oscar and Mary McMains were not entirely cut off from family, however. Not far away on Tinaja Creek his nephew, Robert Fishback, enjoyed success as a rancher and had been joined by William P. Kappes,* his sister Mary's fiancé. And in May niece Mary, now a bride, came out from Indianapolis, followed in August† by her father, William P. Fishback, and the bridegroom's brother, Henry.[24]

In late July the Maxwell case quickened. McMains went to Trinidad to brief Assistant Attorney General John C. Fay and Mr. André Brewster, just arrived from Washington, on the Maxwell north boundary. Then Fay went to Santa Fe to examine public records, while Brewster went to El Paso to question some people allegedly familiar with landmarks on the grant's boundaries.[25]

Trinidad was the center of activity, where testimony was taken before U.S. Commissioner Edward J. Hubbard, commencing on September 18, 1883. Although McMains was called on to testify, his performance was not helpful. It was essential to the government's case that the flat-topped mountain south of Trinidad be shown to be the Raton Peak and not Fisher's Peak, the promontory presumably climbed by Captain Waldemar Fisher,‡ of the Army of the West, in August 1846. The real Fisher's Peak purportedly was farther south near the crest of Raton Pass. Since the Elkins and Marmon north line turned generally westward on the summit of

---

* Kappes also was a lawyer and maintained an office in Raton, sharing quarters with McMains' friend, Judge J. H. Hunt, justice of the peace (*Raton Comet*, April 20, 1883).

† On his own place McMains bought some cattle that summer at $33 per head and sold his lower hay vega for $1,500.

‡ The correct spelling is Fischer, but common usage has changed it.

Raton (Fisher's) Peak. The view is from a point near Trinidad, Colorado, looking south. The peak is allegedly on the north line of the Maxwell Grant. That it is the promontory named for Captain Fisher is extremely dubious.

the peak, its true location would determine the location of that boundary. McMains could not answer directly about the identity of the mountain: he had not been on nor seen the alleged corner as set by the survey.[26]

But other witnesses had been there and were not so vague, providing some very encouraging testimony for the anti-granters. Albert W. Archibald, surveyor and one of Trinidad's first settlers (1861), clearly stated his belief that the original markers of the Maxwell boundary had been moved, an opinion that was rather widely shared. Knowing the region since 1858, he was convinced that the true Fisher's Peak was a few miles to the south near the crest of Raton Pass; grant claimants had boldly moved the marker on it northward to the top of Raton Peak and succeeded in making the altered place-name stick.°

An old trapper by the name of Calvin Jones was familiar with the area from 1846 and had herded sheep for Lucien Maxwell on the headwaters of the Purgatoire River in Colorado. He said Maxwell told him to take the sheep south at once if anyone objected to their running there. Jones felt that the north line was not in Colorado but along the drainage of Red River in New Mexico.[27] That kind of testimony was related to disagreement about the Chicorica Mesa; the Maxwell people insisted that Raton Peak, which they called Fisher's Peak, was a part of the mesa — a contention that was vigorously denied by the grant's opponents.

A major government witness, Faustin Jaramillo, former employee of Lucien Maxwell, was closely cross-examined by Frank Springer, company counsel, concerning his insistence that Maxwell had had a private survey of his north line run along the Red and Vermejo rivers to Costilla Peak in 1867. That line, of course, was in New Mexico, and Jaramillo also testified that in 1854 Maxwell showed him the northeast corner of his claim near the head of Uña de Gato Creek. Unfortunately, Jaramillo could not produce a plat in evidence, but his testimony was not shaken by defense counsel's probings.[28]

The testimony of those government witnesses seriously weakened the affidavits of Wootton and Silva, the primary company attestants. A growing fear of inability to fend off the charges of fraud prompted Maxwell counsel to develop a new defense based on the decision in *Tameling* v. *The*

°As late as the summer of 1974 the writer heard the story that "Uncle Dick" Wootton had admitted that he moved the marker northward, using two yoke of oxen, and that the Maxwell Company paid him $2,000 to do it.

United States Freehold Land and Emigration Company with its argument of a grant *de novo*. It was Christmastime 1883* when McMains first learned of Springer's shift in strategy, which he had fervently hoped would not happen, and Bentley's failure to react quickly and positively against it implanted in McMains' mind doubts about the skill, and even the integrity, of the prosecution.[29]

In early 1884 the government filed an amended bill to limit the Maxwell Grant to twenty-two square leagues within the outboundaries — the way Congress had disposed of the Vigil and St. Vrain Grant. McMains supported this bill but advised that the decision of Secretary Cox, which had made that very point and which was never authoritatively reversed, had not been given sufficient emphasis. Special counsel Bentley, however, was disinclined to give it more weight, although he did mention it. And he said the government would prove, if the court said the grant was valid for all land within the exterior lines, that the company had fraudulently taken over hundreds of thousands of acres outside, including 270,000 acres in Colorado.[30] Such ambience, added to Bentley's down play of the Tameling decision, turned McMains' doubts about him to open distrust.

---

*A personal legal matter also had McMains' attention at the end of the year. He was considering a libel suit against C. F. Martin, editor of the *Colfax County Stockman* published at Springer (Trinidad *Weekly Advertiser*, December 31, 1883).

Chapter 9

❧

The Crow Creek Ranch

THE HON. O. P. McMAINS, representative from Colfax County, arrived a week late for the Twenty-sixth Legislative Assembly, which had convened in the Governor's Palace at Santa Fe on February 18, 1884; but, according to some, Democratic stocks went up three points when he was sworn in. His maiden speech was quite unrelated to land grant matters.[1] In fact, most of his work as a legislator pertained to other problems. He enjoyed considerable public attention as one of seven men who strongly but unsuccessfully opposed a bill providing for a new capitol building in Santa Fe, the measure being one of Thomas Benton Catron's pets.* The valiant seven were warmly praised by the Las Vegas *Daily Optic* as "men of courage," which probably was the only time the *Optic* ever printed a word of approval for McMains.[2]

In mid-March, Edward E. Furman, of Grant County, offered a resolution and memorial pertaining to land grants, but only the unastute could have doubted McMains' authorship. It was a hard-hitting piece excoriating six land grants as

---

*Catron, a major investor in New Mexico land grants, was a member of the territorial council from Santa Fe County.

probable frauds,* and it cited several men (including Thomas Benton Catron) for alleged involvement in those frauds. A newspaper reporter said he would like to be on deck when Catron got hold of it, and McMains was lambasted as a political crank and denounced for taking advantage of his legislative immunity to call men thieves, scoundrels, and other terms.[3] The latter charge was absurd, of course. He had said those things many times as a private citizen. Someone had never been up to Colfax County to listen.

A motion to table the resolution and memorial was passed by one vote. However, the question of land grants could not be disposed of so simply, so a joint committee was authorized to memorialize Congress for an investigation of private land claims and a speedy settlement of those controversies. The members of the joint committee were either pro-grant or neutral; four of the men from the House had voted against McMains' memorial, while the fifth abstained, and Catron was one of the three picked from the Council. In that way the representative from Colfax County was kept from getting a condemnation of the land grant imbroglio from the territorial legislature. His friends made a last effort to salvage something by sending his memorial to William M. Springer, chairman of the House Committee on Territories, to present to Congress, but little hope was placed on that route.[4] The *Las Vegas Gazette* summed up by rewriting a selection from Mother Goose:

> Humpty-dumpty sat on a wall
> Humpty-dumpty had a great fall
> Camp meetin' shoutin' and hard-boiled brains
> Can't resurrect Rev'rend O. P. McMains.[5]

---

* The grants were: the Vigil and St. Vrain in Colorado; the Maxwell and Sangre de Cristo Grants in Colorado and New Mexico; and in New Mexico the Uña de Gato tract, the Mora, and the Nolán No. 39.

The Maxwell and Adjacent Grants

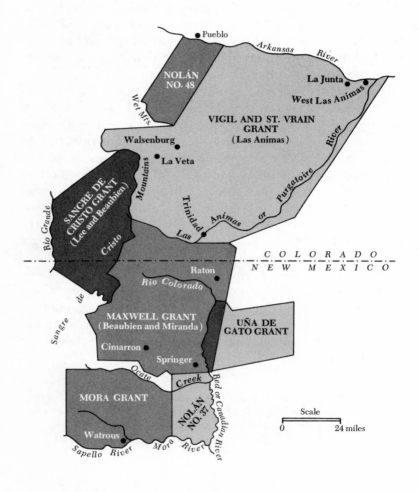

After adjournment O. P. McMains went home to his wife, his constituents, and the Maxwell business. He was apprehensive of his reception by the public because of some criticism and disapproval, which the *Raton Independent* alluded to in coming to his defense:

> The New Mexican REVIEW calls Mr. McMains a crank. This is cruel. But the honorable gentleman has the consolation of knowing that he is not the first Christian to be abused. Yet it does look a little cranky for a man to devote his time and money to serve the dear people, without hope of reward or even thanks in this world, unless we have firm belief in laying up of treasures for the sweet by-and-by.[6]

That helped. The *Independent's* editor, J. C. Holmes, was bound to neither side of the land grant issue but called the shots as he saw them. From afar off came a report giving

---

The Mexican land grants shown here were made in the years 1835–1845, but the boundary lines were set by American surveys in the period 1863–1877. The earliest was the Mora, dating from 1835 and awarded to seventy-six individuals. It was the only colony grant in the group. Five others, all approved by Governor Manuel Armijo from 1841 to 1845, were of indeterminate status under Mexican law because of the ambiguity of the official documents. On June 21, 1860, Congress confirmed, in addition to the Mora, the Beaubien and Miranda (Maxwell) Grant and the Lee and Beaubien (Sangre de Cristo) Grant, made in 1841 and 1843 respectively, but no indication of their size or status under Mexican law was given. In the same act, however, Congress restricted the Vigil and St. Vrain (Las Animas) Grant, made in 1843, to twenty-two square leagues, or ca. 96,000 acres. The Nolán Grant, in Colorado, was made in 1843 and confirmed by Congress in 1870 for ca. 48,000 acres, with the proviso that he forego his claim in New Mexico made in 1845. Allegedly awarded by Governor Armijo in 1839, the Uña de Gato Grant was dismissed as a forgery.

McMains a bit of satisfaction; a synopsis of his land grant memorial had been published in the *New York Sun* — an echo of Tolby associations — and the *New York Times*.[7] The fact that McMains took the initiative did much to allay criticism. At a "rousing meeting" in Raton on the night of April 14, 1884, he "gave the Santa Fe Ring hail Columbia and paid his respects to the Territorial legislature . . . in no glowing terms."[8]

Signs of healthy anti-grantism were widespread. Settlers on the Nolán No. 39 organized and planned how to withstand the claimants. From Trinidad came an editorial that the Maxwell and Vigil and St. Vrain together were the greatest-known obstacles to the development of Las Animas County. But on the other side of the fence, so to speak, a meeting was called at Walsenburg to defend George M. Chilcott, who was attacked in the McMains memorial.[9]

That spring, Charles E. Gast and Frank Springer, Maxwell attorneys, filed a demurrer to the government's amended bill,* and the vacancy on the bench of Circuit Court D, Colorado, was filled by the appointment of David J. Brewer, of Leavenworth, Kansas, before whom the demurrer would be argued.[10] All signs predicted peace and quiet on the grant until then.

Selling his ranch for undisclosed reasons, McMains and his wife moved to Raton. Rumor had them moving to Mora County, but a startling development squelched that and caused the *Daily Optic* to remark that Parson McMains was not always asleep when his eyes were shut.[11]

---

*Government counsel had amended their original (1882) bill of complaint against the Maxwell Land Grant Company et al. in late 1883.

One mid-June day some riders driving a herd of horses appeared at the Crow Creek ranch between the Vermejo and Red rivers southwest of Raton. An excellent spread, the place had been recently acquired by the Maxwell Cattle Company, organized in 1881, to which the Maxwell Land Grant Company had leased the grazing rights on the estate, excepting the Colorado portion. There was no sign of life in the two-story ranchhouse or the stables and corrals, so the strange riders turned their horses out to pasture and moved into the house. McMains had seized the Crow Creek ranch![12]

The news flew far and wide. Within weeks the Maxwell people obtained an injunction from Judge Samuel B. Axell* against "Oscar P. McMains, and his confederates, agents, servants and employees, and aiders and abettors." The document was dated July 10, 1884; two days later it and a subpoena were served on McMains.[13]

Few people saw the reason for the occupation, so a mass meeting was scheduled at Raton to explain. McMains told his audience that he had no intention of heeding the court. Then he proposed something very interesting indeed; he would go to Washington to build up a new case against the Maxwell Land Grant Company. And he asked for a subscription of $500 to defray expenses.[14]

The explanation was simple. McMains had lost confidence in the Colorado case. The possibility that only about 300,000 acres (mainly the Colorado portion) of the Maxwell might be lopped off by the litigation was unacceptable.† His seizure of the Crow Creek ranch anticipated that the company would turn at once to the courts in protest. It did, and

---

*Axtell, the former governor, was appointed chief justice of New Mexico in 1882 and served also as judge of the judicial district that included Colfax County.

†On July 12, McMains wrote a letter to the editor of the *Indianapolis Sentinel* that was bitterly critical of Stephen B. Elkins as the cause of the Maxwell troubles (*Indianapolis Sentinel*, July 16, 1884).

MAXWELL CATTLE CO.,
[LIMITED.]

M. M. CHASE, MANAGER.

P. O. ADDRESS, CIMARRON, N. M.

Range, Western portion of Colfax county, New Mexico.

Range Foreman, MARION LITTRELL.

P. O. Address, VERMEJO, N. M.

Ear marks, grub the right.
Additional brands and marks.

Some cattle branded same as the above cut on right side and hip. ☒ on right side. JWR left side and hip. Various ear marks.

All increase branded and marked same as cut.

Ear mark, crop and split left.
Additional brands.

KLM left side and hip. Some cattle are branded **KLM** on right side. All increase is branded same as cut.

Ear marks, underslope right ear.
Horse brands.

R left thigh.

H left hip; some on left shoulder and hip.

U left shoulder.

H left hip.

+ left hip.

Maxwell Cattle Company advertisement showing the well-known Long H brand.

RED RIVER CATTLE CO.

ADDRESS, M. M. CHASE, CIMARRON, N. M.

Range, Red River, Ocate and Piedra Lumbre.   IRA B. GALE, Range Foreman.   P. O.: SPRINGER.

Additional brands and marks.

Some steers branded thus:

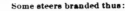

on left shoulder, side and hip.

on the left shoulder, side and hip.

Ear mark, crop the right and overslope the left.

All calves branded same as cut with S additional on the left jaw.

Horse Brand.

 left shoulder, ▬▬▬ left hip.

GILA CATTLE COMPANY.

ADDRESS, M. M. CHASE, CIMARRON, N. M.

Range, Datil, Elk and Luera mountains, in Socorro county.

T. F. MAULDING, Superintendent.
     CHAS. WOODLEY, Range Foreman.

Additional Brands.

 on the shoulder, side and hip.

Horse Brand.

 on the left shoulder and hip.

H. M. PORTER.

P. O. Address, DENVER, COLO., 183 Sherman Ave.
Range, Cimarron and Cimarroncito.

ROBERT DEAN, Range Foreman.
     P. O. Address, CIMARRON, N. M.

Ear marks, old stock, crop each ear; young stock, underslope each ear.

Additional brands.

 only on bulls and thoroughbred stock and only on left hip.

Steer calves of 1884 left shoulder, side and hip.

Horse brand on the left shoulder.

CIMARRON CATTLE CO.

ADDRESS, M. M. CHASE, CIMARRON, N. M.

Range, foot of Staked Plains, San Miguel Co.

T. F. MAULDING, Supt.   P. O.: WAGON MOUND.
G. O. C. McCROHAN, Range Foreman.
     P. O.: LIBERTY, N. M.

Ear marks, underslope left.

Additional brands.

right shoulder, side and hip

Horse brand. on right shoulder.

the injunction proved that the company molested settlers despite an agreed suspension of ejectments while the Maxwell case was in court. The Crow Creek situation, of course, was contrived. The company had let up on most ejectments; consequently, many people refused in this instance to view McMains as a settler hounded by a heartless corporation instead of one who carefully baited the company into an exploitable reaction.

Circuit Judge Brewer decided on the demurrer to the amended bill on July 28, 1884. Defense counsel had argued that mistakes by the surveyors could not be charged to their clients — the owners had purchased in good faith and should not be made to suffer for the government's errors. Brewer denied that the present owners were in the position of innocent purchasers and held that the government could seek a correction of error in a court of equity if a surveyor had gone beyond his jurisdiction, even after a patent was issued.[15] But those points, potentially helpful to the government's position, were made innocuous by his statements that the amended bill did *not* show improper relations between claimants and surveyors, and that *if Congress had intended to limit the Maxwell Grant to a smaller acreage within the outboundaries, it would have done so in the Act of June 21, 1860*, as it did in two other instances.[16]

But the apparent coup de grace given to the Justice Department's suit against the Maxwell patent was Brewer's unequivocal citation of the Tameling case (that Congress had really made a new grant) as disposing of the question.[17] In the face of that, the legal sparring so far, as well as that to come, was purely academic. Brewer actually ruled in favor of the Maxwell Land Grant Company in his decision on the demurrer, but prescribed legal procedures continued the litigation for nearly two more years until a final decision was made.

✺

With his worst misgivings substantiated, McMains looked on the Colorado case as hopeless, but he still firmly believed that the Maxwell patent could be destroyed. Money for another trip to Washington was quickly raised, some contributions coming from settlers on the Nolán No. 39. He relinquished the Crow Creek place to I. C. Showerman, a former train dispatcher at Raton, who also took McMains' horses, giving a promissory note payable in five months.[18]

In the capital city for the fifth time, McMains set to work in the summer heat to halt the downward plunge of the settlers' fortunes. At the Justice Department in August he filed a petition calling for a new suit in New Mexico against the Maxwell patent, based squarely on the Cox decision of 1869. No alleged error or fraud in a particular section of the Elkins and Marmon survey would be claimed. That mistake would not be repeated. A plain restriction to twenty-two square leagues was the goal.[19] And a change of venue might secure a judge who would not regard the Tameling decision as applicable to the Maxwell case — an essential development if relief were still to be sought in the courts.

Attorney General Brewster was not in the city, and S. F. Philips, who had upheld the Dutton recommendation against the first petition, was acting department head. This time Philips did not advise against it, but he evidently hoped to shunt it aside by extracting a new promise from Maxwell officials to observe the ejectment truce. Just what he hoped to achieve by an oblique approach is not clear; however, by letter he said he would deny McMains' application if the company would cease ejectments until the Colorado case was closed.[20] For his efforts he received a sharp reply from Frank Springer: "It is very evident to me that you have been grossly imposed upon by the misrepresentations of Mr McMains, who is, I learn, in Washington urging the bringing of this suit." The Maxwell lawyer went on to say that in only three special instances was the company continuing ejectment efforts, one of them being the injunction against McMains for seizing the Crow Creek ranch:

> McMains seized it without any pretense of right, for the express purpose of provoking legal proceedings against him, to give him a pretext to create a disturbance and riot. . . . McMains wants to have us coerced into an agreement not to disturb possessions, while he is to be left at liberty to go on seizing our lands . . . and publicly inviting people to come and colonize on it. . . . The sworn bill filed by the Government, . . . states in so many words that the grant is good and valid for about 1,030,000 acres.* . . . The recent decision of the U.S. Circuit Court, . . . holds that . . . the only question is as to the exact location of the boundaries of the grant. . . . Yet McMains continuously asserts that the company has no land whatever, — that the whole tract is public domain — and asks your interference because the people, who have invested five millions of dollars in the property, will not lie supinely on their backs until they have been stripped, piece by piece of every foot of land worth taking . . . McMains will not hesitate to deny everything . . . and I solemnly assure you that as to any matter pertaining to the Maxwell Grant, he is incapable of telling the truth.[21]

Springer's anger assisted his eloquence, but the facts suffered. McMains was not trying to obliterate the Maxwell from the map but only to reduce it to ca. 96,000 acres, and the amount embraced by the exterior lines was not really at issue. Springer could hardly have expected McMains to be impressed by the argument that investors had sunk five mil-

---

*Springer's appraisals (both private and public) of the government's position in the Maxwell case fed McMains' doubts about the reliability and sincerity of the government's lawyers. Springer also said, for instance, that "according to the theory of the counsel for the U.S. now in charge of the case [William F. Maury and J. A. Bentley] include a larger area than admitted in the sworn original bill."

lion dollars in the company in good faith when quite a few settlers had taken up land in good faith that it was public domain. And they now stood in danger of losing everything, not just part of their funds.

In 1884 the secretary of the interior was Henry M. Teller, who, as senator from Colorado, had received early anti-grant resolutions, but his own resolution calling for investigation of the Maxwell boundaries had come to naught in the Senate. To Secretary Teller, McMains addressed a letter on August 27:

> I would respectfully inquire if the decision of Hon. J. D. Cox, when Secretary of the Interior, made December 31st, 1869, that the confirmation of private land claim No. 15 [the Maxwell] was to the extent of only twenty-two square leagues, was ever formally reviewed by a subsequent Secretary of your Department, on complaint of error or illegality, and reversed.[22]

McMains hoped for, indeed expected, a reply in the negative, yet, as luck would have it, Secretary Teller was not in Washington either. An answer from Acting Secretary M. L. Joslyn was little more than an enclosure of the 1877 correspondence between Secretary Schurz and Commissioner Williamson concerning the Tameling decision's applicability. Professing to believe that his letter had been misunderstood, McMains pressed the point tactfully again in a second letter.

Joslyn sent that letter to N. C. McFarland, commissioner of the General Land Office, who answered McMains' question, saying that after Secretary Delano's refusal to review Secretary Cox's decision, it remained unreversed.[23] It was the most direct statement on the status of the Cox decision yet, so McMains, very pleased and his funds for room and board about used, headed for New Mexico.

While McMains was still in Washington, he was engaged in concurrent efforts against the Nolán No. 39. In a petition requesting that the plats of the public survey over the Nolán be restored to the land office at Santa Fe, he contended that the private survey by Elkins and Marmon had no legal status,[24] a point that was quite clear in section 4 of the act confirming the Nolán No. 48 in Colorado, passed by Congress July 1, 1870, stating that the confirmed lands "shall be held and taken to be in full satisfaction of all other claims or demands against the United States."[25]

When Acting Commissioner L. Harrison ignored that and advised against restoring the plats because Congress had not specifically disposed of the Nolán No. 39, McMains lost his temper. In a letter denouncing Harrison's opinion, he in effect wrote off the General Land Office as shamelessly corrupt. After his return to New Mexico his frustration was capped by the secretary of the interior's denial of the petition on November 18.[26]

When the Santa Fe train brought McMains home on September 11, 1884, the *Raton Comet* observed that "the old gentleman is looking badly over-worked, but comes home full of hope and says the prospects [on the Maxwell] are now better than ever for his success."[27] Although only forty-five, he had aged rapidly in the last few months, probably well on his way to the white hair and beard which, with his dark eyes, would so distinguish him in later years. He had brought back an authoritative statement that the Cox decision had not been reversed, which lightened disappointment over the Colorado case and gave a chance for a new one in New Mexico. Even his failure against the Nolán Grant, which he reported in a sixteen-page pamphlet, *Conspiracy to Defraud!*, was relieved by a clinging optimism.[28] But always present was the threat of the Tameling decision and its grant *de novo* concept. He hoped that it might be neutralized by a court decision or an act of Congress.

McMains was scarcely off the train before he became embroiled in local politics. The Anti-Grant party had experienced a serious split on September 8. Convention delegates in the dining room of the Moulton House watched a large group, led by J. H. Hunt, leave the meeting because they believed it was packed with men unsympathetic to anti-grantism. Yet the remaining delegates nominated a ticket headed by O. P. McMains for the territorial council.[29] The insurgents chose their own slate of candidates without McMains, only, they claimed, because they respected his decision to forsake politics for the direct anti-grant fight.[30]

Although he withdrew his name from the ticket, no one imagined that McMains would be an indifferent bystander. Nationally the fall campaign was a struggle between Democrat Grover Cleveland and Republican James G. Blaine, the latter nominated mainly through the efforts of Stephen Benton Elkins, former president of the old Maxwell Land Grant and Railway Company.[31]

Renewed conflict over the Crow Creek ranch cropped up. While McMains had been in Washington, I. C. Showerman granted permission to some cowboys to camp and graze their stock. That night the silence was rent by yelling and firing of guns. The cowboys, it turned out, worked for the Maxwell Cattle Company and were supposed to intimidate Showerman and run him off. But he stayed on, and so did the cattle company hands.[32]

Judge Axtell's injunction against McMains' seizure of the place had ordered him to show cause in the September term of court. McMains publicly declared that he would not appear and kept his word. The court issued a decree *pro confesso* — that his failure to appear was an admission of wrong-doing — and a final decree against him came soon after. It was then up to the officers of the law.[33]

The double occupancy at Crow Creek was grist for McMains' mill. Was he not classified as an agitator? Well, then, affairs on the ranch needed a little agitating. His press release called for a protest rally, which he termed an "indignation meeting," on the ranch at noon, Friday, September 26: "As the Land Department admits that the decision of Secretary Cox, of 1869, in our favor, has never been overturned; as therefore the Maxwell Grant Company and its aiders and abettors, the Maxwell Cattle Company, are bulldozing Mr. Showerman, and are lying, and bulldozing generally, I herewith invite the settlers to meet me at Crow Creek."[34] It amused him to use the phrase "aiders and abettors" that had been officially applied to those who had helped him to take over the ranch in the first place.

A large number of his followers accompanied McMains to the disputed property, while other anti-granters came from the hills. The outcome was a failure. The Maxwell men simply declined to move on, and, since neither side was ready to push matters to the point of violence, the joint occupancy continued.[35]

People saw McMains riding through the back country in October, holding meetings and talking on his favorite subject — the Maxwell Grant. On the night of October 26 he was featured at a big political meeting in the Blossburg schoolhouse. The Gate City band went there from Raton,* and candidates from both anti-grant factions attended. McMains was a spokesman for the ticket put up by the group that walked out of the Raton convention.[36]

All but two of the insurgent candidates were the people's choice in the November elections. The posts they failed to gain were those of sheriff and county clerk; John Hixenbaugh, who had thrown his hat in the ring about September 1, was

---

*Gate City was a nickname for Raton, because the town was at the foot of the gate to New Mexico — Raton Pass.

the new sheriff of Colfax County. Nationally Cleveland triumphed over Blaine, and Anthony Joseph,* the Democratic candidate, won the delegate's race.[37]

The Anti-Grant and Democratic victories set off a great celebration in Raton. A long procession headed by the Gate City band marched through the streets in the evening of November 13. The parade halted in front of the *Comet* office long enough to give three cheers for the paper's service against the Maxwell Land Grant Company. In the cavernous Raton Rink, the crowd listened with amusement as A. E. Burnam introduced the "Giant Agitator," O. P. McMains, who gave a very short speech, an unusual performance for him. The gathering was also a public reconciliation of the two antigrant groups, made apparent when Burnam introduced McMains and J. Osfield was seen in the audience. Burnam and Osfield had been leaders in the Raton convention from which Hunt and others defected.[38]

The anti-grant leaders stayed after the meeting to provide a continuing organization.† The breach was solidly

---

*Anthony (Antonio) Joseph was born in Taos in 1846. He served as delegate to Congress from March 4, 1885, to March 3, 1895. McMains had known Joseph as a council member during the Twenty-Sixth Legislative Assembly in Santa Fe, and during the campaign of 1884 had introduced Joseph to a Raton audience (*Biographical Dictionary of the American Congress, 1774–1961* [Washington: Government Printing Office, 1961], p. 1141; *Raton Comet*, September 19, 1884).

† Several nights later a hot-tempered young cowpuncher severely wounded a deputy sheriff, setting off a series of lurid beatings and shootings in Raton and Springer that climaxed about a fortnight later in the deaths of two men and the mortal wounding of a third before the brick and steepled courthouse in Springer. Despite some popular versions of local history, the evidence does not indicate that those events were an integral part of the struggle with the Maxwell Land Grant Company, with one exception.

Appointment of Bat Masterson's brother, Jim, as a deputy sheriff of Colfax County had been generally well received. When a shipment of arms arrived on February 9, 1885, addressed to James Masterson, Captain, Company H, Territorial Militia, most people had never heard of repaired by the election of Burnam as president. In the closed session McMains talked more freely and asked advice on the impossible Crow Creek situation. Deliberation resulted in a resolution asking Manley M. Chase, manager of the Maxwell Cattle Company, to withdraw his men at once; refusal would be looked upon as a declaration of war, although nothing definite was planned in that event.[39]

---

such a company, but they recalled a previous effort by Governor Lionel Sheldon to organize one, which McMains and others had viewed as sponsored by the Maxwell Land Grant Company. The new attempt aroused public wrath expressed in direct, massive action. Masterson and other members of the militia company were brought before a tense meeting of 600 men in the Raton Rink, and then a select committee of fifteen escorted them to the Colorado line atop Raton Pass, where they were turned loose and warned never to return (*Raton Comet*, November 21, 28, 1884, December 12, 24, 1884, January 23, February 7, 13, 27, March 6, 1885; *Daily Optic*, January 26, 1885; Steve Peters, *Incident on Red River and Other True Stories of New Mexico* [Santa Fe: by the author, 1971], pp. 15–27 (fictionalized account); H. B. Hening (ed.), *George Curry, 1861–1947: An Autobiography* [Albuquerque: University of New Mexico Press, 1958], pp. 49–52; William A. Keleher, *Maxwell Land Grant* rev. ed. [New York: Argosy-Antiquarian, Ltd., 1964], pp. 101–5).

Chapter 10

Riding the Crest

THE DEMOCRATS HAD NOT CONTROLLED the executive department since before the Civil War, and McMains shared their elation as he watched Grover Cleveland's inaugural parade.[1] He hoped the new administration would assist him, and he was anxious to move against the Maxwell and Nolán grants as soon as Cleveland made his appointments to the Interior and Justice departments.

Lucius Quintus Cincinnatus Lamar, distinguished Mississippian and former Confederate officer, was the choice for secretary of the interior. Soon McMains appeared with a new version of the old petition to have the Cox decision enforced and most of the Maxwell treated as public land. He was determined not to let that petition end up in the law division of the department, which was, he felt, the burial ground of the others because its staff supported the pro-grant position.

In a preliminary hearing, just as McMains feared, men from the law division tried to convince the assistant secretary that the petition was pointless because the grant company had its patent, the validity of which was then being examined in the circuit court for Colorado. But McMains, adamant and persuasive, won his point to have the petition referred to the commissioner of the General Land Office.[2]

[121]

William Andrew Jackson Sparks was appointed commissioner on March 26, 1885. A former congressman from Illinois, he had made a reputation with his firm stand against a civil service and his advocacy of federal regulation of railroads.[3] He embodied the hoped-for change at the General Land Office, and his response would be critical for the anti-granters.

McMains stayed through the varied weather of a Washington spring. At last on May 30 Sparks reported to Secretary Lamar that McMains' petition on the Nolán No. 39 should be followed — wonderful news to relay to New Mexico. The commissioner's argument closely followed that of McMains' pamphlet, *Conspiracy to Defraud!*[4]

Then on June 10 Sparks clearly stated that the Cox decision had not been reversed and should be enforced against the Maxwell Grant. As for the Tameling decision, Sparks maintained that it was not applicable to the Maxwell but only to similar cases "hereafter." He suggested the impropriety of a survey by the brother of Stephen Benton Elkins, "an alleged principal owner of the grant," and spoke about evident fraud and the ease with which boundary lines could have been moved. Finally he recommended a suit in New Mexico and more vigorous prosecution of the Colorado case. And on the allegation of fraud Sparks said:

> While this question of jurisdiction may not be specially important in this case [referring to the fact that the Maxwell lay in both New Mexico and Colorado], I deem it proper to state that the records of the General Land Office show that nearly all the townships traversed by the northern line of the grant in Colorado had been surveyed and the plats filed long before the survey of the grant; yet this plat of approved survey does not show a single township or section line, and makes no reference thereto, but represents the whole as an unsurveyed region, upon which the marks and monuments purport to have been established by reference to natural and topographical objects, many of the names and delinea-

tions of streams and geographical points being deliberately changed from those already officially reported by
the township surveys and plats.[5]

The report upheld anti-grant contentions right down the line,
but there was a flaw which kept it from being received uncritically except in the most optimistic quarters. Sparks concluded
that "the seemingly improvident issue of patent had placed
the whole matter beyond the power of this Department to
correct."[6] In other words, redress was up to the Justice
Department.

Back in Raton the *Comet* published the full text with
comments that were not an unrestrained paean of victory.
In the Colorado case the prospects of government success
were not strong, and a decision to bring a new suit in New
Mexico rested with the new attorney general, Augustus H.
Garland. The *Comet*'s editor was cautious: "Our readers can
at least say — 'so much, so good,' and patiently await further
developments."[7]

Officers and bondholders of the Maxwell Land Grant
Company felt that the Garfield and Arthur administrations
had been too cooperative with the anti-grant settlers, and
now the Democrats were trying to outdo them. To forestall a
second lawsuit the company exploited an influential business
connection. General Bela M. Hughes,* the Maxwell attorney
in Denver, wrote to Charles J. Canda, trustee for the income
bondholders and a man of importance in Democratic circles,
asking him to get the attorney general to deny such action.[8]

Meanwhile Harry Whigham put minds at ease in The
Netherlands by assuring Dutch directors that Frank Springer

---

* Hughes was prominent in the world of transportation and was a
leader of the Democratic party in Colorado. Hubert Howe Bancroft,
History of Nevada, Colorado and Wyoming [San Francisco: History
Publishing Company, 1890], p. 572.

believed a suit would not be brought in New Mexico while one was pending in Colorado, and, as it was almost certain the company would win the Colorado case, there was little chance of a suit in New Mexico. Whigham dismissed the Sparks report as pure partisan politics: it made Sparks "to any informed person simply ludicrous; but such clap-trap makes capital for the Democratic party with the masses."[9] He did not say why the Republicans took the grant company into court in the first place.

Official testimony on behalf of the Maxwell Land Grant Company in the Colorado case was taken at Las Vegas, New Mexico, before Commissioner Harry S. Clancy, during the spring and summer of 1885. At the same time the affidavits of Jesús Silva and "Uncle Dick" Wootton, taken nearly a decade before, were made a part of the record.[10]

Because his arrival was not known in advance, no crowd greeted McMains in Raton on June 22. The news circulated quickly, however, and his admirers hastened to arrange an expression of their high esteem for him. Plans already existed to invite recently appointed Governor Edmund G. Ross to Raton. What better manifestation of respect and regard could there be for a distinguished local citizen than to transform the arrangements into a joint testimonial? The night of July 3 was picked; Ross wired that he would be there;* and the *Comet*

---

* Ross, the former Republican senator from Kansas whose vote saved President Andrew Johnson from removal from office, was appointed governor by President Cleveland in May 1885. There is no evidence of further association between Ross and McMains, although Ross was a reformist governor and strongly anti-Santa Fe Ring (Howard R. Lamar, "Edmund G. Ross as Governor of New Mexico Territory: A Reappraisal," *New Mexico Historical Review* 36 [July 1961]: 177–209). That probably is explained by the rift that developed between McMains and President Cleveland.

announced "a public reception and banquet is extended to the Governor and Mr. McMains."[11] That should have squelched the editor of the Las Vegas *Daily Optic*, who remarked about McMains' return: "Whether he will be tendered a love-feast or invited to a snipe drive remains to be seen."[12]

Governor Ross was escorted from the evening train to the Raton House for an elaborate supper. Bunting and evergreen decorated the walls and chandeliers, and a profusion of Chinese lanterns glowed brightly. The guests were offered a tempting series of courses, and then a toast to the governor's health. Ross responded that a man who went from United States senator to common printer should not be the governor of a great territory, an allusion, of course, to his political suicide when, as senator from Kansas, he cast the deciding vote against President Andrew Johnson's removal in 1868.

T. D. Mitchell,* representing the Knights of Labor, welcomed Ross in the name of the working people of New Mexico. A toast to "The Future of New Mexico: The Land Question" naturally brought a response from McMains, a specialist in the subject. He was exuberant about a bright Democratic future, observing that the new surveyor general, George W. Julian, was eminently qualified to deal with land titles, New Mexico's greatest drawback.[13] McMains' toast should be viewed in the political context of the occasion in which anti-grant and Democratic interests were closely linked; yet no one knew better than McMains that some of his strongest support against the grant had come from Republican office-holders in Washington. Had he been able to look into the future he would have seen Grover Cleveland as one of the biggest obstacles in the anti-grant path.

Festivities in the hotel dining room were lengthy; one wonders how McMains, a strong temperance man, coped with

---

*Mitchell was the father of Arthur Roy Mitchell, artist, local historian, and friend of the author.

all the conviviality. Following the private libations the select group went to the Rink, where seats had been provided for more than 600, but as many again had to stand. Numerous ladies were present, and over the din and confusion blared music by the Gate City Band.

The master of ceremonies praised Ross's deciding vote against President Johnson's impeachment and McMains' work against the land grant monopolies. After the governor spoke and the band played again, the second feature of the evening was given to the crowd — the Hon. O. P. McMains.

The slight figure, marks of age showing prematurely, was greeted with a tremendous ovation. He began by recalling a song he had heard during the Civil War at Mattoon, Illinois, not Raton,* the lyrics of the ditty beginning: "I feel like I feel like I feel." Being overwhelmed, he could say no more about his feelings. This was not an anti-grant meeting. Thus he did not intend to talk much about the grant; besides he was tired of the subject. With so many ladies present he would rather indulge in gossip pleasing to them, and he gave an interesting description of the inaugural parade, phasing into a tribute to President Cleveland.

But he could not ignore the subject on which his words carried weight. The audience would have gone home disappointed if he had. So he delighted the crowd by telling of how he told Interior Department officials that they would have to enforce the Cox decision if it took the army, the navy, and the Raton militia to do it. His central theme, of course, was the Sparks report and the possible lawsuit in New Mexico.[14]

❧

---

*A play on words, Raton often being pronounced Ratoon.

In July McMains registered and published a cattle brand — MAX — describing his range as the ex-Maxwell Grant,[15] a defiant bit of humor that was soon obscured by publicity given to a letter from Stephen Benton Elkins to Commissioner Sparks. Taking issue with a reference to him in the Sparks report as an "alleged owner" of the grant, Elkins stated flatly: "I am not now and never was an owner directly or indirectly in the Maxwell Grant." He cited a brief association with the old Maxwell Land Grant and Railway Company as attorney and director and said he represented the receiver at the Interior Department at the time of application for the patent "in 1878 or 9." The letter was dated June 22 and was published by the *New York Times** on June 30.[16]

A reason for Elkins to minimize his connection with the grant is difficult to find. He was a stockholder in, and therefore an owner of, the Maxwell Land Grant and Railway Company, and he held that stock during the same years (1872–73) that he was a director. Furthermore, he served as president from October 1873 to November 1875.[17]

When the Associated Press published the Elkins letter, another champion came forth to fight the grant company — William P. Fishback. McMains' brother-in-law sent an exposition of his views on Maxwell matters to the editor of the *Indianapolis News*, who published it on July 4. Blaming the Elkins brothers for a fraudulent survey, Fishback demolished Elkins' point that the validity of the Maxwell had been supported by some of the most distinguished lawyers in the

---

* The *New York Times* showed considerable interest in Maxwell matters. On June 13, 1885, it carried an article summarizing the government's suit against the Maxwell Company and quoted extensively from the Sparks report under the headline: "The Maxwell Land Fraud, A Report On What Is Called the Elkins Steal." And on July 1 the paper discussed Elkins' disclaimer of interest in the grant, stating facetiously that "among those who will doubtless be glad to learn that they have misjudged Mr. Elkins is Mr. McMains."

William P. Fishback (McMains' brother-in-law). A former law partner of Benjamin Harrison, Fishback was editor of the Indianapolis Journal *and then associate editor of the* St. Louis Democrat. *From 1877 until his death in 1901, he served as clerk and master in chancery of the U.S. Court, District of Indiana.*

country. Elkins, he said, was hiding behind opinions given long before the survey of 1877. Nobody denied that there was a grant; the opposition objected to its fraudulent enlargement. Finally Fishback expressed thanks, as a Republican, to the courageous commissioner of the General Land Office, a Democrat.[18]

McMains swung into action with his own letter to Sparks on July 8: if the *Cimarron News and Press* had it straight, Elkins received $10,000 per year as company president, and

as New Mexico's delegate to Congress he violated the law —
no public officer could prosecute, or aid in prosecuting, any
claim against the United States — when he urged acceptance
of the Maxwell surveys of 1870 and 1877. McMains quoted
two letters from Elkins to Commissioner Williamson, then
made his point that probably Elkins was the real owner of the
grant, purchased through other parties at a tax sale. When
Frank Remington Sherwin and others stepped in, the property
was foreclosed, and, if Elkins lost his grant, he did not lose
his investment. This McMains-Sparks letter, carried in the
Comet, was the first time that he signed himself as "O. P.
McMains, *Agent for the Settlers,*" a name and title that would
be synonymous henceforth.[19]

Success in Washington had a by-product — money trouble. Trips to the capital were costly, no matter how careful
McMains was. A few settlers thought that he spent the people's money without much to show for it, or even doubted his
honesty, but most anti-granters did not agree.[20] Confidence
in him was shown, for example, in a call for further public
subscription of funds:

> And now, shall we prove ungrateful to the man who
> has — alone, unassisted and single-handed — secured this
> blessing [the Sparks report] to us? He has a family who
> have claims upon us which we can neither forget nor
> ignore. They [McMains and his wife] were never rich
> and cannot live without support from some source. We,
> who have been the beneficiaries of the time and labor of
> Mr. McMains, and thereby depriving that family of what
> was its just dues, must not fail to, in our feeble way, show
> some gratitude by rendering our benefactor such assis-
> tance as he may need, and lies in our power.[21]

Perhaps embarrassment explained McMains' departure for
Santa Fe that same day to confer with the new surveyor general of New Mexico, George W. Julian.[22]

The summer of 1885 was filled with personal matters for Oscar and Mary McMains. His sister, Mary Fishback, arrived for a month-long visit with her daughter and her family, Mary and Will Kappes, and son Robert, who had settled there some three years earlier.[23] And I. C. Showerman, to whom McMains had relinquished the Crow Creek ranch, was in default on a promissory note he had given McMains for some cattle. When it appeared that Showerman had sold some of the cattle and was about to leave with the rest, the court issued a writ of attachment to Sheriff W. J. Parker for service, which was not made. McMains then sought relief from Judge Vincent in Springer.[24]

Drawing near was the September term of court, when actions against settlers would be prosecuted by the Maxwell Company although the Colorado case was still pending. Their defense had to be planned, so McMains wrote to Surveyor General Julian requesting certified copies of documents "in the interest of the United States" and "for use . . . in resisting ejectments."[25]

Chapter 11

❦

The Vincent Affair

DESIGNATION AS COUNTY SEAT was an advantage sought by hundreds of little towns in the West. Some attained it by forcible relocation, others by chicanery, and still others because of the merits of locale. Springer, Colfax County, New Mexico, was of the latter type.* The Santa Fe Railroad had by-passed Cimarron, the first county town, while Springer was on the railroad and became the terminus of the Springer-Tascosa Trail, serving the big cattle outfits to the east on the plains.

Sessions of court brought a spurt of activity as lawyers, clients, witnesses, jurors, and bystanders crowded into town. The Springer House was booked full; Bob Stepp's saloon and others catered to thirst and chance; the local dance hall was packed. In the steepled courthouse young Chief Justice William A. Vincent, a Cleveland appointee, presided over the court of the first judicial district.

---

*One source says the town was named after Frank Springer, and another says for Frank and his brother, Charles. See *Raton Range*, February 23, 1973; T. M. Pearce (ed.), *New Mexico Place Names: A Geographical Dictionary* (Albuquerque: University of New Mexico Press, 1965), p. 159.

Success did not attend McMains in his personal litigation or in grant settlers' cases. He stated that the sheriff refused to serve a writ of attachment, but District Attorney Melvin W. Mills maintained that he could not serve it because Shower-man had sold the cattle and departed. The judge ruled that McMains had to pay the sheriff's costs.*

The *Maxwell Land Grant Company* v. *George Hixen-baugh* was decided in the company's favor.[1] The defendant operated a sawmill, and McMains expected the Sparks report to be a decisive factor in the case. But the commissioner's opinion did not carry much weight, probably because Secretary Lamar had yet to accept the report and no suit had been ordered in New Mexico.

A local scandal soon involved Vincent, the judge in these cases, in a struggle to preserve his good name and official position. By law the county required five commissioners to select jurors. Two of them — the district and probate judges — were *ex officio*. As district judge, Vincent had the appointment of the other three. Naturally he had to exert careful political and ethnic judgment. The probate judge was a Republican and a Mexican, and two Democrats were not hard to find. For the Republican opening one man had been highly recommended — Stephen W. Dorsey, former senator from Arkansas and a very influential cattleman in the county.†

---

* In 1886 the court ruled against Showerman in McMains' case to recover cattle in partial payment of the promissory note, and a sheriff's sale of fifty head of Showerman's cattle was advertised (*O. P. McMains* v. *I. C. Showerman*, No. 631, Docket, District Court, Colfax County, New Mexico, 1:228, and Record of the District Court B, Colfax County, New Mexico, p. 283).

† Dorsey had been acquitted in the notorious Star Route mail fraud cases. In Colfax County he was suspected of illegal land acquisition. See Arie W. Poldervaart, *Black-Robed Justice: A History of the Administration of Justice in New Mexico from the American Occupation in 1846 until Statehood in 1912* (n.p.: Historical Society of New Mexico, 1948), pp. 133–34; Victor Westphall, *The Public Domain in New Mexico, 1854–1891* (Albuquerque: University of New Mexico Press, 1965), pp. 55–56, 78–79.

After consultations with the attorney general, the clerk of the court, and Frank Springer, Judge Vincent chose Dorsey, who accepted the appointment, and helped choose jurors for the April term. Dorsey then invited the judge, the officers of the court, and several attorneys to his fine home at Mountain Spring Ranch,* east of town.[2]

Apparently satisfied that the Dorsey appointment was a good one, Vincent left to hold court at Tierra Amarilla in Río Arriba County. While there he received a shocking telegram from President Cleveland suspending him from office. Frantically he wired the president asking for an explanation and a hearing, and then hurried back to Santa Fe. From fragmentary reports on the press wire it seemed that the trouble was over the jury commissioners, particularly Dorsey.[3]

All three appointees (the two Democrats and Dorsey) allegedly were much interested in land disputes — disagreements that might be examined by the juries they selected. Asked if he had an interest in the Maxwell or any other grant, Dorsey denied it and dismissed the whole affair as "too miserable to talk about."[4]

The question of how President Cleveland knew so much about details of local government in distant New Mexico was answered in a dispatch from Washington saying the matter had been brought to Commissioner Sparks' attention by William P. Fishback.[5] Satisfying conclusions were quickly reached by some people: the Indiana lawyer, who had invested in cattle in the vicinity of Dorsey's ranches, was the brother-in-law of McMains, and the two of them were trying to make Vincent look like a willing tool of the land-grabbers. When the Agent for the Settlers denied any part in it, the Las Vegas *Daily Optic* outdid itself in extremes of abuse, and when he

---

*The place is often erroneously referred to as the Chico Springs Ranch. See Morris F. Taylor, "Stephen W. Dorsey, Speculator-Cattleman," *New Mexico Historical Review*, 49 (January 1974), pp. 28, 44 n10.

went to Washington a few days later,* Vincent was sure it was "for the purpose of following up and fighting him."[6]

Vincent wired the president twice and finally received a joint answer from Cleveland and Attorney General Garland. That merely added to his consternation, for it said that his successor would be appointed in a day or two. Having done all he could from Santa Fe, the suspended jurist boarded a train for Washington, where he would fight for his reputation and not the office.[7]

The *New York Tribune* suggested that the Vincent scandal opened a major rift in Cleveland's official family over land policy in New Mexico.[8] Intraparty struggles could block a suit against the Maxwell in New Mexico, which explained McMains' departure for Washington better than a vendetta against Vincent. Ex-senator Dorsey, a Republican not averse to fishing in troubled political waters, emerged for the time being as the major spokesman for pro-grant interests. In an interview much suited to the *Daily Optic* line he said:

> Yes, the Vincent matter is still of interest. I have information sufficient to convince me that Judge Vincent's removal was brought about through statements made by vicious and disreputable persons living at Raton. The existence of the person I refer to depends wholly upon lawlessness, agitation, falsehood and willful and unwarranted libel. This fellow without status or credit with any decent man who is unfortunate enough to know him, seems able to mislead an administration — mislead the president of the United States and his cabinet. I am

---

*Fishback said McMains went because of improved chances of action against illegal fencing by big cattlemen (*Indianapolis Journal*, November 17, 1885). Congress passed a law against illegal fencing in February, and President Cleveland issued a proclamation against it in August (Maurice Frink et al, *When Grass Was King: Contributions to the Western Range Cattle Industry Study* [Boulder: University of Colorado Press, 1956], pp. 94, 228–29; Westphall, *Public Domain in New Mexico*, p. 155).

not much surprised at this fact. Stupidity, with a dash of pretentiousness, is generally led by fools. There lives in Indianapolis a narrow-headed crank by the name of Fishback, who in accordance with the fitness of things, is a brother-in-law of the Raton 'sand-lotter' referred to. This Fishback, in his great anxiety for the welfare of the people of New Mexico, wrote Mr. Sparks, commissioner of the general land office at Washington, a letter wonderful in imagination, but not surprising to anyone who knows him and his falsehoods.[9]

The attack on McMains was resumed in a last, long, defensive letter from Vincent to Cleveland dated November 5 and published later. In desperation he used any material that was placed in his hands, including the old murder charge:

> ... Mr. Fishback, of Indiana, who preferred the charge of appointing Mr. Dorsey against me, may be a very reputable man, but he is brother-in-law to a very dangerous, violent incendiary named O. P. McMains, who resides in New Mexico, and has been convicted of murder there, although he escaped punishment on a technicality. I have filed with the Attorney General a certified transscript of his trial and conviction, together with all the evidence given at the trial, and from which you can see that the murder was not only cowardly but cruel in the extreme. During the September term of court, I decided two causes against McMains, at which he was much incensed. Doubtless he caused his brother-in-law, Fishback, to prefer the charge which resulted in my suspension.[10]

After William P. Fishback read Vincent's letter in the *Indianapolis Journal* for November 16, 1885, he wrote at once to the editor, who published his reply in the next morning's edition. Fishback said he read of the Dorsey appointment in a Colfax County paper and that McMains had had nothing to do with his letter to Sparks. What had worried Fishback was the allegation of fraudulent preemption and homestead entries by Dorsey in acquiring control of enormous holdings on the public domain, an allegation made in February in United States Senate Executive Document 106.* He disclosed his opinion about the Dorsey appointment to his friend, Vice President Thomas A. Hendricks, who was in Indianapolis; Hendricks assured him that Sparks would do the right thing.†

Fishback was incensed that the Vega murder charge had been revived against McMains nearly ten years after the court had dismissed it. He also blamed religious bigotry in the indictment of McMains by the Taos County grand jury, yet the people of Colfax County showed they did not believe him guilty when they elected him to the legislature. McMains was regarded as a dangerous and violent incendiary by the great landowners of New Mexico because of his growing success against them. Judge Vincent had learned the hard way the truth of the Shakespearian adage that " 'they that touch pitch will be defiled.' "[11] Perhaps Fishback's disapproval of Dorsey was partly based on personal experience, since the ranching interests of the two men were in proximity on the public domain.

The whole Vincent episode was further proof that land controversies (both on alleged Mexican land grants and the American public domain) permeated nearly every aspect of life in Colfax County and, in turn, could set off reactions in the national political power structure of the Republican and Democratic parties.

---

*48th Cong., 2nd Sess. (1885), Serial 2263, Senate Ex. Doc. 106 contained *Reports upon the Subject of Fraudulent Acquisition of Titles to Lands in New Mexico*. The references to Dorsey were made in a report of Inspector Frank D. Hobbs, dated Raton, New Mexico, June 21, 1884, pp. 312–13.

† Poldervaart, *Black-Robed Justice*, p. 135, suggests that Vincent was an unfortunate victim of circumstances. President Cleveland evidently came to that conclusion several years later when he offered Vincent the chief justiceship of Montana, which he declined.

Chapter 12

Flagging Fortunes

PERHAPS BECAUSE OF THE BAD OMENS in the closing weeks of 1885, a sense of humor emerged. Some wags in Raton produced what passed for a telegram from McMains saying that Governor Ross had been removed and he, McMains, had been appointed.* Apparently some people were taken in. Money was solicited for a celebration, and everything proceeded nicely until the joke was discovered. One newspaper commented that ". . . the hoax had one good effect, in getting opinions from men who are known to be anything for policy. That class are kicking themselves to-day for being so premature."[1]

Not until mid-January was it known that Secretary Lamar had approved Commissioner Sparks' recommendations on the Nolán No. 39 based on McMains' petition. The plats would be restored and the tract thrown open under the public land laws. McMains' detractors refused to give him credit, but the secretary made it clear that the order was based on McMains' efforts.[2]

---

* The basis of the hoax may have been a public remark by Senator Dorsey that he had been offered a committee assignment, which he declined jokingly, saying that if he accepted, Governor Ross probably would be removed (*Raton Comet*, December 5, 1885).

Circuit Court Judge David J. Brewer. Later (1889) appointed an associate justice of the U.S. Supreme Court, Brewer, more than any other jurist, asserted the legal sanction of the Maxwell Land Grant.

To have recovered 575,968 acres for the public domain was a major achievement, although the Nolán case was somewhat simpler than the Maxwell. It remained to be seen whether Frank Springer's private opinion, that Secretary Lamar would never rule against the Maxwell Land Grant Company, would be upheld.[3]

A development elsewhere tempered the Nolán morale booster, but it was not a shattering surprise. Circuit Judge David J. Brewer ruled in favor of the Maxwell Company in the Colorado case. Assigning no importance to the argument

that the Cox decision had not been reversed, Brewer repeated
what he had said so clearly in his rejection of the demurrer
to the amended bill — that the Tameling decision protected
the Maxwell patent.[4]

Despite that, Judge Brewer chose to deal at length with
other aspects of the plaintiff's case, making the broad assertion that the government had absolutely failed to show fraud
in any phase of the Maxwell's history. His uncritical acceptance of the pro-grant testimony by Jesús Silva and "Uncle
Dick" Wootton about the decisive northeast corner, when a
careful examination of their depositions would have revealed
very damaging discrepancies, indicates that Brewer either
prejudged the case or was incompetent. And his rejection of
all depositions by witnesses that challenged the rectitude of
the Elkins and Marmon survey strengthens the case for the
former explanation.[5] In fact, later assessments characterized
Brewer as heavily biased in favor of private property and big
corporations.[*]

In a speech given in the Raton Rink on the evening of
January 27, 1886, the day after Judge Brewer's decision was
handed down, McMains was reduced by the judicial action
to uninspiring reassurances of eventual triumph. He probably
had not seen a full transcript of Brewer's opinion. Once again
stating his belief that the Cox decision would in time be
enforced, McMains digressed on his loss of faith in men

---

[*] For example, ex-Populist, socialist convert Gustavus Myers in his
History of the Supreme Court of the United States (Chicago: Charles
H. Kerr and Company, 1912), p. 603. Editor William Allen White in
his *Autobiography* (New York: Macmillan, 1946), p. 440, said Brewer
"believed in the divine right of the plutocracy to rule." Brewer needs a
thorough biographical treatment; however, for a sketch of his career
see D. Stanley Eitzen, *David J. Brewer, 1837–1910: A Kansan on the
United States Supreme Court*, The Emporia State Research Studies 12
(March 1964), and Robert E. Cushman, "David Josiah Brewer," *Dictionary of American Biography*, ed. Allen Johnson (New York: Charles
Scribner's Sons, 1957), 3:22–4.

because of certain public officials, obscurely criticizing Surveyor General Julian for balking in the matter of the Maxwell plats. With unconvincing bravado he dismissed the Brewer decision as amounting to "simply nothing" and then pathetically pleaded: "If the people will stand by me a little longer, I am so certain of final victory that I am willing to stake my reputation on the matter; yea, more — I am willing to be called infamous, if the people do not win the day."[6]

His virtual promise was based in part on the certainty that the government would appeal the Maxwell case to the Supreme Court. How long that would take was a good question. But his hope of succor from the Court could never be very strong so long as the Tameling case remained a part of the record. Help from the executive branch seemed to be required.

McMains thus proposed the formation of a committee to phrase an appeal to President Cleveland, to be presented through Delegate Joseph and designed to make "unwilling officials do that which is their bounden duty." The committee was appointed then and there.[7] But there was little to bolster spirits when the crowd left the Rink that night, because recourse to the highest executive authority looked like an admission of defeat at the Department of the Interior.

Gloom penetrated to the farthest habitation on the grant, but a small, determined group kept faith. McMains went to Washington with the appeal to Cleveland early in February — his eighth trip.[8]

Many people thought it unlikely that the president would enforce the Cox decision over the opposition of the secretary of the interior and Judge Brewer. For a growing number of anti-granters who had doubts about McMains, their dilemma was where to turn. No one suggested an alternative, and the *Comet*, noting that McMains was still in the capital in mid-

March, observed unenthusiastically: "The last reports from him are that he is sanguine of success. Should success crown his efforts, many a settler will be made happy."[9]

An anonymous letter to the *Comet* commented on the scarcity of news from McMains, concluding that he must have given it up as a bad job. The writer then asked for advice, because some settlers might lease from the Maxwell Company. Francis R. Butler, the new editor and proprietor, weakly suggested unity and expressed sympathy for their exhausting fight against the wealthy, foreign corporation with brilliant talent. Denunciation of Harry Whigham "as the great manipulator for the Maxwell Land Grant Company, a corporation without a soul" also featured in Butler's reply.[10]

Recently appointed as receiver of the Maxwell Land Grant Company, Harry Whigham saw the disorder in anti-grant ranks and persuaded Butler to publish his shrewd exploitation of it.

It is not true . . . that it is the intention of the receiver to proceed to eject settlers off the grant by wholesale. I am directed by the court, which appointed me . . . and I have given notice accordingly. If the lands embraced in the United States patent which the company holds belong to it, the occupants should pay for the use of it. If they do not, I cannot collect rents. . . . You overlook the fact that the patent suit is carried on by the government of the United States, which is certainly as wealthy and powerful as any Grant company. It has for lawyers in the case the attorney general of the United States and his whole force of assistants, besides special counsel, who gives his entire attention to it. . . . It has been decided by a United States judge in favor of the grant company on the law and the facts. . . . And are these gentlemen, who want the owners to wait the decision of the Supreme Court, willing to give a bond that they will pay up all the back rents if it is decided in favor of the company? . . . If these people [the anti-granters] have been misled by . . . the land department in trying to override an act of congress, they would blame the government and not the company. The company bought the land in good faith and paid a very large price for it. . . . The Maxwell Company stand ready to-day, to make a fairer agreement with any settler on the grant than any other owner of private lands in the Territory, and those who try to keep up excitement and prevent any amicable arrangement . . . are the worst enemies of the people most interested.[11]

Whigham's arguments had an aura of reasonableness for some settlers. Company officials saw security in the courts for the same reasons that McMains saw death there for the anti-grant cause. Yet the editor did not demand executive enforcement of the Cox decision but squandered his space to attack Whigham's appointment as receiver as a trick giving an officer of the company the authority of the court. He dismissed Whigham's letter as "just such an argument as a crafty attorney would use to mislead a country jury."[12] Whigham's letter to the *Comet* was public evidence of the skills displayed for many years by the heavy-set, side-burned official* while serving as trouble shooter for the grant company from ca. 1874.[13]

The third annual meeting of the Northern New Mexico Small Cattlemen and Cowboys' Union was scheduled to meet at the Adobe House, Horseshoe Pasture, on the Vermejo on March 31. The meeting turned out to be a big anti-grant con-

---

* Whigham had been a partner in the Cimarron firm of Bushnell and Whigham, dealers in wool, hides, and grain. He was born in England in 1847, coming to the United States in 1862 and to Colorado in 1866, where for several years he was county clerk of Bent County. McMains may have known him there (Interview with Mrs. Lucy Reed Wills, October 7, 1948; Victor Westphall, *Thomas Benton Catron and His Era* [Tucson: University of Arizona Press, 1973], p. 110; Lee Scott Theisen, "Frank Warner Angel's Notes on New Mexico Territory, 1878," *Arizona and the West* 18 [Winter 1976]: 368–69; Charles W. Bowman, "History of Bent County." *History of the Arkansas Valley, Colorado* [Chicago: O. L. Baskin and Company, 1881], p. 847).

clave. Accounts of it caused imaginative people to hear the click of six-shooters and Winchesters when they learned of the new Anti-Grant Mutual Protective Association. Fears were tempered, however, by a committee of six that had been appointed to confer with Harry Whigham — proof that his letter in the *Comet* had been given serious attention.* Those of a skeptical turn of mind were amused by a published squib about an old man who was asked if he were convinced by Whigham's letter: "Convinced! No, sir. Me and Whigham is a good deal like my old woman and me. Fourteen years ago in old Missouri, my old woman caught me in our hired girl's room. For fourteen years I've tried to convince that old woman that my motives and actions was right, and fourteen year more talk won't have no effect on her."[14]

The fact that M. C. (Comp) Reed, one of McMains' closest friends, was on the committee showed that the new protective association was not simply an anti-McMains development. In a meeting at Springer the committee and Whigham agreed that the Maxwell Company would stop proceedings against settlers until the Supreme Court ruled in the Colorado case, and the settlers would pay rent from the date of the decision if it were in favor of the company. The compromise was hailed by people who felt that further defiance would be pointless, and Whigham was anxious that higher company officials should accept the plan.[15]

Five days later the executive committee of the Anti-Grant Mutual Protective Association rejected the terms because the Colorado case would not apply in New Mexico. Here was an unmistakable sign that McMains still had important support;

---

*Membership of the executive committee was comprised of C. B. Ladd, John Holmes, George Geer, Charles Hunt, Joe Lowry, Abe Sever, and M. M. Salazar; members of the special committee were Juan González, Charles Hunt, John E. Lane, Marion Littrell, M. C. Reed, and J. L. Woods (*Raton Comet*, April 2, 1886, and April 9, 1886).

the *Colfax County Stockman* saw a three-way, anti-grant split: pro-McMains, anti-McMains, and compromise. Harry Whigham commented laconically that "we are simply where we started."[16]

In Washington the somewhat discredited Agent for the Settlers was having an unhappy time. Suspecting that Secretary of the Interior Lamar's unfavorable reaction to the Sparks report had been prepared in the law division of the Interior Department, he was certain that Messrs. Britton and Gray, the Maxwell Company's Washington counsel,* were behind it all.[17] McMains, accompanied by Delegate Anthony Joseph, appeared before Lamar; the secretary was indignant at the tactic but promised to investigate. Two weeks later they returned, only to hear a curt announcement by the secretary: " 'I positively decline to have anything more to do with the Maxwell Grant case.' " Angrily McMains strode from the room without waiting for Joseph.[18] Not long after that he heard from home about the near compromise with Whigham and the increasing discord among the anti-granters. Washington matters would have to wait, and the Agent for the Settlers left hurriedly for New Mexico.

McMains did little more than greet his wife affectionately before obtaining a wagon and team and heading into the mountains, where his strongest support always had been. There he castigated the attempted compromise and called for a meeting in Raton on April 24. A strange report came down from the Vermejo that McMains, in a state of great excitement, called for a Clay Allison, who would shake his fist in

---

*The law firm (formerly Britton, Gray and Drummond) specialized in land titles; Willis Drummond had been commissioner of the General Land Office, and A. T. Britton and H. J. Gray were former employees of that agency. See Harold H. Dunham, "Some Crucial Years of the General Land Office, 1875–1891," *Agricultural History* 2 (April 1937): 126; letters of the firm in the Land Grant File, Documentary Resources Department, State Historical Society of Colorado, Denver.

Whigham's face and say: " 'Now stop this thing, or I will put your light out.' "[19] If true, and there is room for doubt, it would be easy to exaggerate his intent. The opposition eagerly picked up anything detrimental to him and then used ridicule to damage him.

A letter to the *Comet*, signed simply "1874," showed some compassion.* The writer approved of the compromise and opposed a lawsuit against the grant in New Mexico. Asserting that everything McMains had attempted from a solution of the Tolby murder to enforcement of the Sparks recommendation was a "catalogue of failures," he told the editor that the Colorado suit had been brought only because an intimate friend of Attorney General Brewster had been paid $500. In attenuation:

> We know that Mr. McMains is honest in purpose, and that he believes every word he utters; and that he has spent many years of unremitting toil in our behalf, and all his worldly goods besides. Yet we must not be deceived and misled by a mirage, although it is painted by the master hand we love so well. Let not the fact that he has been devoted to our interest, even to the exclusion of home pleasure and worldly considerations, interfere with the sober dictates of our cooler judgment.[20]

At the Raton meeting McMains patiently restated his belief that Cleveland would enforce the Cox decision and Lamar had been misinformed by people in his own department in alliance with the Maxwell Company's law firm. He wondered if the lawsuit in New Mexico had been openly promised only to be secretly suppressed. Then the Agent for the Settlers delivered a passionate denunciation of men who he felt had betrayed him. In climax he accused his close friend,

---

* The writer signed himself "1874" probably because that was the year of his arrival in the Vermejo country. Thus he indicated that he antedated McMains and was fully familiar with the course of past events.

J. H. Hunt, of trying to bribe him, through Mrs. McMains, to cease his hopeless assaults against the Maxwell Land Grant Company. Having said that, he attacked Judge Hunt's adherence to Mormonism.[21] To extend the coverage of his speech, a broadside was hastily printed and signed by McMains, but it omitted all the bitter personal references of his oral tirade.[22]

Expected repercussions were delayed for a few days because Hunt was out of town. Then in the *Comet*, of which Hunt's son, Charles, had recently become business manager, the public saw the captivating headlines: "Two Anti-Grant Gladiators Lock Horns in Deadly Combat. Judge Hunt Finds that There is Nothing to McMains But Wind, So He Squeezes Some of It Out, and Then Leaves Him Entirely Collapsed."[23]

After reviewing the lack of success in Washington, Hunt proceeded to the subject of the alleged bribe. With the effect of disclaiming the "1874" letter, Hunt noted that one of Mac's staunchest friends said that although he had worked hard on poor pay, the settlers could not finance him anymore. Some of them could not pay their grocery bills. That same friend and others thought the grant company would pay McMains what he had spent in fighting them if he, in turn, would cease his agitation. Hunt passed that suggestion on to Mrs. McMains, who said she would be glad if such a settlement were reached; she had been trying to persuade her husband to give up and go on the lecture platform. She would not tell Mac, however, because "he would fly to pieces." Needless to say, she did tell him.

The suggestion that McMains interpreted as a bribe was made, Hunt explained, on the supposition that he would give up after his latest defeat. It was offered "in the interest of a much neglected woman and over enthusiastic husband." As for the abuse which McMains heaped "upon those that had done the most for him," Judge Hunt commented: "Such is the action of the professed follower of the meek and lowly Master. He must be hard up for capital to replenish his repeated failures. It is the action of a viper warmed into life by its benefactors, the hiss of the serpent and the sting of the scorpion."[24]

The highly personal exchange between former friends was a spectacular part of a broad split in anti-grant ranks. In the unfortunate collision religion should not have been dragged in, but neither should the implication that McMains could be bought off by the Maxwell Company.

An anti-McMains faction was a reality. But he still had strength in the hill country. A statement repudiating the agreement with Whigham was sent to the Upper Vermejo where it was signed by thirty-one men, four of whom had signed the proposed compromise. McMains rebounded with astonishing alacrity and was on his way to Washington again on May 4, his expenses raised by firm friends.[25]

The wearying miles in a sooty train gave him time to think. If the Cox decision were dead after all, then another position must be made ready. A possible alternative was the old claim that the land in New Mexico and Colorado east of the Rio Grande and south of the Arkansas River had belonged to Texas, for which Congress paid ten million dollars (the so-called Texas Purchase) as part of the Compromise of 1850. Of course, he would have to ignore the generally-held view that Congress had not recognized the claim but simply had paid up to settle an awkward situation. But if official acceptance of the Texas claim as valid could be attained, the props could be knocked from under the Maxwell and other grants on the premise that they were invalid because the land was not the Mexican government's to give. A long article supporting that contention appeared over McMains' signature in the *Kansas City Times*,[26] but he never regarded the argument as anything more than a poor substitute.

The doors of the pillared mansion on Pennsylvania Avenue opened to receive the man from New Mexico. He had made careful preparation with the aid of an attorney. He brought a brief, a petition, and other papers; all was ready for the crucial interview.

O. P. McMains entered the room where the President of the United States waited to receive him. Grover Cleveland saw in the small, rather distinguished-looking Agent for the Settlers little that suggested power of leadership over hundreds of people. Only the intense eyes hinted a faith and unflinching determination. To many prominent citizens he was the scourge of New Mexico, but his manner indicated nothing of a ruthlessness which the president had been told was the mainspring of the offensive against the former chief justice of the territory, William A. Vincent.

Introductory civilities done with, the president and the agent reviewed the status of the Maxwell Grant, McMains explaining that his trouble with the Interior Department came from deliberate mispresentation of his petition. Cleveland examined a copy and then remarked: "Your petition speaks for itself."[27]

That ambiguous comment was interpreted favorably by McMains, who heard more than was actually said. A Maxwell official could have understood the statement as an agreement with Secretary Lamar in denying the petition. Cleveland simply did not commit himself, but McMains, hopeful and excited, left the White House believing that he had an ally in the president. And possibly the Texas Purchase idea would never have to be tested.

At the other end of Pennsylvania Avenue in the Capitol's House chamber Anthony Joseph's approaches to the land grant problem had stopped or slowed down.* Nothing had come of his resolution inquiring about the status of the Cox decision, and Senate action on his House-approved bill for a

---

* Evidently McMains always thought well of Joseph, although some people thought he was like a political chameleon on local issues. See Howard R. Lamar, "Edmund G. Ross as Governor of New Mexico Territory: A Reappraisal," *New Mexico Historical Review* 36 (July 1961): 177–209.

board of commissioners to adjudicate private land claims disputes was awaited.[28]

With the gloom partially dispelled and hope now resting with the chief executive and Congress, McMains arrived in Raton on May 30.[29] It was well that something had rescued his morale, for the trend against him had increased in his absence. McMains' alleged call for a Clay Allison was revived by the *Daily Optic* in a report that Allison, then in Las Vegas, denied any sympathy for "old man McMains" and his agitation against the grant, saying that he had no intention of going after Harry Whigham.[30] And Judge Hunt had picked up the charge of bribery and hurled it back. He blamed McMains alone for the failure of the Colorado suit because he had not come through with promised proofs and witnesses. The Maxwell Land Grant Company must have paid McMains to break his word to the attorney general, he maintained, and it must be keeping McMains in Washington lobbying for the Cox decision and the Texas Purchase, so as to divert the settlers from hiring a good lawyer. McMains had not always been the "strong gladiator" against the grant, according to Hunt, but had in fact offered to "bury the hatchet" when Frank Sherwin first came to Cimarron, if the company would give him title to his ranch and vega — the same for which Hunt and others were ready to fight in 1882.[31]

Hunt's blast was approved by the *Santa Fe New Mexican* as showing up "the Reverend Oliver Patrick [*sic*] McMains in his true colors. The right reverend crank will have to take a back seat hereafter."[32] Mounting press attacks tried to make him into a dishonest laughing stock and stressed a distinction between anti-grantism and McMainsism. The nadir was reached in his old paper, the *Comet*:

> There was an old man named McMains,
> Who possessed more wind pudding than brains;
> He'd flatter like honey
> When talking for money
> To apply to his personal gains.

What has become of old O.P.?
Where he has gone we cannot see.
What has become of him, or how he fares,
Nobody knows and nobody cares;
If he has gone to the realms of love,
We're very sorry for those above;
If he has gone to the lower level,
We heartily pity the poor old devil.

McMains to the settlers said, "Ho!
I tell you the land grant must go;
Just put up your wealth,
I'll go east for my health,
And laugh at you, sabé?" Just so.[33]

Some settlers were certain that they would have to reckon with the grant company and that, in that event, McMains' activities could endanger negotiations. For them he was a liability that must be shunned, even to the point of impugning their honor.

To those who would look and listen, McMains showed the petition to the president and proclaimed his confidence that the Cox decision would be enforced. But despondence had gripped many who had not turned against him personally, with the reported result that an Anti-Grant Mutual Protective Association meeting was canceled because of lack of interest.[34]

Into the midst of all the despair came word that the Senate had rejected Joseph's bill to adjudicate land grant controversies. Worse than that, it was said that Cleveland would not consider the Cox decision until after the adjournment of Congress, so busy was he with the great number of bills on his desk.[35] That seemed like a way of breaking the news that there was little chance of succor from the White House. No anti-granter — pro- or anti-McMains — had reason to be happy.

Chapter 13

The Court Decides

WHILE O. P. McMAINS dropped from the apogee of his influence to a rapid decline, the business affairs of the Maxwell Land Grant Company underwent reorganization. Frank Remington Sherwin had been deposed in 1883, but continuing difficulties finally brought the Dutch investors to take over in February 1885 to prevent ruin. Meeting in Amsterdam on the second day of the month, the board of directors resolved to send Martinus Petrus Pels to America. Nine days later he was appointed by the Maxwell Land Grant committee for the protection of the rights of the holders of the income bonds to be "their true and lawful attorney" in the United States.[1]

Martinus Petrus Pels was forty-eight years old when he arrived. As a young man he was associated with commercial enterprises in the East Indian empire of the Kingdom of the Netherlands, representing the important mercantile firm of Dummler and Company at various places, including Batavia on the island of Java. While in residence there, Pels served as United States consul during the presidency of Abraham Lincoln. Later in Holland he distinguished himself as a member of the Council of Provincial Estates.[2]

Martinus Petrus Pels, general manager of the Maxwell Land Grant Company.

With his Van Dyke and gracious manners, Pels had not been in the United States long before his business abilities were recognized. In New York, Charles J. Canda, trustee of the Maxwell Land Grant Income Mortgage Bonds, spoke of him as a "bright, active man." Charles Fairchild, of Boston's Lee Higginson and Company, said, "We shall have added confidence in the success of the Company, if you will take the management of it yourself."[3] Most fulsome in his praise was General Bela M. Hughes, the Denver attorney assisting Pels: "If he had been put in charge of that Estate when the

Dutch purchased it to-day it would have been clear of debt, clear of silly bargains and of a gang of leeches who have done nothing but to gorge their bellies and laugh at the stupidity of their masters."[4]

Gradually Pels, Frank Springer, and others were able to bring some system to Maxwell affairs. Getting the company on a solid foundation was portentous for settlers on the grant. The Dutch owners planned that settlers could be proceeded against even before the Supreme Court ruled, so good was the company's chance of a favorable decision in the Colorado case.

Imminence of a showdown revived many an anti-grant heart. Men all over the Maxwell desperately wanted to stave off the threat, but without proper guidance their energies might be dissipated: the resurgence needed a rallying point. No first rate lawyer wanted to help. But McMains had not given up his conviction that Cleveland would have to support Secretary Cox's limitation of the grant. McMains' calumniators among the anti-granters offered nothing better, and no one suggested the Texas Purchase argument. And so, in their adversity, first a few and then many settlers sought out "old man McMains." He was spending an involuntary retirement at Raton, except for appearing at the October term of the district court, once as plaintiff and once as defendant.*

It was not difficult to get McMains into harness again. He did not sulk or have to be coaxed, although he did not ignore the enmity of those anti-granters who still refused to

---

* In McMains case against Showerman, the court found for McMains, and a sheriff's sale of Showerman's cattle was set for November 18. In the tax case against him the action was continued by agreement; in 1887 the court ruled that McMains had to pay $14.05 in back taxes on his house and lot in Raton (*O. P. McMains* v. *I. C. Showerman*, No. 631, Docket of the District Court, Colfax County, New Mexico, 1:228, 300; Record of the District Court B, Colfax County, New Mexico, p. 283; *Raton Daily Independent*, October 18, 1886).

Anthony (Antonio) Joseph. Delegate to Congress from the Territory of New Mexico, March 4, 1885–March 3, 1895.

have him. He wanted to resume work for the cause and naturally was gratified to be asked.

The fall political campaign of 1886 offered a reentry into the struggle against the Maxwell Grant; the Democratic and Anti-Grant Party was in the field with Anthony Joseph heading the ticket for reelection as delegate to Congress. At the county convention Joseph was endorsed and Surveyor General Julian commended for his investigation of land frauds, a proceeding which McMains accepted in a speech to the delegates.[5]

A few days later at Raton a similar gathering for ratification of Joseph's candidacy had Will Kappes, husband of McMains' niece, serving as secretary of the meeting. Anthony Joseph that night referred to his own efforts on behalf of Maxwell settlers and then said that President Cleveland would consider carefully the merits of the Maxwell circumstances and give his opinion in a short time. No prediction was made of the president's view, but a favorable inference was drawn.[6]

A reporter said that McMains spoke "in his usual happy vein." In his endorsement of Anthony Joseph he told of his difficulties with Republican officials as contrasted with the cooperation from Democrats.[7] But that was just partisan talk. He would have been hard-pressed to demonstrate that the Cleveland administration, so far, had done any more for the anti-grant cause than that of Garfield or Arthur before it.

Anthony Joseph was returned to Congress, and the Democratic and Anti-Grant party in Colfax County took the offices that were up for election. McMains was happier than he had been in months. Anti-grantism was still a potent force, and he was on the way to reinstatement as Agent for the Settlers, at least for the strong-willed and militant. The editor of *La Flecha*, in Wagon Mound, reminded his readers that McMains "is the person who deserves the credit and thanks of all honest settlers in Colfax and Mora counties for having the so-called Nolán land grant open for settlement."[8]

While waiting for the Supreme Court to act, M. P. Pels revealed something of his plans for the grant company. He would fence the entire estate and develop a big cattle enterprise on it; in other words, the old Maxwell Cattle Company would be made to amount to something. Removal of all non-company cattle was necessary, leaving more than a million acres to herds bearing the Maxwell Long H brand. Settlers could buy or lease the immediate plots that they occupied and often farmed. Later in the year an Englishman by the name of Francis Clutton, who had about fifteen years' experience in Colorado and New Mexico ranching, was hired by Pels[9] as manager of the Maxwell cattle.*

In mid-January 1887 the company hired D. F. Wilkins, assessor of Las Animas County, Colorado, to estimate the values of improvements and livestock belonging to the settlers, and McMains issued leaflets of protest and warning. The new company employee was not cordially received, particularly in the Stonewall country of Colorado. Even when the wind was strong and the cold intense, as it often was in the hills, many people would not invite him into their homes. Others charged him for room and board "like the devil." Nevertheless, he finished his work and crossed over the watershed onto the Upper Vermejo on February 1.[10]

In the snowy mountains around the Rito Leandro, Wilkins "had a hell of a time." Five men barred the way to him and his son. No one along that stream or the Rito Bernal would give information. He had to guess the amount of land under cultivation and gave up counting the livestock. By late February he covered the Poñil drainage and part of Red River, where McMains had a frame dwelling and 400 acres fenced. In early March, Wilkins took his census around Raton, crossed

---

*Clutton and his partner, Henry Hodding, another Englishman, were associated in 1873 with British investors in the Río Arriba Land and Cattle Company, based on the San Joaquín del Cañon del Río de Chama Grant; later Clutton acquired the Urraca ranch on the Maxwell near Cimarron. In October 1887 Clutton was appointed manager of the Maxwell cattle, and in December he became Pels's son-in-law (*Extracts from Reports on the Rio Arriba Ranches* [privately printed, probably 1886]; Lawrence R. Murphy, *Philmont: A History of New Mexico's Cimarron Country* [Albuquerque: University of New Mexico Press, 1972], pp. 136–37).

over the pass, and worked the Colorado side on Chicken (Gallinas) and Clear creeks. He was amazed at the large number of cattle. Because the Maxwell people* seemed bent on forcing reckonings before the Supreme Court acted, Wilkins aroused great antipathy. Pels, alert to the criticism, decided to hold off until then; waiting was not an ordeal because Springer wrote with clear confidence about proceedings before the high court.[11]

Justice Samuel F. Miller wrote the opinion upholding the Maxwell patent. Dated April 18, 1887, it affirmed Brewer's decision on all counts.† Then, as an apparent clincher for

---

*The Dutch Maxwell Land Grant Committee also controlled the southern portion of the adjoining Sangre de Cristo Grant (called the Costilla Estate), and M. P. Pels directed policies of the United States Freehold Land and Emigration Company in addition to his work as the Maxwell manager. Thus his ideas affected developments on ca. two million acres. The United States Freehold Land and Emigration Company, of course, was the victorious litigant in the Tameling case; the Sangre de Cristo Grant originally was the Lee and Beaubien, made to Stephen Lee and Narciso Beaubien, the minor son of Carlos Beaubien, of the Beaubien and Miranda (Maxwell) Grant. Governor Manuel Armijo endorsed both grants, and both were confirmed by the Act of June 21, 1860. Dutch investors acquired the Costilla Estate in 1870, and the company was incorporated by the Act of July 8, 1870 (M. P. Pels to the Maxwell Land Grant Committee, March 3, 1887, Letters March 3–November 7, 1887, pp. 1–5, MLG; U.S., *Statutes at Large*, 16:192).

† The next day two New York papers continued the debate. The *New York Times* (April 19) commented: "But how many men are there in this country, well-acquainted with the nature of land operations in New Mexico, who believe that the Maxwell grant in its present dimensions was honestly procured? The Government submitted no satisfactory evidence, it is said. If this be so, why did it go to court without proof to stand on? The result of these proceedings reflects discredit upon some one, and we hope that responsibility for failure will be fixed where it belongs." The *New York Tribune* (April 22) under the headline, "The Supreme Court Rebukes Slander," defended Stephen Benton Elkins and harshly criticized Commissioner Sparks.

The Maxwell Grant
(Beaubien and Miranda)

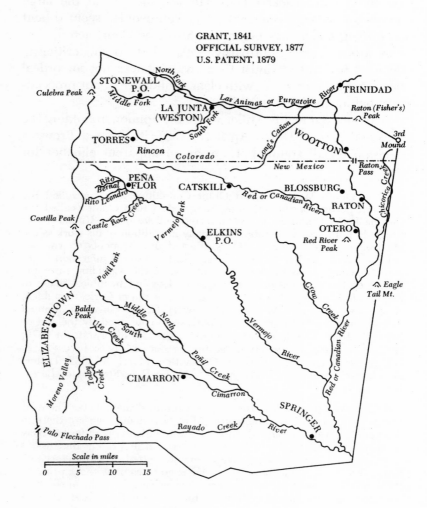

GRANT, 1841
OFFICIAL SURVEY, 1877
U.S. PATENT, 1879

Culebra Peak

STONEWALL P.O.

North Fork

Middle Fork

Las Animas or Purgatoire River

TRINIDAD

Raton (Fisher's) Peak

LA JUNTA (WESTON)

South Fork

3rd Mound

TORRES

Rincon

Colorado

Long's Cañon

WOOTTON

New Mexico

Raton Pass

PEÑA FLOR

Rito Bernal

Rito Leandro

CATSKILL

Red or Canadian River

BLOSSBURG

RATON

Chicorica Creek

Costilla Peak

Castle Rock Creek

Vermejo Park

ELKINS P.O.

OTERO

Red River Peak

Eagle Tail Mt.

Ponil Park

ELIZABETHTOWN

Baldy Peak

Middle

North

Crow Creek

Ute Creek

South

Vermejo River

Red or Canadian River

Moreno Valley

Tolby Creek

CIMARRON

Ponil Creek

Cimarron

SPRINGER

Palo Flechado Pass

Rayado Creek

River

Scale in miles

0   5   10   15

[158]

Location of Maxwell Grant

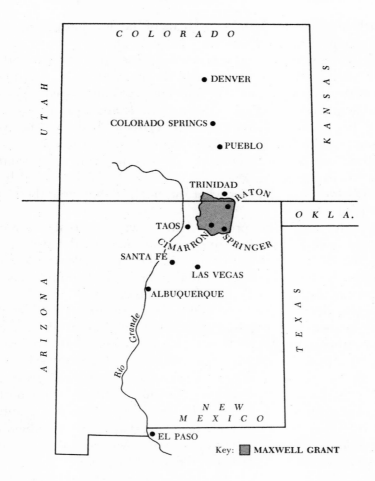

application of the Tameling decision and the concept of a grant *de novo*, in his closing observations Miller cited the constitutional power of Congress to make rules and regulations pertaining to the territory and other property of the United States.[12] Once again, questions of American treaty obligations (also a part of the fundamental law), the veracity of witnesses, and simple justice to ordinary citizens were given little attention, and McMains' fears of the devastating impact of the Tameling decision were substantiated.

Even in the face of this action by the court of last resort, McMains and others insisted that the unreversed Cox decision was the only rule; that the Tameling decision was not applicable to the Maxwell case; that a grant *de novo* was not possible because the United States never really had any title to convey. The failure of the Supreme Court to accept those points was for them evidence of bias and corruption, and McMains hurried to Washington on funds quickly raised by hard-core supporters for what the *Raton Range* described as a "lunatic trip."[13]

McMains' anger prompted him to write a harshly accusatorial, open letter to the Supreme Court justices, dated Washington, May 2.[14] However, he did not then make the letter public because there was still a slight hope of ultimate success for the anti-granters in the federal courts.

At the General Land Office, McMains found high-level acceptance of a proposal to ask the Supreme Court for a rehearing in the Maxwell case. Commissioner Sparks was out of the city, so it fell to Acting Commissioner S. M. Stockslager, with approval by Secretary Lamar, to ask the attorney general to press for a review on the following points: 1. the Court was in error in treating the Maxwell as an *empresario* grant; 2. the Court was mistaken in believing that Carlos Beaubien's mention of fifteen to eighteen leagues was not in reference to his own claim; 3. the Court wrongly assumed that Surveyor General Pelham reported on the extent of the grant, since no survey had been made at that time; 4. the grant had not been confirmed by the Mexican departmental assembly; 5. new and material evidence of fraud had been discovered.[15]

Attorney General A. H. Garland acceded to the request and asked that a rehearing of the Maxwell case be set for March 1, 1888, and a formal motion was submitted to the Supreme Court by Assistant Attorney General William A. Maury on May 12, 1887. The next day the *Raton Range* reported the move by the General Land Office to get the case reviewed,[16] and soon M. P. Pels was aware of the Justice Department's action.*

The grant company manager was "beastly annoyed" and concerned because anti-grant settlers "were picking up life."[17] Telegraphing Charles J. Canda — then national treasurer of the Democratic Party† — Pels asked him to try to head off a rehearing. Canda replied that it had been asked for only "in a perfunctory way" and probably would be refused. However encouraging that was, Pels was not satisfied; he knew that Commissioner Sparks advocated a new lawsuit in New Mexico and that McMains was working on President Cleveland for a public statement in support of the Cox Decision.[18]

Once again using Canda as liaison, Pels tried "to get officials to declare that our property henceforth will not be disturbed by the government," and a second time Canda did not come through, saying simply that he would try "to prevent further adverse action."[19] On a practical basis Pels felt that the grant company could proceed firmly against defiant settlers. He recommended immediate ejectment actions against those who would not meet terms:

> It is the same story as that of the boy who has just been licked, and who is willing to obey, and do everything you want under the recent influence of that punishment; after

---

* In the meantime, McMains, still in Washington, wrote on May 6 to the attorney general requesting a lawsuit in New Mexico against the Maxwell Land Grant Company. Obviously McMains had written off the Colorado case. The next day Garland refused McMains' proposal: "As you do not seem to see the impracticability of what you request, in view of the recent decision of the Supreme Court of the United States in the Maxwell case, it would appear quite useless for me to try to convince you that there is no alternative to submission to the decision of the Judicial Department of the Government." See *Raton Weekly Independent*, February 2, 1889.

† The letter was addressed to Canda as U.S. Sub-Treasurer, Wall Street, New York City.

sometime the impression of that punishment vanishes. Place decision of the Supreme Court in place of punishment, and you will conclude that my comparison is correct.[20]

The high court's decision caused some crumbling of settlers' resistance. A few men, among them the president of the Anti-Grant Mutual Protective Association, went to the company office at Cimarron to inquire about terms. And demoralization was increased when explanatory pamphlets by the Maxwell Company were given wide circulation.[21]

Perhaps McMains heard that the motion for a rehearing was being indifferently handled by the Justice Department. At any rate, while the outcome of that was pending, McMains had another meeting with President Cleveland and came away convinced that Cleveland agreed with him that the Cox decision could not be reversed by inference from a court decision that did not mention it directly.[22] But Cleveland gave no public sign of that, so the Agent for the Settlers returned to New Mexico with only some hope of presidential action and very little expectation from the rehearing.

Chapter 14

Refurbished Reputation

McMains' open letter to the justices of the Supreme Court appeared on May 20, 1887, in the *Raton Range*, successor to the *Comet*. It appeared apparently with his consent;[1] at least there is no evidence that someone filched a copy and gave it to the editor. The timing is still a mystery, since the court had not acted on the motion for a rehearing. When M. P. Pels saw it he commented "that man would be too happy to be placed in jail as a martyr."[2]

The letter was an astonishing production. McMains called the justices a "set of corruptionists" and told them they lied in implying that a commissioner of the General Land Office could arbitrarily revoke the final decision of a secretary of the interior, and they lied in ruling that the Tameling decision overruled the Cox decision by holding that congressional confirmation of a land grant in effect was a grant *de novo*. A postscript switched to the argument that the land had belonged to Texas, not Mexico, thus invalidating the alleged Mexican grant.[3]

Such a public outburst was bad judgment, strengthening the charge that McMains was a dangerous agitator. His opponents were delighted, and the *Range* characterized him

as well-meaning, dedicated, worthy of compassion and gratitude for his time and effort, but inept.[4] That was gentle criticism compared to that of an old detractor, the Las Vegas
Daily Optic, which said the letter reminded one "for all the
world of a maggot trying to vomit on the sun."[5]

McMains ignored the censure and planned a mass meeting in the Raton Rink on the evening of May 24. A large crowd
was there to see and hear. Many were faithful followers, others
were simply curious; but he was still a good drawing card.
Certain he was that his audience had almost begun to look
cross-eyed at his efforts, but he urged another try at enforcement of the Cox decision, saying it would be his last attempt.
He was confident that President Cleveland would answer
clearly if the question were put simply and directly — a comment open to more than one interpretation. A resolution was
passed in keeping with his recommendation.[6]

The Supreme Court on May 27, speaking again through
Mr. Justice Miller, rejected the petition for a rehearing. The
court did respond to some of the points raised, while noting
that it was doing so only because of the importance of the
case. It denied error in treating the Maxwell as an *empresario*
grant, because the decision did not turn on that; the point
was, the court maintained, that Congress knowingly confirmed
a larger amount than twenty-two square leagues — a grant
de novo. Evading the matter of new evidence of fraud, the
justices said they were restricted to the record as it came from
the circuit court,[7] and not even McMains at his most optimistic
could see a chance of a new trial. Their reaffirmation of Judge
Brewer's wisdom and competence raised questions about the
quality of justice in the Maxwell case which have lingered to
this day. At the time it convinced some anti-granters that
McMains' castigation of the Supreme Court was right.

৩৵৩

The prospects for the Maxwell Land Grant Company
were bright. But M. P. Pels, looking back over two harrying

years, expressed some skepticism in a letter to Canda: "I hope that not some other deviltry will be got up now and that we will have rest at last."[8] It was a vain hope; peace was not to be their lot for a long time.

Pels maintained a home and office in Denver, which for him was a good location, because of fairly quick access to the Maxwell and Costilla estates. One day late in May a letter came from Raton with a clipping about McMains' recent mass meeting and plan to importune the president to speak out on the Cox decision. Now it was Pels's turn to belabor Washington officialdom with gusto, the difference being that he did so privately in a letter to Canda:

> ... allow me to suggest that the President be prevailed upon to quickly give such a sweeping answer to the agitator's friends as will end this matter for good. This is only due to the Dutch people even should it injure the "poor Settlers' protecting, popularity seeking President" and the others who parade as landmarks-destroying political iconoclasts.[9]

Pels feared that Commissioner Sparks might succeed in reopening the case for the New Mexico portion.[10] He was grateful for the recent Supreme Court decisions, but:

> ... you know that it does not end as long as a cloud hangs over the 1,500,000 acres in N.M. And as to the President, I wish with you that he might be re-elected; this will give him an opportunity to become, thru' experience, something more of a statesman and will enable him to visit and study the vast empire laying West of New York State; he may acquire a different impression of the "poor Indian and poor, honest squatter" ... I wish he was a shareholder in Maxwell.[11]

Both sides made direct contacts with people on the grant. McMains circulated with his proposal, and Harry Whigham made some of the same rounds to find out who wanted to sign leases with the company.[12]

Audrey and Frank Alpers

Outing on Sugarite (corruption of Chicorica) Creek, 1888. Left to right:
Charles Springer (rancher and brother of Frank); unknown; unknown;
Frank Springer (attorney for the Maxwell Land Grant Company);
Francis Clutton (manager of the Maxwell cattle and Pels's son-in-law);
Harry Whigham (receiver of the Maxwell Land Grant Company); Theo-
dore Schomburg (company employee and Whigham's son-in-law), pull-
ing the shutter cord; Joseph Schroeder, Raton pharmacist.

Not all anti-granters wanted McMains in full command
again; some were convinced that legal counsel should be
retained as well. Consequently a call went out from the Anti-
Grant Mutual Protective Association for a July 4 meeting on
the Vermejo. Rumor had a Santa Fe lawyer, Eugene A. Fiske
(former principal clerk of private land claims in the General

Land Office),° ready to work with the settlers. Pels asked
Henry L. Waldo, former territorial chief justice and prominent
Democrat, to put the damper on Mr. Fiske.[13]

From many cañons and along dusty roads, often little
better than trails, settlers converged on a small meadow in
Vermejo Park in the northwestern part of the Maxwell. Some
of them had traveled for more than a day to reach the Fourth
of July celebration.

Hams and roasts, pies and cakes, pickles and jellies, and
other good things were loaded onto improvised tables. There
would be dancing until the glow of dawn, with bonfires and
paper lanterns lighting the squares and throwing a warm
glow on the pines.

Old timers recalled McMains' first public appearance in
Cimarron on July 4, 1875, and they had often sung with him
his favorite hymn, "Shall We Gather at the River?" His white
hair and beard, his Prince Albert coat, the expression of his
eyes — everything about him was familiar, and they knew
about what he was going to say. Yet as he fervently suggested
the similarity of their predicament to the conflict of revolu-
tionary heroes, his speech was interrupted by noisy applause.[14]

There was some disharmony even so. Those settlers who
wanted an attorney had brought two lawyers to give advice.
However, nothing was accomplished because the lawyers
looked around and concluded that "it was not their picnic."[15]

J. H. Hunt was one of the men seeking good legal counsel,
and through his *Raton Range* he complained about the grant
company, while advising the settlers not to entrust their future

---

°Apparently Fiske resigned from the General Land Office because
of allegations of impropriety in his work (Lee Scott Theisen, "Frank
Warner Angel's Notes on New Mexico Territory, 1878," *Arizona and
the West* 18 [Winter 1976]: 352–53; Victor Westphall, *Thomas Benton
Catron and His Era* [Tucson: University of Arizona Press, 1973], p.
280).

to McMains. His personal feelings towards McMains had softened, although they were still not on speaking terms. The *Range* disapproved of McMains' methods but defended him against those who called him a maniac by describing him as a man "who had already done more at the same time to save and ruin a people than any other man in western history. . . . and the character of his motives has led us to 'glory in his spunk.' "[16] The Hunt-McMains feud was unfortunate; it weakened the anti-grant movement and produced no innovative proposals for action. The *Range*'s opinion that help was most likely from Congress was hardly new;[17] McMains had often used that approach.

The Stonewall country, with its meadows of timothy, cultivated fields, and fat cattle was perhaps the heartland of the anti-grant movement. There men lived who held patents to their land from the United States — later suspended because of inclusion in the Maxwell survey. There McMains enjoyed some of his most ardent support. And there Whigham had met a reception which had convinced him of the imprudence of returning.

In the last week of June, M. P. Pels put up at Pooler's Hotel just west of the Stonewall settlement in Colorado and started to gather "some data about the people and history" before talking with ranchers and farmers. Armed men had tried to waylay Harry Whigham on the Vermejo, and Pels had been advised not to go to Stonewall because McMains had been there and aroused the people.[18]

In addition to plans for developing its cattle department, the company hoped to attract alien farmers onto the estate. Pels favored South Germans, particularly from Bavaria and Württemberg, and arranged to obtain immigrants through the colonization agent of the Santa Fe Railroad. But another reason for clearing settlers from the Stonewall country was the proposal of Trinidad businessmen to develop a summer

resort there.[19] In any case, stubborn anti-granters had some
of the best land on the Maxwell, and Pels made up his mind
that the clique of men holding government papers had to go,
a decision that was a serious blunder.

Pels was not wholly callous to some of the people's problems. In a report to the Maxwell Committee he said: "These
settlers are in a most peculiar position, and if any men settled
on the Grant in good faith, thinking it was Government land,
they did so," and he admitted that "it was not a very pleasant
task to be the chief executioner on the Maxwell estate."[20]
Nevertheless, he believed that their stand against the Maxwell title was untenable and that magnanimity towards the
men with government patents, especially to the extent of
giving them their claims, was not the way to peace.

As a starter, Pels went to see Richard D. Russell, the first
man to receive a government deed (September 5, 1876),
having preempted his chosen tract as early as 1871. Born in
Canada in 1839 while his parents were visiting there from
Illinois, Russell went to California at age sixteen, joined the
First Cavalry, California Volunteers, and came to New Mexico
with that force.* After resigning his commission, Russell took
up ranching.[21]

The interview was dramatic as Pels and Russell walked
beside the rancher's well-stocked lake. At first Russell was
"as quiet as a tomb" and later "damned the whole world for a
few instants."[22] However, he agreed to sell his improvements
and cattle to the company, which would take his cattle in
October.

Agreement with Russell presaged success with the others.
Six soon came to terms, including Robert Vail, whom Pels

---

*Attaining the rank of lieutenant, he married at Fort Union in 1865.
That same year, he and Mrs. Russell were with Colonel Kit Carson at
the establishment of Camp Nichols on the Cimarron Cutoff of the Santa
Fe Trail in the present Oklahoma panhandle.

Mrs. Marion Duling

Lieutenant and Mrs. Richard D. Russell.
(Probably taken at Fort Union in 1865.)

termed "one of the greatest revolutionaries on the Grant."
One influential man held out. Short, stocky, strong-jawed
F. B. Chaplin° "was swearing at the company, at the government, at everybody, and he told me that he would be thankful
if I would eject him, because he would then institute a strong

---

° Frank B. Chaplin came with his wife and family from Nebraska to
Trinidad in 1868, going to Stonewall in 1871 (Notes from E. J. Hubbard
and from Duane D. Finch, Samuel W. DeBusk Collection, Trinidad
State Junior College Library, Trinidad, Colorado).

case against the Government that had given him final papers."
But when Chaplin agreed to think it over, he was informed
next day that Pels would be not available until evening. This
news brought on another outburst: " 'Damn the grant — I will
not hunt or run after grant men.' "[23] Incensed, Pels dispatched
a severe letter to Chaplin by messenger:

> I respect old age: I know that your case is a hard one;
> I have extended a friendly hand towards you in the face
> of the action of the Govt. in olden times; but the Maxwell
> Company insists to be recognized in its rights confirmed
> by the highest Court in the land, and I wish to be treated
> as a gentleman. I therefore have to do my duty, and beg
> to inform you that unless we can come to an agreement
> to-day, I shall have to apply for an injunction in the most
> extensive way, to be followed by a suit for ejectment.[24]

There was no agreement that day, the Fourth of July
(the same day that McMains revived resistance on the Vermejo, not many miles away), so Pels went down the Purgatoire
valley next day to within about seven miles of Trinidad, where
he turned into Long's Cañon. There he had only middling
success.[25]

Resistance on the Colorado portion was slight. The relative ease with which Pels made deals showed the paralyzing
effect of the Supreme Court's decision. Haggling over prices
for livestock and improvements was a minor difficulty.

On July 8, 1887, Pels was in Raton getting ready to leave
for the Vermejo country, where he hoped to be as successful
as he had been in Colorado. The *Raton Range* sounded the
alarm for farmers and ranchers to "Beware of Leases!" Just as
he departed he learned that McMains had written again to
President Cleveland, pleading for an official statement in
support of the Cox decision. While stopping over night at the
home of John B. Dawson, a strong pro-granter, Pels was persuaded to let Dawson try to make arrangements, especially
on cattle options, since a majority of the settlers were cattlemen.[26]

In the New Mexico hill country were pockets of preference for legal counsel as opposed to McMains' leadership. At a meeting on the Caliente, for instance, men from Ute Creek were willing to contribute $2,000 towards hiring a lawyer.

Something had revived determination to thwart the grant company. The announcement of McMains as the principal speaker at a Raton meeting intimated that, and doubts were expelled with the election of Richard D. Russell, of Stonewall, to the presidency of a permanent organization. Elections also chose presidents of districts (giving key positions about equally to Anglo and Mexican settlers) to compile a list of settlers as a basis for a tight network of anti-grant resistance.

Well received as usual, McMains examined the Cox decision and President Cleveland. On the rostrum was F. B. Chaplin, whose remarks were described as "rousing," and before the evening was over other prominent settlers had expressed their sympathetic views.

It was decided to print McMains' remarks in both English and Spanish and give the minutes to the press. Part of the latter was a long manifesto that recapitulated the struggle against the grant, but it incorporated two special points: the record in the Colorado case had not included Secretary Delano's order to treat the Maxwell as public land; nor had it included the public surveys, filings and entries, final receipts, and the thirty-two patents issued to settlers. The second point stated that the Supreme Court did not want to offend the Maxwell Land Grant Company and three railroad companies* by deciding in the settlers' favor, an assertion that was appro-

---

* The Denver and Rio Grande, the Pueblo and Arkansas Valley, and the Atchison, Topeka and Santa Fe railroads were codefendants in the case. See Transcript of Record, *The United States* v. *The Maxwell Land Grant Company, et al.*, Records of the United States Supreme Court, Record Group 267, National Archives, Washington, D.C.

priately reflective of the times — 1887 being the year of the Interstate Commerce Commission Act.[27]

Indeed the resurgence was remarkable, and no doubt incredible to some, especially since it also restored McMains' prestige. How quickly the Maxwell Company's negotiations withered and so much of Pels's work was undone. Of course, several factors contributed.

A prime reason for renewed resistance was the failure to reach an agreement with F. B. Chaplin; Pels believed that "he is for Colorado what McMains is for New Mexico."[28] Also, a feeling of shame existed in the Stonewall country that good men had gone back on their word to McMains, and Chaplin succeeded in recovering those who had strayed. Some men regretted their haste in dealing with the company. R. D. Russell, for one, was having difficulty with Pels over points in his contract.[29] It may be taken for granted that McMains spent many hours of exhortation and persuasion to rebuild opposition to the company. A hard-hitting article in the July issue of the *North American Review*, "Land Stealing·in New Mexico" by Surveyor General George W. Julian, may have had influence through charges of corruption and collusion concerning land grants — with sharp attention to the inflated Maxwell.[30] Finally, the *Raton Range* observed: "It is useless to try to disguise the fact that McMains now has several hundred followers who believe that he is right, that according to law this is public land. It is of no use to tell them that it is no executive officer's place to answer as to the weight of the Cox decision, for no argument, however clear, would change their minds, so fully do they believe in their representative."[31]

Chapter 15

The President's Letter

REINSTATEMENT AS AGENT for the Settlers demanded quick action, but McMains did not go to Washington. A more oblique approach seemed to be called for: strong publicity might bring the requisite pressure. People all over the country should know that the settlers' brief had been misrepresented to Secretary Lamar, that President Cleveland had never said that the Cox decision had been regularly reversed. McMains clearly believed that a favorable decision would be issued eventually, despite all the procrastination.[1]

A letter from McMains to Cleveland, published in the *St. Louis Globe-Democrat*, attracted a lot of attention. In essence it was an urgent appeal to Cleveland to affirm the Cox decision, with this conclusion:

> Long, but in vain, your Excellency, have I offered prayer for the settlers in the dark, secret-keeping, mystery-haunted closets of the nation's houses at the capital city; but hoping this open public prayer, in which the whole nation is expected to join, may meet with better success, be speedily answered, and settlers relieved of heart-sickness, caused by long-deferred hope, I have the honor to remain, very respectfully,
>
> O. P. MCMAINS
> Agent for the Settlers.[2]

The settlers' organization was put in working order, and there were happenings in the hills which indicated that some anti-granters might not continue their docility. M. P. Pels experienced the new flare-up against the Maxwell Company. He started for the Upper Vermejo on August 23 in a horse and buggy driven by Gus, John B. Dawson's son. They reached A. J. Young's place about 1 P.M., and as they approached the long log house they found a small group of men awaiting them. After some talk, Pels saw that nothing would be accomplished and was preparing to leave when Young said that other settlers in the neighborhood wanted to see him. Several of the men galloped up the road and other riders made signals from the promontories. Naturally Pels was uneasy and walked over to the buggy, where he discovered that his gun had been removed. His worry increased when he saw more horsemen coming from the hills until about fifteen were assembled around him.

No direct threat was made by any of the settlers, although their attitude was hardly cordial. W. F. McClure, their spokesman, informed Pels that they had lived on the so-called grant for a long time and had no intention of leaving unless so ordered by the president of the United States, to whom they had written through their agent; he warned Pels not to come to Vermejo Park again. Pels asked for a chance to speak, but they refused and turned on young Gus Dawson, advising him not to bring a grant man there again. Pels and his companion climbed into the buggy and drove off — not up the Vermejo but down.[3]

Nor was that episode the only portent. The company surveyor in Colorado, E. C. Van Diest,* reported that when he drove from Trinidad to the Stonewall Valley he was followed

---

* Van Diest later became manager of the United States Freehold Land and Emigration Company on the Costilla Estate.

for a long distance by at least sixteen masked men on horse-back who prevented him from laying out a ditch line. And in Vermejo Park, settlers told several coal prospectors sent out by the Santa Fe Railroad that no coal leases would be permitted on the grant.[4]

Pels was certain that these interceptions were inspired by McMains and his letter to the president. But two could work at letter writing, and it was about time Grover Cleveland heard the other side of the story. So it was that M. P. Pels, in great indignation, wrote to the president on August 31, 1887. He portrayed McMains as the ringleader in illegal actions and enclosed one of McMains' handbills (probably the one blasting the Supreme Court). As part of the procedure to get Grover Cleveland to state quickly and publicly that the Cox decision was void, Pels again used C. J. Canda as intermediary, sending the letter to him for personal delivery to the president.[5]

Now Grover Cleveland was importuned by both sides to speak out on the Cox decision. But Pels saw no reason to wait for the president's opinion before proceeding against anti-granters. The company seemed safe behind its bulwarks of an act of Congress, a United States patent, and a decision of the Supreme Court. So Pels filed an affidavit with the clerk of the district court at Springer asking for arrest of the men who had denied him the right to travel on the grant. Bench warrants were issued,* and Sheriff Abe Sever set off for the Vermejo country with them.[6]

Word of the warrants leaked out; rumors spread of threats of death to company men. From the Stonewall country came accounts of masked men with blanketed horses waiting for Pels because of the lawsuits filed against R. D. Russell and

---

* The men to be arrested were W. F. McClure, A. J. Young, C. J. Young, George Young, Thomas W. Young, J. W. Parsons, Dudley Shy, Henry Butler, Richard Butler, and William Butler.

F. B. Chaplin. The new legal actions were timed to further weaken the less-determined settlers. Not a few felt there was no sense in holding out if resistance should mean futile violence and bloodshed. Some settlers flatly told McMains they would sell if they could get a fair price. Others urged him again to hire a lawyer, and it was reported that he agreed.[7]

When Chief Justice Elisha V. Long opened court on the September day scheduled for the Vermejo Park cases, all but two or three of those men were there. Other settlers came to Springer to see what would happen. The anti-granters were represented by Santa Fe attorney E. A. Fiske, who had offered his services before; the well-known Thomas Benton Catron, also from Santa Fe and a man much interested in land grants, appeared for the company in the absence of Frank Springer, who was in Europe on company business.[8]

On September 21 Fiske argued a motion to dismiss the proceedings because the judge had no right to issue bench warrants while on vacation and it was a matter for a justice of the peace in the first place. Catron agreed; the cases were dismissed and the defendants discharged.[9] Thus Pels's first move against the recalcitrants collapsed.

But he still had a card or two to play. A grand jury was assembled and the Vermejo Park men brought before it, apparently on new warrants. The settlers were encouraged, however, by the sight of some strong anti-granters on the grand jury and by the judge's mild charge to it.

That night Pels played his trump. He went to see Judge Long ostensibly to apprise the judge of the latest company plans, but incidentally adding that it was very difficult for the grant people to develop their property because of McMains' constant agitation of the settlers. He also suggested that the charge to the grand jury had been too lenient, especially the point that the older settlers had " 'some rights,' " and then protested that the jury was loaded against the company.

Next morning Judge Long informed the grand jurors that if any of them had been involved in the Vermejo trouble they

could not serve; that got rid of W. F. McClure, one of the
"rioters" who had had the unusual experience of questioning
Pels — the man who sought the indictments.* Then the judge
spoke strongly of the need to indict "their own mothers and
fathers" if charges were proved against them. Several settlers
were indicted for assault and menace as a consequence, Pels
believed, of stern talk from the bench.

The indictments demoralized the settlers, so Pels turned
from being the principal witness against them to being their
benefactor. He asked the judge and the district attorney to
dismiss the proceedings, which they did after a seemly interval of a day or so. That the softening-up worked was shown
when a succession of settlers came into the company office
during the week to talk business with Pels, who allowed his
optimism to see agreements with all the settlers in the near
future.[10]

Trying a new avenue of advice, J. H. Hunt and others
sought the opinion of Kansas Senator Preston B. Plumb, chairman of the Senate Public Lands Committee. His letter in
reply was published in the *Raton Range*, September 23, 1887.
Plumb agreed that the Maxwell should be limited to twenty-
two square leagues but saw little chance of it in view of the
Supreme Court's decision. He vaguely talked compromise,
suggesting the government might buy the land and sell it to
the settlers. But why, he wondered, should they not purchase
from the company since they would have to buy their land in
any event? Apparently no one knew that Senator Plumb and

---

*Why McClure was picked for the grand jury is a mystery. After all,
he was one of the Vermejo men for whom the bench warrants had been
issued at Pels's behest, and then he found himself as a grand juror
sitting in judgment on his fellow "rioters," against whom Pels hoped
that bills of indictment would be issued. Pels, of course, was a witness.

Judge Brewer were close friends,[11] and his double-talk simply strengthened those who stood against the grant on principle while reassuring those who would give up.*

Two weeks later the *Range* published a letter to M. P. Pels from President Cleveland dated September 27, 1887. Its platitudes, together with its disregard of the Cox decision, made it of immense propaganda value to the grant company.

> In the matter of the Maxwell Grant referred to in your communication, as in every other, the law of the land must be supreme. The judgment of the Supreme Court of the United States on the subject involved therein is authoritative and conclusive. The judgment must be respected and obeyed. Those who counsel resistance to the law, or by false and inflammatory statements, such as are made in the handbill submitted to me, are the worst enemies of those whom they mislead. . . . If any wrongs are done their redress can be obtained through the peaceful method of the law . . . Its faithful enforcement is due alike to the poor and the weak, the wealthy and the strong.
>
> I sincerely trust the incendiary counsel in the handbill will not produce the baleful effect for which it was

---

*Plumb's position on land grants was enigmatic to say the least. He had been highly critical of Surveyor General Julian's methods against them, yet he had sponsored a bill limiting large landholdings either by Americans or foreigners, which President Cleveland signed into law on March 3, 1887. The senator from Kansas was largely instrumental in securing Judge Brewer's appointment to the Supreme Court in 1889. See Harold Hathaway Dunham, *Government Handout: A Study in the Administration of the Public Lands* (Ann Arbor, Mich.: Edwards Brothers, 1941), p. 298; Howard R. Lamar, "Edmund G. Ross as Governor of New Mexico Territory: A Reappraisal," *New Mexico Historical Review* 36 (July 1961):191; *The Autobiography of William Allen White* (New York: Macmillan Company, 1946), pp. 358–9; D. Stanley Eitzen, "David J. Brewer, 1837–1910: A Kansan on the United States Supreme Court," *The Emporia State Research Studies* 12 (March 1964):29–30.

intended, and those in whose favor the court has determined these vexed questions of title, will not attempt to extend their rights to cases not determined, and that in insisting upon their rights they will deal kindly and generously with those who have mistakenly acted upon an invalid title.[12]

Pels hastened to take advantage of the resulting consternation, going from Raton to Poñil and Vermejo parks, where he was received "most hospitably and kindly." By whom he did not say. That the struggle apparently was over at last he expressed in a letter of thanks to C. J. Canda, saying that McMains had lost much influence.[13]

McMains may have lost influence, but his old vigor recovered fast enough when he read what Pels had released to the press.* He was shocked, angry, and incredulous. Quickly he wrote a scathing piece, and handbills soon poured from the press:

> SETTLERS: You are once more the victim of a trick and fraud practiced upon you by the officers of the Maxwell Land Grant Company. . . .
> Never would President Cleveland commit himself to an assertion, without proof, that the settlers had "mistakenly acted upon an invalid title."† The president would have given excellent reasons. . . . He would not, Pells-like [*sic*], have contented himself with a mere slashing assertion of invalidity.
> President Cleveland never wrote the letter. . . . It is, upon its face, an unofficial letter. It is not headed, as all

---

* It appears that McMains had written to Cleveland again on the same date that Cleveland wrote to Pels (Wilfred I. McPheron, "History of the Maxwell Land Grant" [Master's thesis, Colorado State College of Education, 1936], pp. 79–80).

† The title referred to as invalid, of course, was the U.S. quitclaim to their ranches that the Stonewall settlers had because their claims had been part of the public domain.

the president's official letters are, "Executive Mansion." And that Grover Cleveland ever wrote M. P. Pels an official or private letter on Maxwell grant matters is quite incredible, as that would be placing himself on too familiar terms, for his own good, with the president of the Maxwell grant and the Sangre de Cristo grant — two of the biggest land frauds in the United States.

Never, in a letter to M. P. Pels would Grover Cleveland have lectured a fellow citizen for having made "false statements" statements in a "hand bill" without . . . proving their falsity. . . .

The Grover Cleveland letter is a Maxwell Company trick and fraud, designed to dishearten you, settlers, and force you to capitulate.

Don't be disheartened, settlers, and don't capitulate. "At eve it shall be light." The unreversed decision of Secretary Cox, treated with contempt and defiance for the last seventeen years by Colorado and New Mexico statesmen and a foreign corporation, will yet, and that in the very near future, be respected and enforced.[14]

It is doubtful that McMains, for any length of time, actually thought the letter a forgery. Understandably he took umbrage at the tone of it and was angered that it ignored the Cox decision. And, of course, he was piqued because the president had never answered his letters. However, his headlong rush into print again gave his detractors a highly exploitable item. The *Raton Range* did not miss its chance:

McMains knows and recognizes no defeat. When the Angel Gabriel sounds his trumpet and proclaims that time shall be no more, right there McMains will tell him that he is a fraud and has no authority for such a statement — that St. Matthew made an earlier and authoritative decision which has never yet been reversed and still was law, and that Jehovah had promised him that it should be enforced. . . .

McMains will never give up as long as he lives. . . . Such a man cannot be beaten in his own mind. A man who will find consolation in as many defeats as Mr. McMains has experienced will always be happy.[15]

In the meantime McMains went to the Colorado portion of the grant, and Pels saw flaws in Cleveland's letter because the mention of "cases not determined" had revived hope among some settlers; he wanted Canda to get an explanation from the president.[16]

Someone in Raton thought of comparing the Cleveland signature on the letter with the one on Postmaster Bob Vandiver's commission — a test that appeared to be satisfactory.[17] J. C. Holmes, of the *Raton Independent*, was not content with such simple methods. He wrote directly to Cleveland and asked him to authenticate the letter, also inquiring if the Maxwell Grant had passed beyond the jurisdiction of the departments. He received an answer from Colonel D. S. Lamont, the president's private secretary, dated October 31 at the Executive Mansion:

> The President has received your letter of the 13th instant, which awaited him upon his return to Washington, and in reply you are informed that the printed letter you enclose is a correct copy of the communication addressed by him to Mr. Pels.
> You must find answer to the second interrogatory in the letter itself.[18]

Thus was the element of riddle added, but it was clear by then that no commitment on the Cox decision would ever be drawn from Grover Cleveland.

The president's procrastination needs further consideration. It is difficult to understand his refusal to make a definite statement, either for or against the Cox decision. Perhaps he was reluctant to overrule prominent men in his administration such as Secretary Lamar and Land Office Commissioner Sparks. That might explain his failure to tell McMains, during one of their appointments, that he could not support it. The unfortunate result, however, was an encouragement of optimism in the Agent for the Settlers. And Canda's apparent evasion of Pels's demands that the president take a firm stand may also have been in the interest of Democratic party harmony.

There comes the question of why Cleveland finally responded to Pels's letter with some degree of directness. The McMains broadside, which Pels had enclosed, allowed the president to be morally indignant towards McMains (without mentioning any name), while the Court's decision in the Maxwell case enabled him again to avoid a stand on the Cox decision — implying the court had invalidated it.

Did Cleveland, when he saw the broadside, realize that McMains was the same person who was so sharply criticized by his appointee, Judge Vincent, in that pathetic affair in New Mexico two years before? It is quite likely; McMains' enemies certainly would have pointed out his identity. Whatever the explanation, Cleveland's dilatoriness over the Cox decision was a serious mistake that only exacerbated the bitterness of the Maxwell disturbances. Some people quite naturally took his inaction to mean that he could not in fact say that the Cox decision was inoperative.

Chapter 16

New Irritations

THE SUPREME COURT DECISION upholding the Maxwell patent by no means terminated anti-grant activity on that property. Lawyer E. A. Fiske, for instance, tried to prevent eviction of some settlers because they could claim ten years of adverse possession and undisputed occupancy. In other words, the statute of limitations protected them, but the now pro-grant *Raton Range* contended that the statute's application started with the patent of 1879 and therefore had not run out.[1]

At least Fiske tried to obtain direct relief for his clients, while the *Range* seemed content to publish a feckless interview with Missouri Congressman William J. Stone, who was invited by some former Missourians on the Maxwell to come out and investigate grant matters.* Stone said he knew nothing of alleged fraud but believed that settlers who arrived prior to the Maxwell patent were entitled to damages from the government, adding that Congress probably would not

---

*On a broader front, former Senator Dorsey, the Colfax County cattleman, defended himself and land grant claimants in general (*North American Review* 145 [October 1887]: 396–409) against Surveyor General Julian's attack in a previous issue. It is doubtful that the Stonewall or Elkins post offices handled many copies for local subscribers.

purchase the estate. When told that McMains was aggrieved because the settlers sought outside help, Congressman Stone said he had no intention of interfering, although Commissioner Sparks had urged him to look into the situation. Harry Whigham talked with Stone and came away feeling that compensation for some settlers was a harmless uncertainty; in his opinion the government would do nothing.[2]

Later that month the *Raton Range* carried a long communication from Stone that incidentally pointed to McMains' sagacity in handling the Maxwell problem. Stone said he did not see how the government could make a grant of land it never owned (a grant *de novo*). He thought the Cox decision still had legal force because it had not been regularly reversed, but the Supreme Court's decision seemed to deny Cox's limitation of the grant. In conclusion he said the settlers were "the innocent victims of a shameful fraud accomplished by the connivance of public officials."[3]

Congressman Stone essentially agreed with McMains' arguments (as had Senator Plumb earlier), and twice the anti-granters opposed to him failed to make any headway without him. Yet the *Raton Range* ignored the obvious and continued its attacks on McMains with such statements as: "The last mad fancy of his is to solicit money from the settlers to hire Powderly, the great labor leader, to appear for the settlers at the capital. Dynamite will come next."[4]

Terence V. Powderly was the General Master Workman of the Noble Order of Knights of Labor,* the major union of

---

* McMains already stood in well with T. D. Mitchell and other local leaders of the Knights, and he doubtless knew of Powderly's record of opposition to land speculation. More importantly, McMains must have known that in Las Vegas, New Mexico, the Knights had organized the Las Vegas Land Grant Association to help provide legal counsel for settlers on the Las Vegas Community Grant, who faced possible eviction. See Robert W. Larson, "The White Caps of New Mexico: A Study of Ethnic Militancy in the Southwest," *Pacific Historical Review* 44 (May 1975): 178, 180.

the time with membership of close to a million.[5] In what way McMains might enlist the support of Powderly and his organization is not known specifically, but the idea was in keeping with his goal of making the settlers' battle against corruption known across the land.

The *Range* editorial's reference to dynamite was an allusion to the bombings in Haymarket Square, Chicago, the previous year. It is impossible to say whether the editors were simply expressing general revulsion from such tactics or were trying to thwart any support of McMains by Powderly, who was personally opposed to violence.[6] But there was no doubt that they intended to keep up their denigration of McMains. In September, when the Upper Vermejo men had submitted to the grand jury's investigation, they expressed relief "that the teachings of Herr Most are to have no disciples in the mountains of Colfax County."[7] Herr Johann Most was a prominent German anarchist, who had come to America in 1882 to become the leader of the extreme anarchist faction in this country.[8]

The fanaticism of the *Raton Range* was clear when it reported that McMains said he could blow up the nation's capital with his own hand, and a short time later the paper cast innuendo aside: "Herr Most addressed about three hundred anarchists in New York City, on Monday last, . . . His style of delivery in calling all the court officials hard names and his nervousness remind one of Mr. O. P. McMains. . . ."[9] That technique was no more successful than others employed to separate McMains and his partisans, who raised money to send him to Washington again in the latter part of November. The Agent for the Settlers departed with a flourish, saying he would "break the grant within a week."[10] He did not reveal the source of his optimism.

Harsh treatment of McMains by the New Mexico press reached a crescendo in the spring of 1888, when dispatches from Washington brought the sensational news that he had been arrested on the steps of the east main portico of the

Capitol on April 2, allegedly for firing a pistol. He was handing out tracts charging corruption in Maxwell Grant matters against Secretary Lamar, President Cleveland, justices of the Supreme Court, and former Land Office Commissioner Williamson.[11]

The editor of the *Raton Range* was quick to suggest dementia derived from brooding over grant problems, and he wrote finis to McMains' activities by saying: "His career as a sensationalist in speaking and writing is ended, and the settlers' money he has expended has gone for naught. Alas, poor McMains."[12]

After first astonishment, discerning readers noted two points that toned down the reports. Apparently the gun went off accidentally, and McMains was arrested for carrying arms and distributing circulars. The *Raton Independent* joined the *Range* this time in castigating McMains.[13] Neither paper cited sources, while the *Independent* in its editorial incorporated (almost verbatim) an article from the Washington *Evening Star*,* of April 2, which concluded: "His circular is coherent, and aside from its intemperate charges bears no evidence of crankiness."[14]

---

* "O. P. McMains, of New Mexico, has got into temporary trouble. He appeared at the Capitol early this morning with his arms full of circulars signed by himself as 'agent for the settlers,' charging official corruption against Commissioner of the General Land Office (Williamson), Secretary Lamar, President Cleveland, and the Supreme Court in connection with the Maxwell land grant. While distributing these on the east front of the Capitol his pistol went off, but whether by accident or design is not known. He was quickly taken in charge and sent down to the Police Court to be charged with carrying concealed weapons and distributing documents contrary to law. His circular is coherent, and aside from its intemperate charges bears no evidence of crankiness." A similar presentation was given in the *Washington Post* on April 3, and on the same date the *Evening Star* printed a brief follow-up: "Oscar P. McManis [sic], who created a sensation at the Capitol yesterday by firing several shots, as published in yesterday's STAR, forfeited $5 collateral in the Police Court to-day." Let it be noted that the *Star's* article on April 3 said nothing about several shots.

Even the usually sympathetic Trinidad *Daily Citizen* quoted a Washington dispatch that described McMains as a crank who had conceived the idea that the justices of the Supreme Court should be put to death.[15] But the height of journalistic irresponsibility was reached by the *Independent*, when it quoted an alleged item* from the *Boston Globe*:

> O. P. McMains, a crank from the wild west, stood on the step of the capitol at Washington, the other day, and fired five shots at the statue of Washington. He hoped to get notoriety enough out of it to secure him a place in a dime museum at a comfortable salary. And yet it is sometimes said that the avenues of industry are closed to the rising generation.[16]

The Raton papers were guilty of more than sloppy reporting. They resorted to unconscionable fabrication and went beyond defamation of character in their attempts to portray him as insane.

When McMains left for Washington in November 1887, M. P. Pels was more curious than fearful; ever since Cleveland's letter it had seemed impossible that McMains could ever prevail against the Maxwell Grant. As a precaution, however, Pels telegraphed to C. J. Canda, asking him to keep track of the Agent for the Settlers.[17]

Official support for the anti-granters was greatly weakened by the resignation of Commissioner William A. J. Sparks on November 15 after a difference with Secretary Lamar over

---

* There was no such item in the *Globe* (Letter to the writer from John H. Thaxter, Acting Chief, Serials Division, Library of Congress, August 19, 1955).

a railroad case.[18] The resignation probably caused McMains' hasty trip. A successor was not chosen for some time, and a very cool reception of McMains at the Interior Department and elsewhere was indicated by his newest pamphlet, which opened on this note:

> I herewith charge Hon. L. Q. C. Lamar, Secretary of the Interior, and Hon. Grover Cleveland, President of the United States, with being parties to a trick and fraud, whereby a petition of the settlers on the so-called Maxwell grant to have enforced a valid decision of the Secretary of the Interior of December 31, 1869, has been contemptuously and deceitfully evaded, to the great injury of the private and vested rights of the settlers depending upon said decision of the Secretary of the Interior.[19]

The pamphlet was distributed in Washington,* and copies soon appeared in New Mexico and Colorado, where the press reaction was generally hostile.† The formerly friendly *Raton Independent* joined in the criticism:

> It will no doubt make Mr. Cleveland feel very badly to learn that his intimate friend and adviser "O. P. McMains, agent for the settlers," has gone back on him and that he will no longer be treated to interesting discourses on his duty in setting aside a decision of the supreme court. Poor Cleveland![20]

---

* It appears to have been this pamphlet that McMains handed out on the steps of the Capitol in April 1888.

† He was called an "unmitigated ass" and was advised to come home "and then go off somewhere in the mountains and soak your head." See *Raton Weekly Independent*, December 10, 1887, quoting the *Pueblo Evening Star*.

Even S. W. DeBusk, of the pro-McMains Trinidad *Citizen*, felt he had to backtrack a bit: "Of course Mr. McMains is intensely honest in his convictions, but this is no security against being radically mistaken in his course."[21]

For all their condemnation and sarcasm, however, no one presented an alternative to McMains' persistent faith in the Cox decision except capitulation to the grant company.

Chapter 17

Injunctions and Ejectments

A COMPANY EMPLOYEE, old Tom Boggs,* struggling through December snow in the Vermejo country with a horse and buggy, found a renewed intention to resist: some settlers were excited enough by letters from Anthony Joseph to expect congressional action in their favor. There had been a big meeting on the Poñil to petition Congress, and one for the same purpose was scheduled for the Upper Vermejo. Boggs tried to convince Mexican settlers that help from Congress was only talk, that terms had to be made with the company before January 1, 1888, but, although not threatened with violence, he was subjected to some of the strongest words in the Spanish language.[1]

Boggs worked under strenuous conditions, having to send for the apron of his buggy because it snowed every day and filled the buggy. At a meeting in Cimarron, he and Ted Schomburg (Whigham's son-in-law) had to compete with

---

* Boggs was the widely-known frontiersman and friend of Kit Carson, who was living in retirement at Springer. He had done similar contact work years before for Lucien B. Maxwell, and the grant company hired him for $75.00 per month (M. P. Pels to Frank Springer, September 27, 1887, Letters March 3–November 7, 1887, pp. 425–29, MLG. He resigned as a Maxwell Land Grant agent in 1888. Trinidad *Daily Citizen*, September 10, 1888).

very popular horse races. When finally they were able to talk to some of the settlers, they found them very stubborn. Anti-granter Juan Ignacio Gonzáles deliberately followed them and destroyed what little progress they had made. Schomburg concluded that nothing would happen until a few lawsuits were brought.[2]

In Colorado endeavors to get agreements had about the same degree of success. Pels said he had been threatened and that masked horsemen infested the roads. The company filed a suit against [José] Luís Torres,* an influential man on the South Fork of the Purgatoire,[3] whose case was added to those pending against R. D. Russell and F. B. Chaplin. If Pels expected settlers to be waiting in line to abjure, he was disappointed. They did not respond, and old man Chaplin came to Trinidad before Christmas, denouncing the company and intimating that firm resistance would continue.[4]

But many anti-granters did not belittle the importance of the New Year's Day deadline. The executive board of the old Anti-Grant Mutual Protective Association called a convention to plan for collective action — either to hire legal counsel or send an agent to Washington to press for congressional assistance, the latter proposal evidently approved by McMains, who was still in Washington.[5]

The delegates met in the Raton Rink at ten in the morning, January 27, 1888. Beyond a general agreement that they needed professional legal advice, little of a positive nature was done except to elect a slate of officers.† Not one of them

---

* Born at Ranchos de Taos, New Mexico, August 18, 1854, José Luís Torres was eighteen when he came to the Valle de Los Rancheros, on the South Fork of the Purgatoire (Interview with Emilio Torres, *The Morning Light*, October 22, 1936; Joe V. Torres, *Life History of José Luís Torres* [La Junta, Colo.: La Junta Printing Company, n.d.].

† Allen E. Burnam, president; J. E. Gillum, vice-president; C. B. Ladd, secretary; George W. Cook, treasurer; W. H. Terhune, Arthur Manby, and J. W. Wolf, directors.

was a strong McMains man. And the delegates censured McMains in a supplement to the new articles of agreement, rejecting any more charges of fraud or tirades supporting the Cox decision.[6] The new leadership shunned both the executive branch of the government and McMains.

Pels° and Whigham worked on getting the most influential anti-granters into court by means of a general injunction, thereby giving the settlers "a chance to spend some of the money they seem so anxious to do."[7] Rifts in the anti-grant organization showed when the *Raton Independent* advised settlers to be less concerned, for the moment, with personal lawsuits and concentrate on the new case against the Maxwell patent recently filed by the Justice Department in district court at Santa Fe. Some settlers wanted to hire Congressman Stone; others wished to continue with E. A. Fiske; and a pro-McMains remnant was active.[8]

In Colorado, company men put pressure on the influential Luís Torres, who seemed ready to buy if the lawsuit against him were dropped; then many Mexican settlers probably would come to terms. Special leverage was also kept on Richard D. Russell at Stonewall, but Pels went too far when he sent a registered letter demanding that Russell deliver his holdings as per contract. That was in addition to the case against Russell for cutting timber and milling lumber, because of which Pels refused to take Russell's cattle as they

---

° Pels had become general manager for the Maxwell trustees, and he was having trouble with some new company officers in the matter of getting cash to buy out cattlemen on the grant. Frank Springer supported his disillusionment: ". . . I am heartily sick & tired of explaining the history and situation of Maxwell to new men in order to gain their tardy approval of things that are to me as self evidently necessary as air to breathe. . ." (M. P. Pels to R. V. Martinsen, January 19, 1888, Letters January 1, 1888–January 20, 1889, pp. 181–84, and Frank Springer to M. P. Pels, February 6, 1888, Letters 700, February 20–October 16, 1888, MLG).

had agreed.[9] The chance of removing Russell peacefully from anti-grant ranks was thus lost. And Pels had made a grave mistake.

McMains was still in Washington, working with members of Congress against the Maxwell patent.[10] He, too, had given up on the executive branch, and drew up a petition to Congress, restating the old charges against public officials.

New Hampshire's Senator Henry W. Blair, who was interested in public land problems, introduced a resolution to treat the Maxwell Grant as public land and give relief to the settlers, which was referred to the Committee on Private Land Claims. In the House, Indiana Congressman William S. Holman, another expert on public lands, offered a resolution generally like Blair's but different in detail, authorizing the Committee on Private Land Claims to examine witnesses, compel attendance, subpoena books and papers, and report. From McMains' point of view, the most important part was the requirement that the committee express its opinion as to whether the Cox decision had been regularly reversed. The chairman referred it to a subcommittee of four.[11]

Those intelligences created little excitement among the settlers because the pending trials in Springer and Trinidad were a greater drawing card than legislative maneuvers in Washington.

Judge Elisha V. Long's court at Springer convened on March 15, 1888, to hear arguments in the Maxwell Land Grant cases. Frank Springer — returned from his long absence abroad — represented the company. Counsel for the anti-granters was Assistant U.S. Attorney H. Burns, a new man to most of the defendants, who argued that actions against his clients should be dismissed until the suit against the Maxwell patent had been decided. Springer countered: the Colorado case had settled all question of patent, and the company was entitled to a dismissal in New Mexico. The suit, however, might continue for several years, thus depriving the company of revenues from lands which the Supreme Court ruled had been obtained without fraud.[12]

Springer's brilliant reputation was a deterrent to optimism among the settlers, and a few days later they learned that he had won again. Titles both to Raton lots in the Maxwell North Addition (formerly Boggsville) and to farm and ranch properties were involved.*

The district court's decisions diminished the will to resist the company. Few saw encouragement in the patent case at Santa Fe, that seemed to be based on the old argument that the Maxwell boundaries had been fraudulently extended and using the same evidence that had failed in Colorado.[13] McMains and Springer were in agreement on the futility of it.

Hoping to shore up resistance, McMains and ten others on March 2 filed an action in chancery praying the proceedings be stayed in twenty-two cases until the patent suit had been decided. But it was only a delaying tactic, in fear that meek acceptance of the district court's decisions would be a serious error and in hope that older settlers might be protected by the statute of limitations.[14]

The decisions in Springer against the settlers had considerable approval from local interests who thought that Raton would grow because people now knew where they stood. And there was talk that a colonization scheme would soon develop, now that land titles were no longer cloudy.[15]

In Trinidad a jury tried Richard D. Russell on March 22 and 23 for cutting timber and sawing lumber on the Maxwell. There had been difficulty empaneling a jury; several men

---

*Of the former was a case against McMains to recover Lots 23 and 24, which premises he had entered on June 1, 1887. In the court's opinion the improvements belonged to him (*Raton Weekly Independent*, March 31, 1888, p. 4; *Russell Marcy et al.* v. *O. P. McMains*, Records of the District Court, Colfax County, New Mexico, No. 911 [1887]).

frankly said they were very sympathetic to the defendant. The jury returned a verdict in favor of Russell, whereupon James M. John, counsel for the grant company, suggested a change of venue in the Chaplin case and advised that all future cases against settlers on the Colorado portion be brought in a federal court. He was amazed at the popular sentiment in Las Animas County against the Maxwell Land Grant Company.[16]

General Manager Pels was greatly relieved in May when a $300,000 company fund was set up for cattle purchases. Many outsiders — ranchers on the fringes whose cattle grazed both on and off the grant — had high-grade cattle, which they sold at rarely more than fifteen dollars per head, while some settlers asked twenty because the company had offered that to Stonewall men. The lower prices accepted by the outside men were used as a lever against the settlers, who were worried that injunctions against running their cattle on the grant would leave them high and dry if the company refused to take their cattle. Pels reported that the squeeze was working.[17]

Most of the older settlers did not scare that easily, so the company set the spring roundup as the deadline after which only cattle from other ranges would be purchased. Also the company offered grazing land leases for one year at seventy-five cents per head. The limitation offered no security, while the company could change the terms when a lease expired. No "old timer" could be expected to fall for that one, but the alternative was hardly more attractive. He could sell his livestock at fifteen dollars for "good cattle" with that year's calves thrown in.[18] If a man accepted neither proposition he could clear out or expect court action against him.

On the New Mexico portion of the Maxwell a few men ignored legal action against them and cut down trees for lumber and railroad ties. Harry Whigham expressed his anger: "It is a little tough to have these fellows rubbing it into us

this way.... The more we exert our authority in the neighborhood [on the Vermejo], the more those fellows will respect
us. Force is the only influence they have any regard for."[19]

In the Stonewall country and elsewhere on the Colorado
portion, company representative Richard B. Holdsworth*
encountered some resistance. He informed Pels: "That Russell
defeat [of the company in a timber case] has been a great
misfortune & can only be counteracted by vigorous measures,
in my opinion."[20]

McMains finally returned from Washington about May 1,
predicting that the subcommittee of the House Private Land
Claims Committee favored enforcement of the Cox decision.
Said the *Raton Range*: "The settlers are growing weary of
opening these wormy chestnuts which the agitator gleans
from the alleys of the national capital."[21]

The Settlers' Anti-Grant Mutual Protective Association
received a mortal though not unexpected blow on May 12.
In Santa Fe the federal court dismissed the government's
suit to vacate the Maxwell patent. The association had
decided to stake its life on the case; that its demise would
strengthen McMains' position was not foreseen.[22]

Success in Santa Fe signaled Pels and Whigham to go
after the remaining anti-granters in earnest. There was no
reason to temporize, and Pels wanted to block possible escape
through the statute of limitations. A handful of old line opponents refused to deal with the company but most of the cattlemen would. In fact, so many of the latter came into the
company's office — recently moved from Cimarron to Raton —
that Whigham hardly knew against whom to get injunctions
for running cattle. But he closely watched a small cattlemen's

---

* Holdsworth, an Englishman and partner in real estate of J. W.
Shryock in Trinidad, was hired by Pels in the summer of 1887 (M. P.
Pels to the Maxwell Land Grant Committee, July 16, 1887, Letters
March 3–November 7, 1887, MLG).

association in Vermejo Park known as the Quoquors,* some members of which were inflexible anti-granters.[23]

Pels went to Raton in late May to assist in the swelling volume of cattle purchases, which peaked out just before the spring roundup deadline. By then the company had acquired 18,000 head, of which 4,500 had ranged on the grant. About fifteen men in the parks and the Moreno Valley declined to sell, so Pels asked Springer to get injunctions against them.† They were not all die-hard McMains men.[24]

Although McMains was personally popular with most of the Mexican settlers, many of them came to terms, discouraged by the waning strength of the anti-grant movement and the increased legal pressures applied by the grant company. Pels was delighted to have an agreement with Juan Antonio Valdez, "one of the worst old timers on the Vermejo where the Rito Leandro comes in."[25] Others were holding out until Judge Long ruled in the case of the formidable Jacinto Santistevan. For the leading Mexican opponents of the grant it was a very distressing time. Their group's cohesion was breaking up, as was that of the Anglo settlers, and there were no signs of closer coordination of the remnants of the ethnic groups.

In Colorado, R. B. Holdsworth tried to make separate arrangements with settlers of Spanish surname, especially on the South Fork of the Purgatoire where they occupied some of the best lands. He raised the price beyond their ability to pay, offered them reasonable sums for their improvements, and threatened them with ejectment actions if they did not

---

* The origin of the name of this small group is not known. Occasional mention of the Quoquors was found in the *Raton Comet* and the *Raton Range*, and Mrs. Lucy Reed Wills referred to it.

† They were William H. Terhune, Frank Terhune, J. E. Gillum, John Gallagher, the Manby brothers, J. J. Lane, A. J. Young, the Irwin brothers, Claiborne Young, Manby and Raynor, Thomas Young, William Honey, James Scully, M. C. Reed, and John E. Codlin.

submit by May 23. Some gave way, and Holdsworth was proud of selling 320 acres to Juan Matías Durán, treasurer of a recently formed organization to resist the company.[26] Others, as in New Mexico, did not budge.*

In early 1888 the real estate firm of Shryock and Holdsworth was given the management and development of 5,220 acres acquired by a syndicate of businessmen from the Maxwell Land Grant Company for promotion of a summer resort in the Stonewall Valley.[27] That project was a new irritant in anti-grant country.

F. B. Chaplin and a man named Kelly jumped some of the syndicate's land. Injunctions against them for trespass were obtained and company officials decided to move in quickly for a final showdown in the Stonewall Valley. Attorney James M. John filed ejectment actions in the U.S. Circuit Court against F. B. Chaplin and R. D. Russell, the other mainstay of anti-grantism.[28]

Arrival of the Agent for the Settlers augmented the chance of serious trouble on the Colorado portion. He talked to men individually and addressed quickly called meetings. He could offer only his old belief in the ultimate enforcement of the Cox decision, and some clung with him to that slender reed against the alternatives offered by the grant company.

In early July, Holdsworth carried back to Trinidad an ominous warning that only anti-grant men would be tolerated

---

* It is impossible to assess the influence of the highly secretive Penitente Brotherhood, although bits of evidence indicate that the religious society had a part in the resistance. Several years later Mexican diehards took courage from the somewhat terroristic *Las Gorras Blancas* (the White Caps), an organization that spread northward from San Miguel and Mora Counties in the early 1890s (M. P. Pels to Chief Justice Smith, August 20, 1894, Case A, File 17, MLG; Robert W. Larson, *New Mexico Populism: A Study of Radical Protest in a Western Territory* [Boulder: Colorado Associated University Press, 1974], p. 67; interview with Mr. and Mrs. Hugh McKee, April 9, 1948).

on the Colorado portion. On the day the Maxwell agent returned to town, a deputy U.S. marshal rode into the Stonewall area to serve ejectment notices on twenty-four settlers. Holdsworth wrote to Pels that it "will stir up a very pretty hornet's nest for a time, but I believe it will be the means of bringing nearly all of them to time before their cases come up for trial. . . . I have an idea of going up there for a couple of weeks, to show them that they have not the field to themselves, what do you think of it?"[29]

Pels also believed they would capitulate before long, but he did not underestimate their temper at the moment. In answer to Holdsworth he said: "I would rather be excused from advising about the desirability of going up there yourself, unless you have any business to do there."[30]

About the time that the federal marshal served notices in Colorado, the sheriff of Colfax County, New Mexico, carried injunctions against thirteen settlers for grazing livestock on the grant.[31] This time there was none of the secrecy of the bench warrants' incident; their names were published.*

The darkening aspects of the future prompted Samuel W. DeBusk, editor of the Trinidad *Daily Citizen*, to remark gravely: "It is coming to the old story of evicting settlers from their homes by violent means. We need not say what will happen. All who know the history of such matters can foresee the ugly result."[32]

---

* Henry Butler, Richard Butler, William Butler, C. B. Ladd, William McClure, Juan José Martínez, J. W. Parsons, Nicholas Pasini, Dudley Shy, A. J. Young, C. J. Young, George Young, and Thomas W. Young.

Chapter 18

◑❦◐

Prologue to Violence

THE FARMERS' ALLIANCE (Southern) started as a local protective group in Lampasas County, Texas, during the 1870s. Developing into the Texas State Alliance, it was set on a rapid course of expansion through the South and Southwest in 1886 under the leadership of Dr. C. W. Macune, who built on the discontent of small farmers and ranchers. The organization stood against alien land ownership and control of the public domain by big cattlemen.[1] To many anti-granters the Southern Alliance seemed a natural ally.*

B. W. S. Overstreet organized the Colfax County Alliance No. 31 in 1888, and soon new alliances spread in Colfax

---

* McMains' attempt to link up with the Knights of Labor had failed, probably because his detractors had convinced the peaceable Powderly that McMains was a flaming radical. And the remoteness and ruralness of the anti-grant scene may have prevented enthusiasm as well. The association of Knights' assemblies in San Miguel County with the secret masked society known as *Las Gorras Blancas* (White Caps), which later frightened Powderly, was in such a preliminary stage that it probably had small influence. See Robert W. Larson, "The White Caps of New Mexico: A Study of Ethnic Militancy in the Southwest" *Pacific Historical Review* 44 (May 1975).

County and over the line in Colorado.[2] But alliance membership was not exclusively anti-grant, so that the organization
was never a primary weapon against the Maxwell. At the
same time that the members of the Colfax County Alliance
and their families met in July in a large cottonwood grove
near A. J. Young's home, an anti-grant meeting, with McMains
as speaker,* was being held about a quarter of a mile away.[3]

A great picnic was set out at noon on a table 100 feet
long. Following an afternoon session, feasting resumed about
6:30, and dancing began in the early evening. Great bonfires
and Chinese lanterns illuminated the platform and grove, and
during the dance "many eyes followed the Misses Lucy Reed†
and Lotta Young, the brown and blue eyed belles of the occasion, who wore a smile for everyone, and moved with perfect
grace in the dance."[4]

While bonfires glowed on the Vermejo, M. P. Pels was
on the Poñil, watching other flames — signal fires — flaring
on the mountains. Sheriff Sever was in the cañons to serve
injunctions. Many whom he sought were at the Farmers'
Alliance meeting. What better opportunity to serve the
papers? But when he reached Vermejo Park, McMains and
the anti-granters were ready for him — forewarned by signal
fires and riders. With overwhelming odds against him and his
personal sympathy for the anti-granters, Sever did not press
the point.[5]

---

* In fact, the real spark of anti-grantism was McMains himself; he
recognized the inherent weakness and tried to broaden the base. Attendance at his speech in Vermejo Park was large; one editor remarked that
"hundreds continue to hold Mr. McMains very high and right in their
estimation." But it was questionable if hundreds would follow him on a
new path of resistance if Congress, the current hope, refused to limit
the Maxwell under the Cox decision. He and a few others recognized
the value of securing the Alliance as a pressure group in Washington
(*Daily Advertiser*, July 28, 1888).

† Mrs. Lucy Reed Wills, whose recollections have been so important
in preparing this work.

Audrey and Frank Alpers

Meeting of McMains (on horseback) and anti-grant settlers east of Raton.

On the third day of the big gathering a courier on an exhausted horse rode into the grove, with a message that aroused extreme agitation. George Blosser and his family listened grimly as he related that deputy sheriffs had gone to their home, the old Willow Springs place formerly occupied by W. W. Boggs,* and set their household effects outside.[6]

"Do something about it! Show those Dutchmen a thing or two!" Demands for quick action drowned out the voices

---

* It appears that Blosser jumped the place after Boggs was evicted, which was extremely galling to Maxwell officials. A little over a year later Blosser was evicted (Trinidad *Daily Citizen*, September 10, 1889, and September 18, 1889). Blosser had another place about fourteen miles southeast of Raton, just off the grant (T. M. Pearce, ed., *New Mexico Place Names: A Geographical Dictionary* [Albuquerque: University of New Mexico Press, 1965], p. 18).

of caution. With Friday's dawn seventy-five to a hundred men (one source simply said over sixty) saddled their horses, and Blosser hustled his family into their covered wagon. An arbitrary, and to many a cowardly, act had fanned the cooling embers of anti-grantism; and the wrathful cavalcade, led by the Agent for the Settlers, descended from the hills and rode into Raton about 8:30 in the morning.[7]

Routine business was interrupted by the beat of hooves, the creak of saddle leather, and the rumble of Blosser's wagon which headed the procession along First Street. McMains rode immediately behind the wagon, the rest following in a double column. Prominent among them was Comp Reed with a white plume in his hat à la Jeb Stuart, the Confederate cavalryman, and someone dragged the Dutch flag through the dirt of the street. Whistles on Santa Fe engines in the yards cheered them, and astonished townspeople trailed the parade to the Blosser place.[8]

Accounts differed. In one version, the man who had bought the place from the company was put off and told "particularly, yet politely, not to interfere with Blosser in the future."[9] Another told of Winchesters much in evidence; that McMains was abusive and frothed at the mouth; and that two anti-granters escorted the man off the place, telling him to hide out or risk getting killed. The Blossers' belongings were set back in the house and the torn fences repaired. About noon the horsemen departed in an orderly manner but warned that if they had to come again, so much the worse for the company.[10]

Most of the riders waited around Raton for a meeting of the Farmers' Alliance that night. They made camp in the McMains pasture south of town. The meeting was not harmonious. After electing J. E. Gillum, of Red River, and R. D. Russell, of the new Stonewall Alliance No. 1, as president and secretary respectively, a strong condemnation of the day's action suffered defeat. A statement released to the press

Locations of Prominent Anti-Granters
on the Maxwell
1875–1890

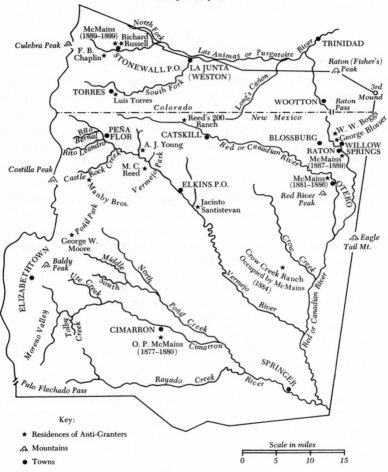

Key:

★ Residences of Anti-Granters

⚠ Mountains

● Towns

Scale in miles

0 5 10 15

focused on the failure of the House subcommittee to report. It had McMains' style, asserting that no attention would be paid to injunction papers until Congress or the president told them the Cox decision had been legally reversed by the Department of the Interior or the courts.[11]

M. P. Pels arrived in Raton two days later. He was alert to the crucial split in anti-grant ranks when Tom Gillum, brother of J. E. (Ed) Gillum,* arranged to sell out, as did William McClure, another long-time opponent. According to Pels, they said that many others would sell out if they were not bulldozed by McMains and his friends.[12] That confirmed Pels in his opinion that the removal of McMains was the sine qua non for peace. The Agent for the Settlers was tireless, undaunted, and for some anti-granters, irresistibly appealing. Pels wrote:

> Whilst preparing to take most stringent measures by causing the arrest of Mc'Mains and others, I am nevertheless well satisfied that these rioters are unhappy over the situation and when the influence of Mc'Mains is removed from them they will disintegrate, and one by one make terms with the company.[13]

Then he revealed what he thought would be necessary to break the anti-granters of McMains' persuasion:

> But we do not want to risk to enforce the orders of the Court, nor does the Judge, unless backed by U. S. troops which will end matters for good. Unfortunately the laws

---

* There were five Gillum brothers, and they were related to Mrs. M. C. Reed (Interview with Mrs. Lucy Reed Wills, October 4, 1948).

of the Territory do *not* give discretionary powers to use these troops and the President & Secy of War have to be applied to. It would be very desirable, if you have influential friends at Washington, (same as I had in Canda) to let them request the President who wrote me such a good letter last year to inform the Settlers that, unless they submit to orders of the Court and if they interfere with the same, U. S. troops shall be sent.[14]

He urged Governor Ross to issue a proclamation against the rioters and was told that the governor wrote to the secretary of war. M. W. Mills, at Pels's bidding, asked Judge Long to use his influence on the president and Indiana Congressman William S. Holman, sponsor of the resolution that created the subcommittee.[15] And Pels instructed Springer: "We wish Mc'Mains arrested in the following charges: Contempt, both for standing off the sheriff, and for disobeying the injunction which stands against him, Riot, Assault with words, and any other charge which you can think him guilty of."[16]

Judge Long's new writs of ejectment, giving thirty days to answer, were the first direct action. The settlers responded by calling a meeting and assuring every man the right to reach agreement with the company or not, as he saw fit, a serious wavering that suggested a decisive company move might bring the collapse of anti-grantism at last. A court ruling against Jacinto Santistevan, a step that Pels considered as next to McMains' arrest in importance, probably would bring Mexican resistance to an end.[17] But Pels felt he needed a much freer hand within the company, which he demanded of the Maxwell trustees: "You must approve beforehand all I do, and can discharge me if I don't do it well, but I must be able to act when once there — Trustees or not — these are no times to be afraid of burning our hands in cold water." He saw the settlers in the mountains as "uneasy, restless & afraid of the consequences, tho' having 300 armed men at their disposal all bound by a pledge."[18]

But Pels had no clear plan. He wanted to drive Chaplin and Russell from the grant sooner than the ejectment writs could be enforced, but he recommended only constant, petty annoyances — whatever that meant.[19] If his figure of 300 armed men bound by a pledge was close to reality, then minor harassments were not likely to succeed.

A warning against his return to Raton made McMains bristle with contempt and announce he would board the next train for New Mexico. He thought his arrest might help the settlers by forcing public attention to their predicament, but he abandoned the idea.[20] Of what use would he be twiddling his thumbs in the Colfax County jail?

On the day after the Farmers' Alliance meeting at Raton, the Agent for the Settlers went by train over Raton Pass to Trinidad to avoid any attempt to arrest him in New Mexico. McMains met Holdsworth, the Maxwell agent, on the street in Trinidad, and McMains proffered the information that he was leaving for the East on a Santa Fe train that afternoon. Holdsworth relayed the news to Pels as fast as the U.S. mail could carry it. But, instead, the Agent for the Settlers went west into the mountains of the Colorado portion, withdrawing deep into anti-grant country. Feelings ran high against the grant company at Stonewall, where the lid might be blown sky high at any moment.[21]

Holdsworth posted notices that a $1,000 reward would be paid for the apprehension of anyone killing Maxwell cattle. A member of the summer resort syndicate saw a placard on the fence of E. J. Randolph, a pro-granter near Stonewall, threatening death unless he cleared out within forty-eight hours.[22]

In a stirring speech given in the South Fork schoolhouse, McMains exerted an amazing pull on a rapt audience. And in New Mexico about thirty anti-granters came to the Vermejo

Park schoolhouse to hear "McMains, the prophet, the priest, the king of the settlers [who] was present to strengthen hearts and brace knees." During the meeting they "devoted some words to Mr. Pels, agent of the grant, whose aristocratic bearing and birth across the sea invite the sharp remarks of the yeomanry of the mountains."[23]

While at Stonewall McMains heard that Judge Long and Governor Ross had been in Raton to investigate the matter of Blosser, the ejected settler, the judge saying he would push for a subcommittee report — using his acquaintance with members of the Private Land Claims Committee. McMains approved in a letter published August 7:

> I am further informed that warrants are in the hands of officers for the arrest of the Blosser reinstaters — myself, of course, included. That we may aid Judge Long and Gov. Ross in procuring a report from the Private Land Claims Committee we hereby give notice in behalf of the settlers that for once they will refuse to be arrested by the regular officers even though backed by the militia. It is, I find, the opinion of the settlers, as a mass, that they can get away with any force of militia that may be projected into the mountains against them, even if they are compelled to call into action their reserved force on the Sangre de Cristo and Mora grants. Hence it will become necessary to order out United States troops; but before President Cleveland will order out United States troops he may . . . examine into the matter and ascertain who is the trespasser, the settler or the Maxwell Grant Co. This examination, of course, can have but one result; . . .[24]

Both McMains and Pels were caught in the same maddening impasse caused by the dilatory subcommittee. Each was optimistic that a report would be in his favor; each was plagued by the chance that it might not. Both felt that federal troops might provide the ultimate solution.

Just what the settlers would do if regular troops were sent, McMains did not say. Nor did F. B. Chaplin in a letter to the *National Tribune,* a Washington paper, although he explained the settlers' exasperation:

> The people are enraged at the delay of Congress, and have resolved to ignore and resist the so-called civil authorities, claiming that the courts who send them have not jurisdiction.... At this writing there are about one thousand men [undoubtedly the number included men on other grants], well armed, and determined not to give one inch until that committee reports. If the committee will report, all will be well; but if they will not, then the scoundrels must desist further persecution or bloodshed will be the result. Who is responsible for all this? Answer. The chairman of the sub-committee; the other members are ready and willing to report.[25]

Chaplin's letter was published on August 18. About ten days later Anthony Joseph introduced a resolution asking that the Secretary of the Interior report on every adverse claim by Maxwell settlers to indemnify them for expenditures incurred in good faith.° It also called for suspension of ejectments during the investigation. Texas Congressman Joseph D. Sayers, chairman of the subcommittee of the Private Land Claims Committee, asked leave to report at any time, and there was no objection.[26]

The resolution was offered on August 27. Joseph and Sayers did not know that two days before the circumstances on the Maxwell Grant had been radically changed by a violent collision of anti-granters and sheriff's deputies at Stonewall.

° In December the subcommittee favorably reported on reimbursing settlers who held government patents (*Daily Citizen,* December 12, 1888, and December 18, 1888).

Chapter 19

⟨❧⟩

The Stonewall War

THE RAIN FELL in a heavy downpour. A man, driving a team and wagon, came up the muddy road to the Stonewall Valley. His horses plodded in the ooze past Storz's mill, through the little cluster of the Stonewall settlement, and on a short distance to the Stonewall Hotel, a two-story, frame structure of sixteen rooms, operated by Shryock and Holdsworth for the summer resort syndicate.* After putting his team in the barn across the road, the man stayed in the hotel the rest of the day, Thursday, August 16, 1888.

Next day the rain continued, and he walked to George Lounsbury's store in the settlement. There he chanced upon Richard D. Russell, to whom he gave a letter of introduction that said he was Thomas J. O'Neil and he hoped to jump a Maxwell Company ranch. "Well you are the kind of man we want," Russell said and introduced the newcomer to James Cox, the conversation turning naturally to the grant. O'Neil

---

*Originally called the St. Cloud Hotel, the place was popularly known as Pooler's Hotel, because Mr. and Mrs. Robert Pooler ran it for several years. Occasionally it was called Coe's Hotel for the family of J. P. Coe, who were in charge for the syndicate.

learned that the settlers could be assembled within six hours after trouble started and that they were hopeful of attracting the government's attention to their predicament. O'Neil and Cox talked further after Russell left, Cox agreeing to show O'Neil some of the ranches the next day.

It was late afternoon when the two men returned. They had ridden about twenty miles through the mountains along the north line of the Maxwell, and O'Neil found a place to his liking. He told Cox he would jump it. Early that evening at Lounsbury's store he made the acquaintance of F. B. Chaplin. A leader in the religious life of the little community, Chaplin invited O'Neil to attend Sunday School on the Sabbath morning. O'Neil went, and even taught a class of children that day.

O'Neil told his new friends that he had left his wife in Trinidad until he could find a place, and that now he would fetch her. Tuesday at midday he reached Trinidad and called that evening at the home of the grant agent R. B. Holdsworth. Holdsworth agreed that O'Neil should take his "wife" to Stonewall to avoid suspicion.

On Wednesday, August 22, 1888, detective Thomas J. O'Neil made his report to James McParland, superintendent of the Denver office of Pinkerton's National Detective Agency.* McParland was a formidable figure in that line of endeavor, having become nationally known for his part in squelching the actions of the Molly Maguires in the Pennsylvania coal fields.[1]

---

* Pels's decision to employ O'Neil was a kind of compromise with Mills's warning against hiring a number of Pinkerton agents. At the time Pels was intrigued by the idea of using an agent provocateur. McParland achieved national notoriety for his part in breaking up the Molly McGuire movement in Pennsylvania (Robert W. Larson, *New Mexico Populism: A Study of Radical Protest in a Western Territory* [Boulder: Colorado Associated University Press, 1974], p. 61.

While the Pinkerton detective secured the confidence of the Stonewall men, someone destroyed much of the three-mile fence on an upper Red River ranch leased by Dr. I. P. George from the Maxwell Company. Pels professed belief that McMains planned the action in his attempt to get federal troops onto the scene. The grant manager's irritation was extreme. His own hope for federal troops was no closer to fulfillment, and he was disgusted with New Mexico lawmen. It seemed that he would have to go ahead, alone, to protect the property in his charge, and he convinced himself that he could have 500 to 1,000 Pinkerton men out from Chicago within three days. If bloodshed resulted, he reasoned, that fault would lie with the courts and the government for having procrastinated.[2] He confided as much in a letter to District Attorney M. W. Mills and then wrote privately to the president of the Maxwell Land Grant Company:

> Has your Board no influence at all at Washington or shall you consider it after I am *shot*? Can you not make the Prest. write a letter stating that unless the law is obeyed, he shall send U. S. troops . . . and make that Congress Committee state publicly that Cox decision has no force? But you don't seem to care & all I have from you is an occasional telegram![3]

Mills replied with clear disapproval and sound advice:

> Your Pinkerton brigade will result badly, it will devastate the country and ruin your property, you would not have in a short time a hoof on the range. Do not organize any such foolish thing as a lot of Pinkerton Detectives would be. . . . it would take a hundred Pinkerton men to every settler. The settlers know this country and are fighting for their places, the Pinkerton men are fighting for a few dollars.[4]

Mills passed on to Pels Governor Ross's advice to go slowly. Their plan was to allow more and more unserved writs to accumulate until an aroused public opinion forced the courts to act.[5] Mills evidently brought Pels back from the wild tangent of his thoughts.

The public had not long to wait for developments on which to pass judgment. Jefferson W. Lewelling, a contractor digging an irrigation ditch for the summer resort syndicate at Stonewall, sent to Trinidad for guns and ammunition because settlers had warned him and his men to get out. And E. J. Randolph, manager of the Maxwell cattle in Colorado, asked the sheriff for protection because a large number of riders went to his house one night when he was away, ordering his wife to clear out before a certain date or they both would be hanged.[6]

Pels tried to assist Randolph and any others in similar trouble. He succeeded in having Sheriff William Burns deputize six men to keep watch at Stonewall: William Hunn, John Sells, Frank Lewis, John Hannan, Edward Brown, and George Howard. On August 23 the deputies left Trinidad in a mule-drawn wagon, and Pels entrained for Denver that night.[7]

At one o'clock the next afternoon Lewelling rode into Trinidad and told of being forced out of the Stonewall country. Accosted by a large number of riders, whom he described as "mild but determined," no personal threats were made — only objections to the outfit for which he was working.* Lewelling parleyed with them. At first they agreed that he could remain for a while, but later they told him to leave that evening. In a final arrangement Lewelling and his party started for Trinidad at 4 P.M. the next day. Two groups of horsemen followed, five in one band and six in the other.

---

*Lewelling later said that about 107 masked and armed men surrounded his camp, using rifles and pistols as persuaders. He was sure force would have been used had he resisted (*Daily Advertiser*, October 5, 1889).

Before they came to the town of La Junta (Weston), the six had disappeared, and the others did not continue beyond the settlement. The contractor's caravan traveled through the night and camped about twelve miles above Trinidad while Lewelling came in and reported.[8]

The townspeople were absorbing that news when the E. J. Randolph family reached Trinidad at 4 P.M. on the Stonewall stage. Because of threats, the Randolphs had stayed with a neighbor and watched night riders apply the torch to their home.* Nothing was salvaged but the clothes on their backs.[9]

In the excitement and alarm there was talk of sending the Barela Guards, the local militia unit, but the sheriff had no authority to call them out. By 3 P.M., Saturday, August 25, the sheriff's office in Trinidad was jammed with some sixty men asking to be deputized. Twenty-five were sworn in, ten of them to be paid by the county and fifteen by the grant company. Taking with them a baggage and mess wagon, they planned to leave that night and go as far as they could to Stonewall, while the moon was high, to join the six who had left two days before. Their leader, Deputy Sheriff Alex Taylor, hoped to return by Monday.[10] No one in Trinidad knew that the plans were too late.

Thomas J. O'Neil reached Stonewall with his alleged wife and two children about 12:30 P.M., August 24. Some settlers were at Lounsbury's store in seeming expectancy of the deputies, who drove up about half past two and went on to Pooler's Hotel (the Stonewall) west of the settlement. The detective,

---

* F. B. Chaplin said Randolph set fire to his own house and tried to make it look like a job by anti-granters (*Trinidad Daily News*, November 2, 1888).

sure that his identity had not been guessed, took the woman and children to the home of Mrs. Mollie Morgan, where they would room and board. At the store that evening he saw quite a few horsemen. A feeling of exciting preparation prevailed. But by 9:45 it was comparatively quiet, most of the riders having disappeared.

Shortly after that James Cox told O'Neil that Richard Russell and Sam Bell distrusted him. His arrival just ahead of the deputies had created their suspicion. Either Cox did not share it or felt it did not matter, because he told O'Neil that riders were in the mountains to give the alarm that the deputies were at the hotel. Russell and Bell had ridden east; young George Russell had headed west; someone, whose name O'Neil did not recall, had gone north; and "Frenchy" Girardet was on his way to New Mexico.[11]

McMains was in New Mexico, on Red River, when he received the news. He saddled up and headed for Colorado, while riders continued to spread the information through the New Mexico portion to the Poñil and beyond. Comp Reed was sick in bed at his Red River cow camp, but his son Ollie and George Young rode swiftly towards Colorado, meeting others on the way.[12]

From the four points of the compass groups of riders, lone horsemen, and men in wagons converged on Stonewall, and by early morning of Saturday, August 25, some of them had tied up in front of Lounsbury's store. At 9 o'clock about fifty armed men were there, Thomas O'Neil among them, and Richard Russell made it a point to introduce him to Sam Bell. It was a critical moment for O'Neil as he stood with the two men who suspected he was a spy. No one batted an eyelash when Bell allowed that there might be trouble and invited O'Neil to join them. O'Neil replied that he "was with them at any stage of the game."[13] It was too dangerous not to bluff.

A contingent of settlers was expected from New Mexico at any moment. They would come from behind the Stonewall

*M. C. (Comp) Reed's cow camp, called the 200 Ranch, on upper Red
River.*

along the road across the valley, past the hotel and on to the
settlement. Sam Bell mounted and galloped ahead to watch
for them, while the others rode about 200 yards and dismounted, sending Luís Torres on a little way to watch through
a gap for Bell's signal, while they waited out of sight from
the hotel.[14]

When Torres waved they rode around the shoulder of
the ridge and saw a large number of horsemen, well in front
of whom rode a solitary figure, approaching the hotel. Impec-
cably dressed, his garb set off by a stiff-brimmed black hat
and gloves, O. P. McMains, Agent for the Settlers, led the
cavalcade.

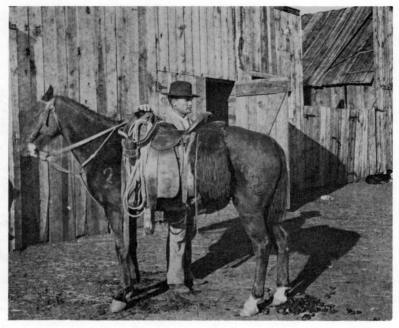

Olliver [sic] *Lee Reed. Comp Reed's son is shown with his horse in front of Taylor and Butler's livery stable in Catskill on upper Red River. The town flourished as a lumber and charcoal center in the early 1890s, after the anti-grant troubles on the Maxwell had notably subsided.*

The two groups, totaling about 200 settlers, met before the frame hotel with a great clatter and flourish.* William Hunn and another deputy stood between the fence gate and the entrance. The Anglos were masked, except McMains and Russell, and McMains alone was unarmed.[15]

---

*Estimates range from more than 100 to about 400, with around 200 being the consensus.

In the first confrontation McMains spoke for the settlers. Russell was with him, their horses being pressed up to the picket fence by the riders crowding from behind. Described as extremely nervous and excited, McMains demanded that William Hunn and his five men hitch the mules to their wagon and get out. (Someone in the crowd loudly suggested that they shoot the sons-of-bitches.) Hunn said he would see what the others thought, perhaps seizing a chance to get back into the hotel.[16]

Russell dismounted and walked to the door with McMains and one or two others. Hunn met them, telling them in a loud voice that the deputies would not leave. McMains shouted to the anti-granters to surround the building, and at that critical stage someone* in the crowd fired a six-shooter.[17]

The shot touched off the fight,† apparently as McMains walked towards his horse. Russell and another man‡ stayed

---

*All available sources agree that the first shot came from the crowd outside, although there was later controversy over the person's identity (Affidavit of T. J. O'Neil, MLG; Reed-Wills; interview with George W. Moore, May 22, 1948; testimonies of deputies, and instructions to the jury, *People* v. *O. P. McMains et al.*; *Daily Citizen*, September 12, 1888, and September 13, 1888; *Daily News*, November 2, 1888).

† Deputies' testimony indicated that McMains ordered the anti-granters to "take them," meaning the deputies, and that two shots were fired. One deputy said that Alphonso Chaplin fired the shot.

‡ Who was the man with Russell? Ollie Reed said his name was Petacia — a man often seen with Russell, but the only surname close to Reed's spelling was that of Vicente Pretica, an Italian. Detective O'Neil identified him as "Frenchy," probably Adrien (Frenchy) Girardet, a Maxwell company lessee and one of the riders warning of the deputies' arrival. O'Neil may have been right. In any event, Girardet later was named with McMains in a criminal indictment growing out of the encounter (Reed-Wills; Affidavit of T. J. O'Neil, Case A, File 17, MLG; telegrams from J. W. Shryock to M. P. Pels, August 26 and 27, 1888, Letters 700, February 20-October 16, 1888, p. 632, MLG; M. P. Pels to the Maxwell Land Grant Committee, Letters March 3-November 7, 1887, pp. 231–46, MLG; *People* v. *O. P. McMains et al.*, passim).

close to the hotel, and return shots from inside caused them to stand with their backs against the building. Russell was between the door and a window on the right, his gun pointed towards the window, and his companion was between the door and the left window, aiming at the door.[18]

Soon after the shooting began, Richard Russell was mortally wounded. Deputy William Hunn later was quoted as saying that Russell was shot about an hour after the fracas commenced. However, Hunn viewed the fighting as starting with the gathering of horsemen under Russell's direction at Lounsbury's store, then his timing pretty well agreed with that in O'Neil's sworn affidavit. In other words, it appears that Russell was wounded not long after the first shots.[19]

Mattresses were placed against the windows* by the men inside, but whether before or after the fight started is not known. Russell was hit in the top of the right shoulder by a Winchester rifle bullet, which passed down through his body and came out on the lower left side. The bullet came from above, either over the top of a mattress at a main floor window or from the second story. Either way disposes of statements that Russell was shot by someone standing in the doorway of the hotel.[20]

Who shot Russell? There is no firm answer. Three contemporary sources accuse Hunn. He denied it, saying that Russell was too close to the hotel for the deputies to see him, but the angle of the bullet's course through Russell's body would seem to refute that contention.[21] From his horse in the front rank of the settlers, O'Neil, the Pinkerton detective (hardly an anti-grant source), "heard a report and a window crash, the east window of the hotel, and saw Russell fall apparently shot."[22] Corroboration came from McMains, who said that the shot came "through a window near which he

---

* The Reed-Wills Manuscript says that furniture and other articles were piled across the windows.

[Russell] was standing."[23] There is thus no reason to doubt that the fatal shot came from inside the hotel.

After Russell fell, a rangy, red-headed young man named Martin Kephart, Sam Bell's brother-in-law, took over as leader of the settlers.[*] The anti-granters withdrew to less exposed positions, except the man who was caught with Russell close to the hotel. He emptied his gun at point-blank range, practically shooting the casing off the door. Then he lay flat on the ground near the wounded man, gradually inching his way on his belly to a dry irrigation ditch, along which he reached settlers who were bunched behind a large barn across the road. Others were down the road behind the ridge.[24]

Several horses were killed in the first firing, and some men sought protection from the picket fence. From that semi-concealment, Ollie Reed and George Young watched Happy Jack, an Irish bronco-buster who worked for the Reeds, walking slowly up and down the road. The shell extractor on his rifle being broken, he looked for a stick to pry out the empty shells. To their amazement he escaped, as did a settler who shot out the few unbroken windows with a slingshot. Reed and Young finally made a successful sprint to the rear of the barn.[25]

Around midday a flag of truce was displayed at the door of the hotel. McMains and Kephart approached and were told that several men, employees of the hotel trapped there, wanted to leave. Permission was granted, and probably during the lull Russell's friends picked him up and took him to his home. A youth of eighteen, surnamed Valerio,[†] had been instantly killed by a bullet through the head, his body in all

---

[*] This is an assumption based on the fact that Kephart was the ranking defendant after McMains in the indictment. Unfortunately no more data has been found to give Kephart a clearer identification.

[†] His name was Rafael Valerio, and he may have been the son of Antonio Valerio, first reported as killed.

likelihood also being recovered during the same inaction. Under the white flag there was discussion with Deputy Sheriff Hunn about terms for ending the conflict and letting the deputies depart. Talk failed and shooting resumed.[26]

The Vermejo or the Poñil could have been the site, but it was the Middle Fork of the Purgatoire. Pooler's Hotel turned out to be the pinpoint on the map where emotion took over from reason, where anger and impatience dominated restraint.

At 4 o'clock that afternoon a messenger rode hard into Trinidad and gave an account from an eyewitness at Stonewall. No longer was the posse, which was to go upriver that night, limited to twenty-five men; every willing man was accepted, and they would break their ride only to rest their horses. Again it was rumored that the Barela Guards would march, but calmer minds managed to control the excitement.[27] Hoping to forestall folly, the *Daily Citizen* warned that "ten men on those mountain sides could, with their needle guns, pick off a regiment in time," and "if these settlers stick to their hills and trails as many of the bush soldiers did in the civil war, there will be time enough for all who yearn to see service."[28] When emotions died somewhat, caution prevailed, aided by widespread sympathy for the settlers. So instead of a big posse or a company of militia with "bright suits, guns and cartridge boxes,"[29] only two men started for Stonewall late that day — County Commissioners Duane D. Finch and Richens L. ("Uncle Dick") Wootton,* who hoped to intercede in behalf of the beleaguered men in the hotel.[30]

---

* This was the same man who swore he was present when Cornelio Vigil set up the third mound (northeast corner) of the Beaubien and Miranda (Maxwell) Grant in 1843. He had lived on the Colorado portion of the Maxwell since 1865, when he established his tollgate in Raton Pass.

Shooting was sporadic during the afternoon. Dwindling ammunition worried the deputies, while, unbeknown to them, some of the besiegers planned to set fire to the hotel after sundown. About 8 P.M. the man who was with Russell when he was hit crawled slowly back through the darkness and was close to the hotel when the big barn across the road suddenly burst into flame, revealing him as the would-be arsonist. But the deputies were more interested in what the blaze concealed than in what it exposed. The rear of the hotel was enshrouded in deep shadow, giving them a longed-for chance. Their own dangerous exposure by the burning barn distracted the settlers, and the great uproar among men and horses allowed the deputies to escape through a coal shute into a grain field behind the hotel. Flat against the ground, they worked their way through the grain and an irrigation ditch until they came to a gulch, which afforded cover. Keeping in the hills they headed in the general direction of Trinidad,* arriving there late Sunday afternoon.[31]

Unaware that the deputies had eluded them, the settlers took up the siege again with some scattered shooting during the night. Sentinels on the Stonewall road early next morning spotted the fast approach of a horse and buggy with two men, a white handkerchief tied to the buggy whip. County Commissioners Finch and Wootton found the anti-granters surrounding the hotel, some of them pumping bullets into it. Lack of shots from within was attributed to an ammunition shortage, but the men outside showed no disposition to rush the place. Finch and Wootton talked with McMains and others and finally were given permission to speak with the

---

* Ollie Reed stated that they commandeered a wagon and team, requiring a farmer to drive them to Trinidad. M. P. Pels believed the barn caught fire from a carelessly dropped cigarette (Reed-Wills; M. P. Pels to Harry Whigham, August 29, 1888, Letters 700, February 20-October 16, 1888, pp. 647–49, MLG).

deputies. The commissioners came out of the hotel in a very few minutes with the astonishing report that no one was inside. Incredulous, six or eight of the settlers went in to see for themselves. The flight of the deputies also brought into focus the disappearance of Thomas J. O'Neil and his "family."[32]

Reinforcements arrived that morning from other land grants in Colorado and New Mexico, and a four-horse wagon loaded with grub and ammunition labored through the mountains from La Veta to the north. The ranks of anti-granters expanded to 400–600 men, who reportedly ate three Maxwell beeves a day.* The hamlet of Stonewall was crowded with grim men, and many campfires flickered in the valley. Sharp eyes kept watch down the Purgatoire for a sheriff's posse or a military company. Vigilance increased when it was learned that two cases of rifles and more than two thousand cartridges, consigned to the Maxwell Land Grant Company, had reached Trinidad by train from Denver, and that Colonel Benjamin F. Klee, commander of the 2nd Infantry Regiment, Colorado National Guard, was there as well.[33]

Richard D. Russell died on Monday afternoon August 27, 1888, at his home just north of the settlement. The Anglos assembled at Stonewall three days later under the presidency of F. B. Chaplin, with Martin Kephart as secretary. Expressing their sentiments in resolutions, they blamed Russell's death on the United States government for ignoring the Interior Department ruling that the Maxwell Grant should be treated as public land. Mrs. Russell was extended sincerest sympathies, and the settlers proclaimed their intention "that the dead shall not have died in vain" and that circumstances "shall be carried forward to a successful close and beneficial

---

*About August 1, the Maxwell Company had begun to advertise a $1,000 reward for evidence leading to the conviction of anyone for killing company livestock (*Daily News*, January 3, 1889).

conclusion."[34] They demanded enforcement of the executive
order of 1874 (upholding the Cox decision) and the implications of the Texas Purchase as well: "Until this demand has
been complied with, all peaceful methods having been
exhausted, the United States government cannot expect us
to do better than the honored gentlemen who figured in the
tea crate business in Boston harbor."[35]

Mexican settlers had a special commemoration for Rafael
Valerio. They asked for the satisfaction "that his blood may
speak for us to the United States government for the enforcement of the law that requires the Maxwell Grant be treated
as public land."[36]

There were other casualties at Pooler's Hotel. One
Lorenzo Griego was wounded by a bullet striking his skull,
glancing from the temple. First reports had Griego going
around in a daze, but later it was said he had become quite
mad. Unconfirmed stories told of wounds to several others,
and it became known that one of the deputies had had his
thumb shot off.[37]

The camps of men from other grants did not break up
after the fight. When word circulated that a lone deputy U.S.
marshal would come up from Trinidad the first of the week
to serve papers, a contempt and bravado was bred that
brought on further direct action.

A reddish glow on the sky that night grew bright and
faded as Pooler's Hotel was destroyed by fire.[38] Burning of
the barn was considered as accidental, but destruction of the
hotel was another matter. Many anti-granters and their sympathizers deplored a wanton act that would damage the
cause. S. W. DeBusk, whose Trinidad *Daily Citizen* had con-
sistently spoken in their favor, commented: "The settlers find
themselves in a dilemma. First they are resisting a great
wrong, and in this they have the sympathy of all. Secondly,
some of their number are drifting into arson and other lawlessness, and these will receive condemnation only, from the great
jury of the people who have no personal interest."[39]

Chapter 20

Aftermath

THE EMBERS STILL SMOLDERED at Stonewall when more reports and speculations ruffled the peace of Trinidad. Holdsworth, the Maxwell agent, had left town in fear of his life and was cautioned that it was yet too dangerous to return. Many of the townspeople favored the settlers; there was talk of forcibly releasing any anti-granters who might be lodged in the county jail. Imaginations were stimulated when Commissioner Finch told of an improvised fort at Stonewall called "Defiance" and of military drills by the anti-granters.[1]

A significant segment of opinion was pro-grant, however. Pels had conversation with men attending a political convention in Trinidad. They felt the Maxwell Company had taken the only possible course, and they thought the settlers would not resist federal troops. Pels reported that "Meantime they say that all these troubles . . . reflect unfavorably on Colorado and especially on Las Animas County . . . they suggested to me that it might be a good plan for . . . Congress . . . to buy the Maxwell Grant. . . . I said that, of course, the Company should be entirely out of this move . . . because otherwise it might be construed that the Company was creating a fight in order to entice the Government into just such a scheme."[2]

New York papers carried stories about settlers who held government deeds to their lands, and impressions in other quarters were not good for the grant company.* One of the company's immigration agents was concerned, and Pels tried to minimize the problem:

> The trouble on the Maxwell Grant is confined to a small portion in the mountains of Colorado . . . , and has nothing at all to do with the valley lands and the foothills in New Mexico where we want to locate settlers, there being a distance of fifty miles between those two spots. This is an old trouble, and I think the end will be that the United States will send troops there to settle the matter *for good.*[3]

Publicizing the Stonewall War produced no positive Washington reaction in favor of the anti-granters. The House heard of it but made no response to a resolution introduced by Anthony Joseph to provide indemnities to those settlers who had taken land on good faith that it was public domain. The House Private Lands Committee received the resolution.[4] Missouri's Senator George Vest wrote to one of the settlers, it was claimed, that federal troops would not be sent if he had anything to do with it; such a tactic was unthinkable, especially since the House committee had not yet acted. DeBusk, of the *Daily Citizen*, then suggested that no word came from the subcommittee to which the investigation had been assigned because its chairman, Joseph D. Sayers, was the brother-in-law of Wilson Waddingham, one of the great

---

* Support for the grant company was expressed occasionally. For example, one well-known publication said that if the settlers did not surrender, "Uncle Sam will send some of his valiant troops to bring them there, putting the rightful owners in possession" (Leon Noel, "The Largest Estate in the World," *Overland Monthly* 12 [November 1888]: 482).

landholders of New Mexico formerly involved in the Maxwell Grant.[5] And there was a local angle. To accept compensation would be an admission of the validity of the Maxwell's million and a half acres — something a true anti-granter could never do.

The *Daily Citizen* in Trinidad and the *Albuquerque Citizen* were the only regional papers that took a position approaching what McMains wanted to see in headlines across the country. The latter paper protested the idea of sending New Mexico militia into an obviously federal matter, maintaining that no citizen of Bernalillo County would join an expedition against anti-granters in Colfax County.[6]

Astonished and angered at the influence still exerted by the Agent for the Settlers, Pels pressed for his arrest in Colorado and for a writ of extradition from the governor of New Mexico. But the grant people were not at all sure what kind of charge to prefer against McMains in order to get him behind bars. The most unusual proposal was made by Harry Whigham: McMains could be seized for murder in some degree because he had led a riot in which two of his followers had been killed.[7]

A coroner's jury at Stonewall found that R. D. Russell had been feloniously shot by Billy Hunn, leader of the deputies, aided and abetted by the five others. In a second verdict the jury held that Rafael Valerio had been killed by the deputies, but it failed to state (inadvertently no doubt) that it was feloniously done. The coroner issued his warrant for arrest of the six men, and Pels thought the company was obligated to help them with their bond.[8]

Incidents in New Mexico warned that tempers among the settlers were still warm. L. S. Preston, surveying for the grant company in Vermejo and Poñil parks, was confident he had "made friends with nearly every family." But on the last day of August a man appeared at the surveyor's camp with a note that was unsigned and succinct: "You are here by the members of the Ponil Association requested to leave this Park."[9] And next day work was interrupted by a settler named Richard Youst, Winchester in hand, who watched them all afternoon from the pine woods. Being stalked made "three defenceless young men a little nervous to say the least," and it accomplished what the colorless ultimatum of the Poñil Association failed to do. Preston and his men suspended their work.[10]

Another incident occurred on October 9, after survey work had been resumed. Preston went to A. J. Young's house to purchase some eggs for his noon meal. While there, he talked to Lena Young and May McClure, both of whom were attired for riding. About 4 P.M. the surveyors saw a cavalcade of riders led by a woman stop at Young's house. Soon fourteen masked riders — a majority Mexican — formed a semicircle around Preston and his men. The leader was dressed in black with a small cap and black mask and had a low voice, which Preston was certain he would recognize again. Second in command was a large, heavy set man with an iron-gray beard showing beneath his red and white handkerchief mask, whom Preston believed was Comp Reed. All carried Winchesters or revolvers or both. And they made it quite clear the survey work would stop: " '. . . We claim this country and intend to hold it. We have lost one of our best men by the hands of this Grant Company and we feel it, and we don't intend that the Grant shall have anything to do in here.' " Growing irritation among the riders prompted the surveyors to pick up and get out.[11]

Pels did not mind hailing any man into court, but "as soon as young girls become riotous, the matter becomes difficult!"[12] He felt certain that only federal troops could break the impasse, and U.S. Marshal Zeph T. Hill accepted Judge Moses Hallett's advice to make a strong effort in Washington to obtain troops.[13]

In the mountains the will to resist remained strong, but after more than a week in September with no move against the encampments at Stonewall, many men went home for harvest. A few more than a hundred men stayed on, but a prearranged signal would send an alarm through the cañons to regain the settlers' full strength quickly.[14]

In Denver, Pels gave way to great exasperation in a letter to Marshal Hill:

> Some time ago when the cowboys stole horses from Indians, who very justly retaliated and when the Sheriff could not serve papers on the Indians, all Colorado wished to uphold the majesty of the law and Gov Adams said in a speech at Meeker that the law and the service of legal papers should be enforced, should it take all the forces of the State and the U. S.! And what has he done, or his Sheriffs or officers, in this Stonewall matter? Are we not owners of the property? do we not pay taxes? have we ever been aggressive? If so, how long shall we have to wait for justice in this lawless country and see our property burnt and destroyed and settlers killed as regular troops under the eyes of the Government![15]

Pels was angry also because a scheme to get McMains was not carried out. Whigham's suggestion that McMains be arrested for the deaths of Russell and Valerio was tried with modification. Instead of murder the charge was manslaughter, and warrants were obtained for his arrest together with those of his accomplices. No one from the Las Animas County sheriff's office tried very hard to apprehend the accused, and Pels was certain that no one intended to.[16]

O. P. McMains was angry too. Putting the blame for the two deaths on him was an attempt to show him as the irresponsible ringleader who promoted an attack on the deputies — a correct interpretation of Whigham's intent. And concurrent with the news of the warrants, the truth about Thomas O'Neil* burst upon the scene.

---

* Pels regretted employing the Pinkerton agent. He questioned the use of O'Neil's affidavit in court because detectives were not looked upon favorably, although railroads employed them constantly.

In a letter to the *Raton Independent*, McMains told of the Pinkerton detective and his deceptions, and how on the morning of August 25 "O'Neil's first work was accomplished by his seemingly accidental shot which led to the firing and served as an excuse for killing 'the leader.' O'Neil's next work, after taking in the situation fully, was to strike out for Trinidad."[17]

Sometime between September 6 and 11 the Agent for the Settlers rode south to the Red River country to avoid arrest in Colorado. He stayed a few days with Comp Reed at his cow camp and then went down through the hills to Raton. The governor of New Mexico had not signed extradition papers, so McMains returned to his wife and home.[18]

McMains' role as dramatic leader in front of the frame building beside the Purgatoire obscured his stratagems in the marble building along the Potomac. But his real mission was recalled when he released another letter to President Cleveland about the status of the Cox decision. If it had been regularly reversed, he assured Cleveland that the settlers would give "peaceable possession" to the claimants of the Maxwell Grant.[19]

The letter was sent to Dr. C. W. Macune, then president of the National Farmers' Alliance and Co-operative Union of America, to be forwarded to the White House, presumably with a covering letter of his own. But McMains' continuing effort to use the alliance as a lever in Washington probably was doomed to failure.[20] Perhaps he misread the Farmers' Alliance (and the Knights of Labor) as more radical than it really was, and his own tactics scared them off.

In Springer a grand jury investigated the interference with Sheriff Sever and the reinstatement of George Blosser, as well as interruptions of Preston's survey work. But, since there were only a few indictments, Maxwell officials left the sessions unsatisfied. Indeed, Frank Springer despaired of any

help from the courts of New Mexico, calling on the company
to "rely on our own resources — getting in the settlers one by
one, by individual negotiations, selling lands to them, or buying improvements — preferably the former in many cases, so
as to get active allies, instead [of] useless improvements,
which will tempt the rioters to destroy it."[21]

Judge Long was loathe to do anything before elections.[22]
Anti-grant issues had been in the political arena before, and
a possible recurrence was one reason McMains returned to
Raton. In Colfax County, where the sharpest line always had
been drawn, the Democrats campaigned under the tag of the
Anti-Grant Democratic party, while the opposition forsook
the Republican label and became the People's party — a
Republican-Maxwell Grant combination nonetheless. In Colorado, the Las Animas County Democratic convention merely
passed a resolution favorable to the anti-grant settlers.[23]

McMains had no connection with the Springer grand
jury, nor did he allow himself to be subpoenaed by the one
in Trinidad that was examining a possible indictment of himself and others for manslaughter. In Colorado no U.S. marshal
had stirred up things yet; even R. B. Holdsworth felt safe
back in Trinidad.[24]

But the relative peace of the late September days ended
when the Agent for the Settlers suddenly published a strident
call for resistance. Headlined "DEFIANCE!" it was a rallying
cry to anti-granters. The piece was studded with invectives,
but a fairly subdued paragraph told the old tale:

> The war is on; the precious blood of the settlers has
> been shed; and we must fight it out on this line. No quar-
> ter now for the foreign land thieves and their hired assas-
> sins, who, in defiance of the Secretary's *valid* decision, are
> attempting to evict American citizens from their homes,
> ranches and mines.[25]

Release of the broadside was timed by leaks from the
Trinidad grand jury foretelling indictments of McMains and

DEFIANCE!

And Contempt for that which is Contemptible.

SETTLERS—Your case is won.

The Interior Department admitted, March 6, 1888, that the decision of Secretary Cox, of December 31, 1869, upon which your property rights depend, had not been reversed by a direct proceeding. The LAW says it cannot be reversed by an *indirect* or collateral proceeding. *Hence,* the Secretary's decision is valid—it is *law*—and it must and shall be enforced.

After having, for several years past, exhausted all peaceful remedies to induce public officers to compel the Maxwell Grant Company to respect the authority of a Secretary of the Interior, you have at last said to that law-defying, thieving corporation :

"Hands off! Get out of these mountains!"

And from Stonewall, Colorado, to Marino Valley, New Mexico, no Maxwell Grant thief dare show up.

The war is on ; the precious blood of settlers has been shed ; and we must fight it out on this line. No quarter now for the foreign land thieves and their hired assassins, who, in defiance of the Secretary's *valid* decision, are attempting to evict American citizens from their homes, ranches and mines.

The result of your uprising against a law defying corporation, and the public officers who are aiding them in their high-handed lawlessness, cannot be doubtful. The people of the United States, aroused at last to the enormity of the crime that is being committed by unlawful evictions, will demand, in their indignation, that these eviction proceedings be stopped, the valid decision of Secretary Cox enforced, and your rights dependent upon that decision protected.

In your name, then, SETTLERS, I hurl defiance at the foreign corporation. I say to those foreign evictionists—Your Supreme Court decision, purchased at so great a price, is a contemptible legal abortion ; it is entirely too *collateral* ; the Secretary's decision, in spite of it, is still law ; so, then, you bloody-handed Dutch, English and American corporate land thieves—you government-defying, court-corrupting, assassination-plotting scoundrels—hands off, git, or be gotten.

O. P. McMAINS,
Agent for the Settlers.

A McMains tract published ca. October 1, 1888.

others, despite the freak fact that the district attorney opposed the indictment. The broadside appeared on October 1. Two days later the grand jury indicted and issued warrants for O. P. McMains, Martin Kephart, F. B. Chaplin, John L. Hagen, Alphonso Chaplin, Joseph Hagen, George Hagen, George Russell, Sam Bell, William Hadden, Ale Kelley [*sic*], O. B. Abbott, James Cox, A. Girardet, A. Duling, Joe Duling, one McGarty, and one Harness, Senior.[26]

Nobody from the sheriff's office volunteered to serve the warrants. None of the indicted men were taken into custody for a long time, although they made no great effort to conceal themselves. McMains, for instance, was in and out of the Stonewall country; there he wrote a letter to the *Raton Independent** charging that the burning of Randolph's house, two nights before the Stonewall fight, was a put-up job by Maxwell sympathizers to look like the work of anti-granters.[27]

The Stonewall War accomplished no substantive change in the circumstances of the settlers against the grant, except, perhaps, to make each side extremely wary about a second collision. That McMains and Pels both verbalized their frustrations helped them personally. The potential for more violence, however, was there, although the controversies were quickly moving again into the courts and the political arena — in the latter without much of the old gusto.

---

* F. B. Chaplin wrote similarly to a Trinidad paper. In his opinion the killing of Russell was premeditated (*Daily News*, November 2, 1888).

Chapter 21

The Beales Grant

POLITICS DOMINATED THE ATMOSPHERE as election day 1888 approached. It was a presidential year, with Democratic incumbent Grover Cleveland running against Benjamin Harrison, the Republican. But national issues were of secondary importance to many voters in Colfax County, N.M., and Las Animas County, Colorado. The Anti-Grant Democrats in New Mexico endorsed Anthony Joseph for reelection and pledged to work for a law preventing ejectment if a man had occupied his land for six years and for a statute of limitations operative from a grant's confirmation rather than its patent — a difference of nearly twenty years in the Maxwell instance. An alternative was indemnification of those ejected after six years, to the value of their improvements and with 160 acres of public land without charge.[1]

Some Democrats in Colfax County had bought or leased land from the Maxwell Company, so they could hardly be actively opposed to it. In Colorado the official stand of the Democrats opposed land grants in principle, so the party faithful in Las Animas County had a hard job accepting Dr. Michael Beshoar, a leading Democrat, as a promoter (with Charles Goodnight, the Texas cattleman and Democrat) of the enormous Beales claim.

[235]

In Colfax County, Maxwell officials worked for the People's party ticket, but in Colorado they supported one Democrat, Julius C. Gunter, for the district judgeship.* O. P. McMains plunged in as a Democrat, but he could hardly have been enthusiastic about Grover Cleveland. Benjamin Harrison was formerly the law partner of McMains' brother-in-law, William P. Fishback. In Colfax County he endorsed the reelection of Abe Sever as sheriff, while in Las Animas County his choice for district judge was Julius C. Gunter, a preference that some settlers criticized.

Cleveland was defeated, but in the two counties the Democrats made a much better showing. Grant men were pleased that Gunter was elected in Las Animas County, but Colfax County voters disappointed them. The Democratic Anti-Grant party won by a small majority. Harry Whigham had predicted a close contest, and he attributed the failure of the People's party to unexpectedly small majorities for it in Raton and Blossburg.[2] He commented: "We have met the enemy and we are theirs."[3]

For all the political activity the land grant controversy was no nearer to solution. Again surveyor Preston was driven from his work on the Vermejo. Deputy U.S. Marshal Walker had papers to serve on about a hundred settlers in Colorado; he went about it casually, serving a warrant when he chanced to meet the man concerned in Trinidad. Pels disapproved of that method and urged Walker to show up at Stonewall to perform his duty.[4]

---

* He had been retained on occasion by the company, and settlers opposed him for that reason. R. B. Holdsworth, Maxwell representative, approved of Grover Cleveland but there can be no doubt about his endorsements on the local scene.

Washington reports suggested that Congress might bestir itself. In mid-December the House subcommittee agreed to report favorably on a joint resolution looking to the settlers' relief.[5] But nothing was said about the Cox decision; it had been killed in committee.

At year's end the deadlock on the Maxwell Grant still held. Spanish-speaking settlers, led by the unrelenting Jacinto Santistevan, held a "junta" on the Vermejo, where some of them agreed to no dealings with the company. Only on the middle Vermejo, however, was Santistevan able to keep most of them in line, and he had called on the Anglos to run a man out of the area, only to be refused. Harry Whigham argued that resistance could be destroyed by evicting Santistevan, but nobody dared to try — not even Whigham.[6]

Anti-granters at Stonewall did not greet the Christmas season with much joy. They were " 'waiting for the final roll call,' " as F. B. Chaplin put it.[7] Just before the new year, Deputy Marshal Walker appeared with forty-three notices of eviction, delivering several before militant settlers convinced him to leave.[8]

Early in January 1889 residents of the Stonewall country commemorated their loss in the death of R. D. Russell. The Stonewall Farmers' Alliance No. 1 published resolutions of respect in memory of the late lecturer of the alliance. A committee, of which McMains was a member, prepared the tribute.[9] But most attention was directed to the future; time favored the Maxwell Land Grant Company. More Mexican settlers on the Poñil and the Upper Vermejo° were ready to come to terms.[10]

° The court ruled against Santistevan in the September term, but he did not relinquish his place until May 1889. See *Maxwell Land Grant Company* v. *Jacinto Santistevan*; Records of the District Court, Colfax County, New Mexico, No. 974 (1888).

For some time the future had portended a supreme irony that might sweep away the Maxwell and other grants in northern New Mexico and southern Colorado. A lawsuit had been filed against the Maxwell Land Grant Company on January 20, 1888, by the Interstate Land Company, pressing claim to about 60,000,000 acres of something called the Beales, or Arkansas, Grant. Allegedly made by the governor of Coahuila-Texas in 1832 to John Thomas Beales, an Englishman, and José Manuel Royuela, the alleged *empresario* claim would absorb the Maxwell and Sangre de Cristo Grants, grazing ranges of the great Prairie Land and Cattle Company and the huge XIT ranch of the Capital syndicate in Texas, to say nothing of numerous townsites and countless farms, ranches, and other claims.* A principal sponsor of the Interstate Land Company was the important Texas cattleman, Charles Goodnight, who had been a claimant to the Nolán Grant No. 48, in Colorado, before the Panic of 1873 wrecked him and sent him back to Texas.[11]

It is difficult to believe that anyone really took the Beales claim very seriously — even those seeking its confirmation† It was more like a big gamble that, if successful, would be

---

*A man named Hodges claimed he was a rightful owner of a thirty-mile-square claim called the Corpus Cristi Grant, allegedly a Spanish grant dating from 1685. Its 698,960 acres supposedly lay in New Mexico and Colorado, but the claim was officially listed as in Colorado (*Daily Citizen*, November 4, 1888; Richard W. Bradfute, *The Court of Private Land Claims* [Albuquerque: University of New Mexico Press, 1975], p. 246).

†This may be inferred from the fact that Goodnight's biographer, J. Evetts Haley, in *Charles Goodnight: Cowman and Plainsman* (Norman: University of Oklahoma Press, 1949), did not mention the Beales Grant or the Interstate Land Company.

truly spectacular, but if it did not, little would be lost. In the wheeling and dealing world of land grants in the 1880s, it was another chance worth taking — to the Supreme Court, if necessary.

McMains' reaction to the imminent lawsuit bore out the general doubt that the enormous claim would be sustained. When he wrote to the editor of the *Raton Independent* from Stonewall on January 5, 1889, rather than discuss the merits of the Beales Grant he presented it as further evidence, if valid, that the Mexican state of Coahuila-Texas and the Republic of Texas extended to the Río Grande — circumstances that made it impossible for the governor of New Mexico to have made any grants east of that stream. And then he explained why he thought no court would affirm the Beales Grant at such a late date: because claimants had not protested what in effect was their dispossession by the Texas Purchase of 1850,* and the *empresarios* had not brought in any families to colonize, which they were supposed to do under Mexican law.[12]

About a month later in a clever piece also published in the *Independent*, McMains put the old arguments against the Maxwell patent in the mouths of counsel for the Interstate Land Company. Then with enviable skill he had the judge (no name mentioned) parody the grant *de novo* argument used by Judge Brewer and Justice Miller in the government's case against the Maxwell, saying that Congress would not do such a vain or foolish thing as enlarge a grant by more than a million acres over what it was entitled to have under Mexican law, because it would be put in a ridiculous light.[13]

McMains was aware that Judge David J. Brewer, who had upheld the Maxwell patent on the basis of the grant

---

*Congress paid $10,000,000 to Texas to relinquish its claim to New Mexico east of the Río Grande.

de novo concept, would be the circuit judge hearing *Interstate Land Company* v. *Maxwell Land Grant Company.** When Alexander Graves, one of the Interstate lawyers, appeared before Judge Brewer in Kansas City on March 11, his arguments were essentially those McMains had predicted.[14]

Judge Brewer handed down his decision in favor of the Maxwell Company on December 20, but in it he made no reference to his first favorable Maxwell decision in 1886. Instead, he focused on the *empresarios'* failure to fulfill their colonization contract. Because of that, no title had been conveyed to them under Mexican law; the most they could now claim was eleven square leagues each.[15]

That decision must have been one of the last things Brewer did as circuit judge before being translated to the Supreme Court that same month. In 1891 the Supreme Court upheld his decision,† the second time the high court sustained him in a Maxwell Land Grant case.[16]

McMains was intensely annoyed that some of his friends succumbed to the blandishments of the Interstate Land Company; he thought they were simple opportunists. He was not in tune with a yearning for plain, simple living after years of insecurity. Completely dedicated, he professed not to despair of destroying the Maxwell, a faith that was fast waning among other anti-granters. Trying to beat the Maxwell with a bigger and prior claim seemed to him like trying to fight fraud with a hoax.[17]

---

* The Interstate case was argued concurrently with *Maxwell Land Grant Company* v. *Vicente Pretica et al.*, which sought to restrain Interstate Company tenants from occupying Maxwell land.

† The Supreme Court's opinion was written by Justice L. Q. C. Lamar, the former secretary of the interior, whom McMains had so harshly criticized. Lamar went to the supreme bench in 1888. In his opinion against the Beales Grant, he reaffirmed the unassailability of the Maxwell patent as protected by the Tameling decision, which introduced that insurmountable obstacle — the grant *de novo*.

Chapter 22

⊙━⊙

Twice Arrested

McMains was arrested in Trinidad on a charge of manslaughter on the same day that his latest anti-grant article
appeared in the *Raton Independent*.[1] He was arrested because
he wanted to be. When he voluntarily showed up, arrest
occurred soon after word got to the county courthouse. More
than once he had thought his detention might do the anti-
grant cause some good, and now seemed the time to find out.

Never had hopelessness been greater, with no help for
the settlers from the usual sources, public or private. There
seemed to be only an outside chance that the Harrison
administration, to be inaugurated a month hence, might be
attracted by the notoriety of McMains' incarceration. The
Agent for the Settlers and the anti-grant cause were reduced
to that.

Some people attributed McMains' extreme action to
vanity, believing that his "ambition has seemed to be to cover
himself with glory by leading armed resistance to the law."[2]
It would be silly to suggest that McMains derived no personal
satisfaction from what he was doing. He was not without
conceit, nor was his judgment beyond reproach; but a decade

of service supported an impersonal explanation in the best interest of the cause, as he saw it.

The sheriff said the amount of his bond was $5,000, and the Agent for the Settlers replied that he would go to the "calaboose" before he asked his friends for such a sum. When they reached the jail, "that full pen, so uninviting, was looked at closely, and the papers again inspected." The perusal revealed that the sheriff had misread the figure — it was only $500.[3]

Sam Bell and Anderson Duling helped McMains obtain the money. Those Stonewall men, also under indictment for the death of R. D. Russell, thus made their presence in Trinidad known (perhaps so planned with McMains), and they were quickly served with similar warrants.[4] Duling was one of the men recently criticized by McMains for dealing with the Interstate Land Company.

The trial would not be held before the March term and perhaps later. So the Agent for the Settlers went to Fort Worth, Texas, to lecture on the Maxwell Grant, and the *Fort Worth Gazette* carried a three-column article by him on the struggle of the anti-grant settlers.[5] After his return to Raton, the Supreme Court upheld former Secretary Lamar's order, based on McMains' petition, to treat the Nolán No. 39 as public land.[6] That was a pleasant reminder of better days.

Three days after President Benjamin Harrison took office McMains sent him a petition in behalf of the settlers through an intermediary, the brother of the slain Richard Russell. Charles Russell had gone to Chicago to publicize the Stonewall War through a series of public lectures, hoping to enlist support against the Maxwell Company among organized labor groups. At the same time an announcement of the new petition circulated in a McMains broadside entitled "The Fight Is Still On."[7]

In the Colorado district court at Trinidad, district attorney W. W. Dunbar doubted that the indictments of McMains and others for manslaughter could be sustained, and he secured dismissals and submission of the question to another grand jury. This time the grand jury looked less directly at Russell's death and more towards the intent in the attack on the deputies in the hotel. Ten indictments were returned against O. P. McMains, Martin Kephart, and others unknown. Nine were for "assault with intent to kill and murder" William Hunn and others, and the tenth was for arson in connection with the barn on the night the deputies escaped.[8]

After McMains was arrested a second time in Trinidad, his bond again was a matter of confusion. Either he could not or would not secure the $19,000 called for, so he spent a night in the county jail. The editor of the *Daily Citizen* was vividly critical:

> McMains has never been a criminal by intention. His purpose has been to resist wrong as he understands wrong to be. We question his choice of methods; think some of them unwise. But he is a sober man, a moral man, a man of much kindness of disposition. When he slept in the lousy, fetid cells of the jail last night, we think it was a shame — a travesty on the dear old flag that we all stand pledged to contribute life to if necessary.
>
> McMains' bed among vermin and rags last night weakened the Maxwell grant people wonderfully in the public esteem.
>
> Another night will give a thousand majority against Mr. Holdsworth for city treasurer, we fear.
>
> The American spirit will not permit American born citizens to lie in jail on this issue. The methods of McMains compare most favorably, indeed, with the methods of Chaffee, Elkins & Co.
>
> The men who now own the Maxwell grant paid their good money for what they had reason to believe was property with unquestioned title. The parties who sold the grant to the present owners we believe to have been thieves and the present owners should, for this reason, proceed cautiously. But McMains will not be in jail to-night! It is un American, you know.[9]

As editor DeBusk* predicted, McMains did not spend a second night there. It turned out that $19,000 was the aggregate on all the indictments; the amount required of him was $5,000: $4,000 for assault with intent to kill and $1,000 for arson. (His bonds were signed, interestingly enough, by Alex Taylor, the deputy sheriff who headed the posse that was to have rescued the deputies in Pooler's Hotel.[10])

On the evening of March 27, McMains boarded a north-bound Denver, Texas and Gulf train. The Stonewall settlers on whom the deputy marshal had served ejectment papers were before the federal district court in Pueblo, and he wanted to be on hand. Judgment was obtained against the settlers in all cases except that of R. D. Russell, which was held over to substitute his heirs as defendants. Only in the action against F. B. Chaplin was there a show of fight; that intrepid man made the Maxwell attorney go to the time-consuming trouble of submitting strict proof of title.[11]

After failing to fend off ejectment, the settlers returned with McMains to the Stonewall Valley, where he remained through April and the first week of May. That part of the world seemed more like home to him of late. Little was left

---

* DeBusk was strongly anti-grant and the only area newspaperman to speak up sharply in McMains' behalf, but he did not advise continued settlers' resistance: "In justice to themselves and their children they should end it as best they can, and like the poor old Mexican who was wronged but not well able to fight, turn the matter over to God to punish" (*Daily Citizen*, March 21, 1889). Harry Whigham, whether he believed it or not, took the position that DeBusk really was not himself. "To try to inflame a mob by misrepresentations and demagoguery, is beneath the character of such a man as Mr. DeBusk" (Harry Whigham to J. W. Shryock, August 29, 1888, Letters 7, July 5–September 14, 1888, p. 379, MLG). To Pels, Whigham wrote: "That fellow DeBusk is going crazy. I have asked Shryock to ask him if he won't 'come off' " (August 29, 1888, ibid., pp. 367–69, MLG).

for him and Mary in New Mexico, and the mountains of the Colorado portion were more agreeable to that unobtrusive woman. He had very close friends on the Red River and on the Vermejo, but now access to them seemed just as easy from Stonewall as from Raton.

General despondency subdued most of the anti-granters. Someone rustled Maxwell cattle in New Mexico, taking them into Colorado's San Luís Valley. A number of grant opponents disapproved, and Comp Reed tipped off the Maxwell people as to whom he suspected, for which Pels had the grace to say that Reed was "after all an honest man though a violent anti-granter."[12]

George Blosser still held out, but Harry Whigham heard that settlers in the mountains would not ride down again and that another writ of possession would drive Blosser out for good.[13] The will to resist approached its nadir.

Then came a taunting echo from the past. The *Colfax County Stockman* published a letter from William Pinkerton, the Nolán claimant recently turned down by the Supreme Court, saying that Secretary Lamar had acted "on the petition of a man named McMains, a man who had been convicted of murder, who now lies under indictment for manslaughter."[14] The ghost of Cruz Vega joined those of Richard Russell and Rafael Valerio.

Chapter 23

Days in Court

To quit was not in McMains' nature, so he prepared another petition to President Harrison for the Maxwell settlers and those on the Mora and Sangre de Cristo grants as well, stressing the invalidity of those grants because of the Texas Purchase, which seemed to be the only argument left that might be accepted. Again he worked through Charles W. Russell, who was now secretary of something called the National Anti-Land Grant Association, with an office in Chicago.[1]

In Trinidad McMains walked along Main Street on the evening of May 31 and was stopped by R. B. Holdsworth, of all people, "proffering to shake hands and talk for a few minutes. Mr. McMains was averse to doing either, declining with some emphasis. A little irritation arose which resulted in both gentlemen clinching one another. The altercation ended at this interesting stage."[2] As a matter of fact, Holdsworth's use of the direct approach was a problem for his employers. A few days later he insisted on interviewing Comp Reed and another man who refused to deal with him. Harry Whigham was greatly annoyed because there was hope that tact and patience would finally bring those men around.[3]

Oscar and Mary McMains in mid-June 1889 pulled up stakes in Raton and moved to Stonewall. Their departure attracted no public notice except that the *Raton Range* jeered good riddance that McMains "finally left New Mexico" where "his agitation and labors have resulted disastrously for himself and those who entrusted their cases with him."[4] For a parting shot it added: "As old age is fast overtaking him and his following is scattered, he moves away from the scene of former victories to avoid seeing the disputed territory peacefully peopled by earnest and industrious farmers who had no interest in the contest."[5]

A little house at Stonewall, belonging to the Russells, received them, and there Holdsworth discovered they were "quietly" living. McMains was only fifty, a rather advanced age to start thinking about security. Even then the problem did not fully preoccupy him. He acquired an interest in some mining property near Stonewall[6] to do a little prospecting and stake some claims.*

For many people the summer of 1889 was a time of preparation for the fall terms of court. Well over one hundred prosecutions of settlers were planned in New Mexico alone.[7]

The Colorado case against McMains was very special so far as the Maxwell people were concerned. The criminal action was brought, of course, by the state, but company men assisted in every way they could to develop a strong case against him. As Holdsworth put it: ". . . if the thing is well managed I think we shall get rid of him for about seven years."[8] All of McMains' anti-grant newspaper articles and

---

* McMains brought in some samples of copper and silver ore from the headwaters of the Purgatoire River, but nothing came of it (*Daily News*, July 27, 1889).

broadsides were collected. Pels had made a good start by keeping a scrapbook of many of them, but attorney James M. John had doubts that any of it would be admissible as evidence except that having direct bearing on the Stonewall collision.[9]

General Manager Pels naturally took a radical view of the prosecution: "He has given us too much trouble to be lenient with him in any way. At the time of the decision in the Molly Maguire cases,* the courts in Penna. decided that a man who instigated murder was even more guilty than the man who accomplished the deed, and this McMains has been doing all the time."[10] That accusation was absurd, but Pels lost his objectivity when he thought about the man. Of course, no one better knew the impact of McMains' opposition.

At a sylvan spot beside the South Fork of the Purgatoire, settlers from both sides of the state line assembled on August 12. McMains attended the meeting that was under the presidency of Comp Reed, Urbano Vigil serving as secretary. Once again the anti-granters restated their time-honored contention:

> Be it resolved, That we will not submit to eviction by the Maxwell Grant Company and its bribe polluted courts; that not until the Interior Department can show that its order of 1874 is no longer law, will we permit an overbearing bulldozing act of foreigners to evict a single settler with impunity; that lawful eviction we will not oppose, but the unlawful eviction proceedings of the Maxwell Grant Company and its Long courts† we will resist to the last extremity.[11]

---

*A reference to the terroristic "Molly Maguire" groups which operated in the anthracite coal fields of Pennsylvania in the 1870s.

†Long courts referred to Chief Justice Elisha V. Long of the New Mexico Supreme Court and judge of the district which included Colfax County.

A certain admiration is due those men who persisted when most people thought "the last extremity" had been reached in front of Pooler's Hotel a year before.

The first judicial move in Colfax County was an order by Judge Long on September 19 to arrest George Blosser for contempt. The judge was angered that when the sheriff had tried to serve a subpoena Mrs. Blosser had threatened to put a bullet through him. He called her bluff and served the paper, but her husband was elusive. McMains blasted the order, maintaining that the statute of limitations vested title in Blosser.[12] But not even the Blosser case was a drawing card like the trial of McMains in Trinidad.

In the afternoon of October 2 the case of *The People* v. *O. P. McMains et al,* was called. James M. John assisted the district attorney, while Caldwell Yeaman and James Martin, Trinidad lawyers, represented McMains and Martin Kephart. The Hon. Julius C. Gunter was on the bench. The job of empaneling a jury* took until noon the next day.[13]

The trial carried on for eleven wearisome days. At first spectators were numerous, but lengthy testimony and cross-examination soon cut down attendance. Defense attorney Yeaman contended that the deputies sent to Stonewall were agents of the grant company rather than public officers, the company having put up money to arm them. Other defense arguments held that the settlers had not gathered with intent to do violence, and that Tom O'Neil fired the first shot as a prearranged signal for the deputies to start firing.[14]

---

* The jurors were: J. T. Larson, C. H. Schwatzel, Regino Archuleta, Manuel J. Ma. Vigil, William Milliken, Jesús García, J. A. Bell, B. F. Gumm, Gabino Vialpondo, A. Roland, George Schornhorst, and W. S. Richards (*People* v. *O. P. McMains et al.,* Records of the District Court, Las Animas County, Colorado, Nos. 1618, 1619, 1625 (1889). Judge Gunter later was Democratic governor of Colorado, 1917–19.

Yeaman felt that the defense was sound enough without calling McMains or Kephart to testify. For the summations the courtroom was crowded, Messrs. Yeaman and John being admired for their oratory.[15]

When the jury came in at eleven o'clock the next morning, October 12, the foreman proclaimed McMains and Kephart not guilty. Friends crowded around, excited in their congratulations and praises of the jury.

While the joyous demonstration continued, Deputy U.S. Marshal E. C. Currier pushed his way through the crowd, went up to McMains, and arrested him yet again on a federal charge of conspiracy in inciting and aiding resistance to the service of official papers.[16] A strange silence followed the first astonishment of the men around McMains. But he faced the shocking development with resignation. Moments later he observed that he was " 'out of the frying pan into the fire,' " and then with a smile, " 'It is the heavenly will.' "[17]

The will of heaven, perhaps, but implemented by the general manager of the Maxwell Land Grant Company. Pels, anticipating acquittal, had arranged with federal authorities for McMains' arrest on a complaint sworn out by R. B. Holdsworth.[18]

It was thought that McMains would have a hearing before a U.S. commissioner in Pueblo, but the marshal took him to Denver, where he was jailed. His friends in Las Animas County were refused as bondsmen, and it took time to find sympathizers in the state capital who would arrange for his release. Lodged in a common cell with assorted wrongdoers, McMains remained there until October 17, when he was released to appear before a grand jury in November.[19]

The arrest was bad enough, but the unseemly haste with which McMains was whisked to Denver endangered the progress the Maxwell Company had made with settlers. He was back in Trinidad on October 18, telling an *Advertiser* reporter that he did not expect new violence, nor did he think the grand jury would indict him. His condition — thin, half sick, despondent — made a strong impression on his interviewer, who published the consolation that "he has friends in this county who will cheer him up and no doubt in a day or two his spirits will be renewed and he will appear the same cheerful, genial talker that it is natural for him to be."[20]

The Agent for the Settlers knew that the backbone of resistance was broken, a judgment substantiated by events in Las Vegas, New Mexico. Ejectment actions against fourteen Anglo and Mexican settlers had been taken there on change of venue, and Pels hoped to settle with them out of court. The wish was sterile, but he perked up when he learned that Comp Reed, J. E. Gillum, and one or two others were on their way from Red River. Perhaps they were ready to make a deal.[21]

Those anti-grant stalwarts (such as Reed, Gillum and the Youngs) decided their chances of getting the better of the Maxwell Company were slight. Their lawyer advised compromise, and, taking his advice, they agreed to sell their improvements. They would lease their ranches for two years and then leave the grant, also agreeing to try to convince others to come to terms. To company officials in New York an elated Pels expressed confidence "that we can easily dispose of the remaining settlers and that peace, and as I hope prosperity, after twenty years of struggle, will henceforth reign on the Maxwell Grant."[22]

Peace was much closer as Vermejo Park and the Red River country declined as anti-grant strongholds. But there were a few diehards; on Red River two or three men fumed and threatened and warned Whigham not to press matters too fast. One of them gave Whigham such a rough time in Raton that it seemed they "would have a fight before he got out of the office." He was bearded, barefooted Bill Harness, who demanded a price for his ranch the grant people thought exorbitant. If he failed to get his price, Harness promised a flaming defense of his place, causing his son-in-law to beg Whigham to accept before Harness left town. Whigham came within a hundred dollars of the sum asked and was greatly relieved when Harness accepted.[23] Serious trouble was thus averted, leaving only two Red River men holding out.

Extremely gratifying for the company was Whigham's deal with George Blosser, who accepted a down payment of $100 for his improvements and a balance of $300 to be paid when he vacated on March 1, 1890. By Christmas, resistance seemed to be restricted to a few settlers, mostly Mexicans, in the more remote canyons. Whigham was optimistic, but not so Pels, who disliked the Harness compromise, he said, because it might encourage the holdouts to bully the company.[24]

In Colorado the Chaplins, the Russells, the Torres family, and a few others had not left their ranches, and just before New Year's Day 1890, a deputy sheriff went to Stonewall to serve papers on ten men, who allegedly had jumped company properties. Pels doubted that there would be a serious disturbance, the growing desuetude of anti-grantism having been increased by Judge Brewer's decision against the Interstate Land Company, with which some of the Stonewall people had tried to do business.[25]

When finally the grand jury investigated the conspiracy charge against McMains in mid-December 1889, Samuel DeBusk, editor of the Trinidad *Daily Citizen*, sent the following observations to his paper:

> If I were in McMains' place, I would take off my hat to the Maxwell Grant, and tell them that while my heart might not have changed radically on the subject at issue, yet realizing that life is too short for such a contest, and especially being a trifle knocked about in the fray, I should like to quit if they would. Were I in Mc's shoes I would try to impress upon that corporation (soulless of course) the duty of quitting. But ten to one the old

man will decline to take that view of the case. Unless he can effect a timely surrender, I fear that some of his doings, well-meant at the time, will be taken away from all local surroundings tending to mitigate and excite sympathy, and viewed in the cold light of the law and the evidence, may bring troubles to his grayhairs at a time when he should enjoy peace.[26]

The federal grand jury indicted McMains on December 21 in a true bill that accused him and others of conspiring to prevent federal officers from serving summonses and subpoenas dated June 26, 1888, and August 22, 1888, and of trying to deny certain citizens and a certain corporation equal protection of the laws. Used in evidence against him were his "violent and inflammatory address" at the South Fork schoolhouse, his threat to resist militia and his broadsides, "The Texas Purchase" and "Defiance!"[27]

Very prejudicial to McMains was the charge that he and others caused "a large number of persons to gather together with guns and pistols in a loud and tumultuous manner and with threats of violence" which prevented the deputy marshal from serving papers. In other words, the encounter before Pooler's Hotel was part of a conspiracy to obstruct a federal officer. Nothing in the data suggests that anything other than the arrival of the sheriff's deputies at Stonewall brought the massing of anti-granters. The claim of interference with a federal officer did not square with the facts of the Stonewall War. Later in his own defense McMains insisted that the relevant papers were not in the marshal's hands before August 27.[28]

While the grand jury was in session McMains was at home, but early in January 1890 he came down through the winter landscape to Trinidad, where he published a new broadside — a personal gesture of defiance — entitled: "My Case Against the United States." A few days later he went to Denver to stand trial, but on the last day of the month U.S.

District Attorney J. D. Fleming secured a transfer of the case to the district court at Pueblo for the March term.[29] McMains returned to Stonewall under the dejection of anticlimax.

In February, twenty-four settlers in the Red River country sold out to the Maxwell Company and then issued a public protest against the pressures put on them to sell,[30] a tactic that showed how barren the anti-grant movement had become. Another ineffective protest was the burning of three abandoned homes of former settlers near the head of Red River. The incendiarism was attributed to Mexican settlers, because next day about thirty of them broke up a surveyor's camp on the South Fork of the Purgatoire. But Harry Whigham blamed a group of Anglos, who had made terms, accusing them of doing as much damage as possible before their leases expired. That version could be used against McMains, and Whigham passed the idea to Pels,[31] who used it in a letter to the U.S. attorney:

> I am sorry to see that this lawlessness seems not to end, and I agree with Mr. Whigham when he writes that certainly McMains who lives among those men is at the bottom of this new outrage as everywhere in New Mexico the most perfect order exists.... I think it my duty to give you notice of these facts as in my mind there is a close connection between them and the man Mc Mains who se [*sic*] whole life has been spent towards inciting to riot, destruction and contempt of the law.[32]

Pels did not quote Whigham exactly, and he had no proof of McMains' implication. The gratuitous information was in the prosecutor's possession when McMains arrived in Pueblo to stand trial in late March, but the case was again postponed to the October term.[33]

Flames leaped once more on the New Mexico portion early in April. Two haystacks and an unoccupied house on Red River, three places on the Vermejo, and two houses on the Poñil became charred ruins. Whigham was aghast.[34] Pels's "perfect order" was shattered. By this time McMains had become a natural and convenient scapegoat on whom to place the blame for much of the discord on the grant, with attribution of responsibility to Mexicans not far behind. In instances of the latter, grant officials either were unaware of, or ignored, the infiltration by *Las Gorras Blancas* (the White Caps) into the remnants of anti-grantism. However, it is impossible to measure the degree of its involvement.

In the spring and summer of 1890, McMains worked hard to reanimate the anti-grant movement by probing for help from the Fifty-first Congress[35] and continuing to demand support from the General Land Office.* Many anti-granters finally leased from the company, but company officials were under no illusion that leases meant conversions to the pro-grant side. So anti-granters on the Maxwell, together with some on the Sangre de Cristo, sent McMains to Washington again. The renewed confidence touched him deeply; it was like old times when he climbed aboard a Santa Fe train in Trinidad, telling a reporter: " 'The settlers have decided to make one more appeal to Congress and have sent me on for that purpose.' " Asked if he expected difficulty in securing a hearing, he replied:

No, sir, not in the least. Nor of getting a committee appointed to make the investigation. It is the sub-committee in every instance that thwarts our efforts. The chairman of the sub-committee is always captured and no report is ever made to congress. I shall get the matter

---

* The *New York Times* published a letter from McMains to the commissioner of the General Land Office.

before the house and either the committee on private
land claims or a special committee, though I prefer the
latter, then I will ask the Alliance people who are in
Washington to keep the matter stirred up until a report
is made. That is all we want. Congress is favorable to
the settlers and a report means a victory for us.[36]

His eleventh trip kept the Agent for the Settlers away
from home until late August. During his absence the first and
only issue of the *National Anti Land Grant Monthly* appeared
in Chicago, but editor Charles W. Russell's office address was
listed as Trinidad. The monthly featured an eye-catching page
with a silhouette of a bullet and a caption, "The argument
used to silence R. D. Russell's objections to ejectment, Stonewall, Colorado, August 25, 1888."[37]

Several Colorado settlers received ejectment papers on
July 7. F. B. Chaplin ignored his and announced that he was
"still doing business at the old stand,"[38] while Comp Reed
warned any trespasser to bring two coffins with him — one for
himself and one for Reed. When old settlers with leases complained about railroad construction across their fields and pas-
tures, Pels agreed that they had legitimate complaints of open
gates, strayed cattle, and damaged crops. All were mollified
except Comp Reed, who was described as walking around
with a brace of pistols and a Winchester. Pels also made other
agreements, including one with the Manby brothers at Castle
Rock.[39]

McMains returned from Washington with the doleful
admission of failure. Congress had not budged. One local
editor said that "the Elkins ring was too much for the old
man,"[40] a meaningful allusion, although Stephen Benton
Elkins long before had shifted his economic and political base
to West Virginia.

Wild stories in the hill country had McMains telling
Spanish-speaking settlers, who had given money for his recent

trip, that when the senators in Washington paid no attention to him he fired three shots in the Senate chamber, making those distinguished gentlemen listen carefully and promise to break the grant.[41] Shades of the doctored newspaper dispatches published several years before.

Congressional indifference assisted the grant company. Comp Reed gave up and relinquished his ranches before his leases expired — a grand piece of luck for Pels.* However, Reed's friendship with McMains did not founder; in fact, no one who made terms with the company was shunned by McMains. But he could not bring himself to do the same.

For the first time in several years the anti-grant issue was not a part of the fall political campaign, so the pending ejectment suits on the New Mexico portion were not pushed. In Colorado, company counsel won judgments in quite a few cases, securing others by default. Richard Russell's heirs were granted a new trial, however, along with ten others including F. B. Chaplin. At year's end Frank Springer reported a total of sixty-two cases in 1890 — judgments obtained for the company in sixteen, fourteen dismissed pursuant to agreements with the general manager, and thirty-two pending.[42]

The conspiracy case of *The United States* v. *O. P. McMains* was, for M. P. Pels, an intense preoccupation, almost an obsession. He saw the Agent for the Settlers as an evil genius. ". . . He is not a crank but is thoroughly dangerous and remains and ever will be an agitator unless placed behind bars. . . . the man McMains whose whole life has been spent and is being spent towards inciting to riot, destruction and contempt of the law."[43]

---

*According to his daughter, Mrs. Lucy Reed Wills, Reed was offered $50,000 by the Maxwell Land Grant Company at an earlier time to get out, which he indignantly rejected as a bribe to betray his anti-grant colleagues (Interview with Mrs. Lucy Reed Wills, February 12, 1948).

McMains took a Denver, Texas & Fort Worth train to Pueblo on the last day of September. Some of the older residents remembered him as the builder of the first Methodist Church and recollected the Pueblo *Chieftain's* strong defense of him in the Cruz Vega murder case. The *Chieftain* on October 9, 1890, published his poem, "Miss Nell Snow, A Stonewall Romance,"[44] recalling days when poems and chatty articles by A. Bach were features of the paper.

Pels had the intense satisfaction of seeing McMains caught at last. The court dismissed defense motions to quash the indictment, and for several days the jury heard testimonies and arguments. Judge Hallett gave a strong charge to the jury, terming the violence at Stonewall "the worst in the history of the State."[45] The jury came back in a few minutes with a verdict of guilty. Hallett denied a motion for a new trial and suspended sentencing until the next term of court, allowing McMains his freedom on $500 bond. That indecision baffled attorney James M. John, who could explain to Pels only that the judge did not know what to do because he believed McMains to be a lunatic. For his part, Pels thought that Hallett held off so as to hold a sword of Damocles over McMains for the next six months in order to see how McMains would behave.[46] At any rate, McMains now had several months away from the court. He must have welcomed the respite.

Chapter 24

❦

The Populists –
A Bright, New Hope

WHEN THE SIX-MONTH SUSPENSION of McMains' sentence elapsed on the morning of April 17, 1891, Judge Moses Hallett sentenced him to six months in the common jail of Pueblo County, the cost of the trial to be paid by the prisoner.[1] A deputy marshal delivered him into the keeping of the county jailer.

About all Oscar McMains had left were recollections of service for the welfare of others. His own future and that of his cause looked bleak. Mary, who stood quietly by him during the hectic times, was a real comfort. He looked forward from one visiting hour to the next. Once in a while old friends dropped in to see him, but it was a long way from Stonewall or the Vermejo to Pueblo. Slowly the months ticked away, the monotony relieved only by visits and reading.

Regarded by some as having paid his debt to society and by others as a maligned man, McMains was released from jail in October. Imprisonment had not extinguished his will to challenge the land grants, and his spirit was replenished by trends he saw in the country.

Encouraged by new political colorations,* the Agent for the Settlers resumed his crusade against the grants. He distributed handbills that were critical of the Supreme Court and arranged for public meetings. On the night of October 21, 1891, only days after his release from jail, he addressed a large gathering of laboring men, a few businessmen, and others in Pueblo's Board of Trade Hall. His special object for excoriation was former Land Office Commissioner Williamson. And McMains sought expanded support by contributing articles to the labor press.[2]

Agrarian discontent and labor unrest created hopes that rejuvenated the anti-grant spirit to an old response — raising money to send McMains to Washington. There he used the fortuitous development that put Kansas Populist John G. Otis in the Fifty-second Congress and on the House Private Land Claims Committee, and Otis (a Harvard Law School graduate, Kansas Free Soiler, and leading Granger) was much more than politely receptive. The congressman on March 5, 1892, introduced a smashing resolution to revoke the confirmation of several big ones: the Maxwell, the Vigil and St. Vrain (already limited to 96,000 acres), the Nolán No. 48 in Colorado, and the Sangre de Cristo[3] — the most momentous support McMains had received since Commissioner Sparks stood squarely behind him in 1885.

---

*A political convention, representative chiefly of farmers and organized labor, had met in Cincinnati, Ohio, and planned for a national party in the presidential election of 1892. The movement had already won some congressional seats in the mid-West, and by 1891 the Populist (People's) Party had eight representatives and two senators, to say nothing of nominal Democrats and Republicans who sympathized sincerely or expediently. See John D. Hicks, *The Populist Revolt: A History of the Farmers' Alliance and the People's Party* (1931; Lincoln: University of Nebraska Press, 1961), pp. 211–16; Solon J. Buck, *The Agrarian Crusade: A Chronicle of the Farmer in Politics* (New Haven: Yale University Press, 1920), p. 140; Louis M. Hacker and Benjamin B. Kendrick, *The United States Since 1865* (New York: F. S. Crofts and Company, 1938), pp. 301–2.

The four grants had been dealt with by Congress, a fact that placed them outside the jurisdiction of the Court of Private Land Claims that Congress had created about a year before. Generally stressing their invalidity because they were not in the Mexican Cession of 1848 but were in Texas, the Otis resolution had the immediate goal of getting the Private Land Claims Committee to investigate the need for protection of Maxwell settlers in Colorado who had government papers to their lands. On April 13 Otis introduced a joint resolution to revoke congressional action on the four grants. A little over two weeks later he brought out of committee H.R. 8474, concerning the intent of Congress in former acts relative to former Spanish and Mexican grants. With it he submitted a comprehensive report on land titles in New Mexico and Colorado, stressing both the validity of the Cox decision and the invalidity of Mexican grants east of the Río Grande. The bill was referred to the House calendar and ordered to be printed.[4]

McMains worked again at the Interior Department, getting in touch with Secretary John W. Noble and Thomas H. Carter, commissioner of the General Land Office. Secretary Noble, in a letter to McMains (March 31, 1892), declined to enforce the departmental order limiting the Maxwell to twenty-two square leagues, saying it "has practically been a dead letter from its issuance." Using another approach with Carter, McMains argued that the Colorado portion really was within the outboundaries of the Vigil and St. Vrain Grant, but Carter in effect said that it was too late — the land was within the patented limits of the Maxwell.

Although McMains met with obdurate refusals, Frank Springer, then a member of the Maxwell board of trustees as well as company counsel, had expressed a different view of people in the Interior Department. About a year before, the Maxwell board asked for Springer's advice on a proposal to recover about 100,000 acres north of Uña de Gato Creek (which surveyor W. W. Griffin had included in his survey of 1870 and that had been excluded from the officially accepted

Elkins and Marmon survey of 1877). Agreeing that the attempt could be made, Springer felt that it would be extremely unwise and would have no part of it. To reopen the question of the Maxwell survey and patent would, in his opinion, probably only result in the exchange of the much larger Colorado portion for the Uña de Gato, although Springer believed that both parts legitimately belonged in the grant. He said, in other words, that no commissioner or secretary would permit a new survey to include land north of the Raton Divide, so great was the latent resentment in the department against the Maxwell people,[5] for having secured nearly 300,000 acres north of the Colorado–New Mexico line in their patent.*

Of this residue of opposition to the Maxwell at the Interior Department, McMains was unaware. Support for the grant in that former bastion of anti-grantism now seemed obvious to the Agent for the Settlers. His strongest ally was Congressman Otis, who offered another resolution calling for a seven-man committee, with subpoena powers, to investigate alleged unlawful procedures and conspiracy of public officers relating to the Maxwell and other grants.

An objection was raised to immediate consideration, so the resolution was sent to the Private Land Claims Committee. Securing favorable action there, Otis reported on July 9 to the House, which referred it to the Committee of the Whole House on the State of the Union and ordered it to be printed. Such marvelous progress had hardly been equaled in the history of the anti-grant movement. Nonetheless, when McMains arrived in Trinidad on August 25, the fourth anniversary of the Stonewall War, he could not flatly say that success would

---

* One wonders if Springer's warning against disturbing the patent of 1879 expressed a fear that it might collapse to ca. 96,000 acres, as Secretary Cox, Secretary Kirkwood, and Commissioner Sparks had advocated.

come in the second session of the Fifty-second Congress. He brought the committee report with him, but it made slight impression. Even the local papers made no reference to the report's fulsome recommendations.[6]

In the Stonewall country McMains' reception was slightly more cordial. When anti-grant settlers heard him and read the report there was a faint resurgence of the old spirit — weak because so few were left. Rents due the Maxwell Company suddenly were hard to collect, and in one or two instances company ranches were jumped. Although a handful of men believed the chances of breaking the grant were the best ever, Pels and Whigham treated the incidents as petty annoyances. Nor was Frank Springer, recently made president of the Maxwell Trustees, afraid that Congress might act affirmatively on the committee's recommendations. His certitude was correct. Any worry that he might have had was dissipated when John G. Otis failed to secure renomination for a House seat.[7]

The Populists featured the free silver issue in 1892, but they also called for an end to corporate and alien ownership of land, a stance that encouraged hope of final success against the grants. Las Animas County received a strong dose of Populist doctrine; Democratic presidential electors were removed from the Colorado ballots and replaced by Populists on instructions from the Democratic national headquarters.[8]

The election results were surprising. Although Democrat Cleveland returned to the White House after an absence of four years, the Populists gathered over a million votes across the country and captured twenty-two votes in the electoral college. (Populist strength lay mainly in Kansas, North Dakota, Colorado, Idaho, and Nevada, much of it in fusion with the Democrats.) In Colorado they made a clean sweep of the entire Republican state ticket, one of the two Populist congressmen being John C. Bell,* whose district included Las Animas County and hence the Colorado portion of the Maxwell Grant.[9]

Fatigue kept McMains quietly close to home during the campaign. Christmas at home had not been a regular occurrence for him for many years, so that pleasure pervaded his little house at Stonewall during the Christmas season of 1892. Christian reverence was still very important to him, and the holy day was, for him and Mary, a time of sincere observance and great joy.[10] As the mountain winter wore on, McMains varied routine by turning again to poetry.[11]

The absence of John G. Otis from the Fifty-third Congress would terminate, temporarily at least, anti-grant leadership on the Washington scene. The significant Populist gains in the elections of 1892 were generally encouraging, but it would take a while to find individuals who might carry on in the Otis tradition — if indeed they were there. John C. Bell, the new representative from Colorado's third district, was an unknown quantity. Grover Cleveland's return to the White House was no cause for anti-granters to celebrate. He had not lifted a finger to help them before, and there was no reason to think he might do differently in his second administration. Moreover, the state of McMains' health plus the difficulty of raising funds made it unlikely that he would reappear in the capital as the anti-grant spokesman. An unmistakeable sign of how moribund anti-grantism had become in Washington was the failure of the Fifty-second Congress to act on the Otis report before it adjourned on March 3, 1893.

---

*Actually Bell was a Populist-Democratic fusion candidate.

Chapter 25

❦

The Last Optimism

A MEASURE OF PHYSICAL STRENGTH came to McMains with the warmth of summer, and with it anti-grant hopes began to revive in his growing belief that the new Populist governor of Colorado, Davis H. Waite, might be the key to renewed effort against the Maxwell Grant. Waite's polemics against the common man's subjugation to Wall Street and the big corporations made him kindred in spirit. McMains took a familiar first step, sending him a petition to open the Colorado portion of the Maxwell as public land and requesting the governor to forward it to the General Land Office in Washington.

Waite's gratifying response on September 28 was full compliance and a public announcement of his sympathy with the prayer of the petition. Remarking that he believed the Maxwell to be " 'a fraud from the ground up' " and citing his inaugural address reference to fraudulent entries, Waite revealed he had asked the commissioner of the General Land Office to remedy the situation as justice demanded.[1] But McMains had been in that state of affairs before, only to find the petition emasculated by Interior Department lawyers.

The Panic of 1893 seized upon the nation, and in Colorado many people blamed the Populists for the economic breakdown of the state. However, that did not prevent a startling maneuver in Las Animas County in October — a fusion of the Populist and Republican tickets. So strong was the desire to dislodge the long-entrenched Democrats in the county that the unusual combination had a chance to work.[2]

McMains publicly argued the Populist cause and pleaded that Waite's stand against the Maxwell Grant not be dismissed lightly by old settlers. If anyone suspected that Waite endorsed the anti-grant cause only for political reasons, it is not of record, but the editor of the Democratic *Daily Advertiser* said he assumed McMains was not aware that one of the leading fusionists was James M. John, the Maxwell attorney who had done so much to secure imprisonment of the Agent for the Settlers. Furthermore, there was no real Populist ticket because the fusionist leaders were corporation tools.[3]

McMains was committed to the Populists in principle, so he regarded political association with a pro-granter as an inconsequential detail — a rather surprising and opportunistic rationalization. The coalition won.[4]

Shortly before year's end McMains' petition against the Maxwell was rejected. Hoke Smith, Secretary of the Interior, wrote at length to Governor Waite, explaining the rejection and why Waite's appraisal of the Maxwell was in error. He insisted that the Supreme Court's 1887 decision ended the controversy, and that McMains' argument that the Colorado portion was a part of the Vigil and St. Vrain Grant had been negated by the Court's decisions in the Maxwell and Interstate cases. Smith concluded:

> If this department were to disregard the confirmatory act of congress, and the repeated decision of the United States supreme court, and restore to the local office the plats of public surveys for [filings] and entries, the only result would be to mislead innocent parties into making entries of lands to which the department would be wholly powerless to convey title.[5]

For McMains those familiar reasons were excuses, not explanations. He was as sure as ever that the Cox decision was valid and enforceable. The Populist party, he felt, was the one great hope against corrupt Republican and Democratic administrations alike.

In 1894 McMains was chosen as Populist* committeeman for Precinct 3, Stonewall, and his improved health also was indicated by his return to an old avocation, the lecture platform, where he discussed various public issues.[6] That September, the Pops, as the opposition press usually called them, chose McMains to head their county ticket as candidate for representative in the Colorado General Assembly. Whether his nomination was staged or spontaneous is not known. The *Daily Advertiser* remarked that "the pops met and 'popped out' on an unsuspecting public the following list of nominations" and referred to the head of the Populist ticket as "O. P. McMains of New Mexico."[7] Another editorial skirted the edge of the old Vega murder in its derogatory comments about him:

> ... [McMains] came to the Rocky Mountain country nearly thirty years ago preaching "Christ and Him crucified," but in an evil hour he turned his back upon Christ and has left him to shift for himself ever since. Why he was nominated no one seems to know, but it was done through another who was a standard bearer of the Lord, but of late years has allowed the sacred banner to trail in the dust. It was done, no doubt, through a fellow feeling that "we worldly minded ex-Reverends must stand together."[8]

The other "standard bearer of the Lord" was Samuel W. DeBusk, county commissioner, ardent Populist, and former

---

*The Populist-Republican fusion in Las Animas County had not survived.

A. R. Mitchell

O. P. McMains at Stonewall.

preacher for the Methodist Episcopal Church, South. Like McMains, he had given up the ministry, and he had defended McMains in his *Daily Citizen* during the anti-grant uproars of 1887–1889.[9]

McMains' candidacy may not have been a wise move. Although a man of ideals and a fine speaker with legislative experience (albeit in New Mexico), many voters knew him best as the Agent for the Settlers — a distasteful recollection to quite a few, especially those who feared actions that might depress real estate values and scare off investment capital. That he might use legislative office against the Maxwell Grant doubtless was a suspicion with substance. And he was criticized for not being familiar enough with the entire county (a very large one), his experience being almost exclusively with people in the foothills and mountains of the west end.[10]

Minimal outside support came to McMains when the Prohibitionists, who did not name their own slate in Las Animas County, endorsed both McMains and his Republican rival.* The Las Vegas *Daily Optic* picked that up with undiminished spite: "Up at Trinidad Rev. (?) O. P. McMains, the land agitator, with more mouth than brains, has been nominated by the Prohibitionists for representative in the legislature from Las Animas County. He has no more chance of being elected than he has of going to heaven when he dies."[11]

McMains was not physically up to a vigorous campaign, but on one occasion he joined his fellow candidates on the stage of the Jaffa Opera House in Trinidad to give support to, and gain endorsement from, Governor Davis H. Waite,

---

* The Prohibitionists, a splinter party, often endorsed candidates of both major parties so long as they were temperance men; in many local situations that tactic seemed the best way to assure getting temperance men into office.

who defended his administration for two and a half hours.[12] In view of election results, locally and across the state, McMains' espousal of the Populist leader was a liability.

The Republicans took the governor's office, but the Populists retained control of the state senate. In Las Animas County a poor third place was the Populists' lot, while the Republicans won. McMains ran next to last among the six who sought the two legislative seats, his Populist running mate coming in last. Of the total 13,047 votes for the six, McMains received only 1,900. The precincts where he either won or made a good showing were areas in which coal miners were strong. Farmers and ranchers gave little support. That reflected a state-wide trend against "Waiteism." The governor carried only three of the ten counties that in 1891 had been regarded as very strong Farmers' Alliance counties.[13]

McMains won not a single ward in Trinidad, while the Stonewall precinct, which the Republicans and Democrats conceded to him, gave him an astonishing 55 votes out of 430. He trailed the Republicans by a few votes, but the Democratic winners received 104 and 106 votes respectively. La Junta (Weston) gave him only three votes even though the place had once been an anti-grant hot bed. Only on the South Fork of the Purgatoire did he make the grade along with one of the Democrats.[14]

In Las Animas County, then, rural residents relinquished Populist doctrines to the miners, the railroaders, and other working men, and opposition to the Maxwell Land Grant Company was no longer a potent tactic.[15]

Winter closed in. McMains stayed quietly at Stonewall. The news came to him that Martinus Petrus Pels had resigned as general manager of the Maxwell Land Grant Company, effective January 1, 1895, although he may not have known that Pels did so under pressure from the company directors and Frank Springer, president.[16]

On May 30, 1895, Justice David J. Brewer (on the supreme bench since 1889) wrote the Supreme Court's opinion against the plaintiff in the case of *Marion Russell* v. *The Maxwell Land Grant Company.* Since, as circuit judge, he had already supported the Maxwell Grant in three cases, the opinion had no element of surprise, even though some people may have wondered why he did not disqualify himself in the Russell case. The long litigation of the Russells came to an end, and the family came to terms with the company* for a part of their claim at Stonewall.[17]

The anti-grant movement was moribund to say the least, but McMains was implacable. He had expected the adverse decision and once more had turned to Grover Cleveland, asking the president to at last take a firm stand against the grant before the court acted. Cleveland made no acknowledgment of McMains' request, although an answer of sorts came on October 12 when Secretary of the Interior Hoke Smith replied that the department had no authority to reopen the controversy.[18]

As incredible as McMains' persistence was the fact that people still solidly supported him, and for the fourteenth time money was scraped together to send him to Washington. He left Trinidad on January 6, 1896. In the Fifty-fourth Congress were six Populist senators and seven Populist representatives, including John C. Bell of Colorado's Second District, from whom help might be received.[19]

Changing his approach, McMains aimed for impeachment of a high public official. Although the sources do not say whom, he probably meant the Secretary of the Interior

---

*A few months later F. B. Chaplin signed a lease with the company for 160 acres on March 23, 1900 (Las Animas County [Colorado] Miscellaneous Deeds, Book 109, p. 223).

(but his intended target may have been President Cleveland). His strategy was new but not strong. Congressman Bell refused to introduce the necessary resolution. McMains retaliated on February 10 with an open letter to the Speaker of the House, setting forth five complaints against Bell. The charges added up to saying that the congressman was not performing his duty, was forgetting to uphold the Constitution, and was bringing reproach upon the House. There was a mild hint that settlers might use force against unjust convictions, and the letter concluded:

> Mr. Speaker, permit me to state that settlers on the Colorado portion of the alleged Maxwell grant have received many a cruel stab from public officials during the fifteen years that I have acted as their agent; but the fact that their petition for impeachment, as a bar to their unlawful eviction, should be shut out of Congress by their own Populist representative, is "the unkindest cut of all."[20]

Congressman Bell responded by introducing two resolutions: one called for information on the secretary's action and the other sought an investigation of the Colorado portion of the Maxwell.[21] Both died in committee.

Chapter 26

❦

"I Can Do No More"

THE LETTER to the Speaker of the House was a last, fading blast on a trumpet that was also off-key. It had none of the old verve and assurance, and there were few to rally. Nearly everyone but McMains accepted the impregnability of the Maxwell Grant.

Early in 1896, McMains suffered a physical breakdown, diagnosed in the terminology of the day as shattered nerves and catarrh of the stomach.[1] Doubtless it was related to exhaustion and despondence incurred in the anti-grant cause. Even without bodily infirmity, fifteen years of failure, the Nolán No. 39 excepted, was enough to stifle a stout heart. McMains was only fifty-six, but his hair and beard had been white for a long time.

Except during the time of heavy snows Stonewall was not an isolated spot. Cool and beautiful in the summer, the mountain valleys were favorites with hunters, fishermen, and outing parties. In the summer of 1898 a professional photographer did a brisk business at Stonewall. A friend stopped by McMains' house and suggested that "Mac" have his picture taken. As a further inducement, the friend said he would pay for it. The notion was agreeable to McMains, but when he saw the picture he was sorry. Mary wanted to send a copy to her brother in Illinois, but Oscar would not permit that. It looked " 'awful' " in his opinion; his hair was long and bushy, and his clothes hardly presentable. He did it on the spur of the moment and did not think "to fix up a little," he said, a sad change from pinning up the tails of his frock coat so that they would not be wrinkled on the saddle.[2]

That winter McMains felt so miserable that he went to Trinidad to be within easy reach of a doctor. Getting no relief, he went on to Denver.[3] In the Colorado capital the state of his health was not his only concern. McMains just had to take another crack at the Maxwell Land Grant Company. The twelfth General Assembly convened in January, and one of the representatives from Las Animas County, J. P. Dunlavy, respected him enough to listen to the Agent for the Settlers.

On January 26, 1899, Dunlavy, at McMains' request, introduced a resolution containing three allegations: 1. that the public surveys over the Colorado portion of the Maxwell were lawful because that tract was within the outboundaries of the Vigil and St. Vrain Grant; 2. that the General Land Office treated the Colorado portion as public land by granting school sections to the state and homestead patents to coal companies; 3. that the General Land Office, however, refused to grant homesteads to bona fide settlers. It passed, and a special committee was appointed to investigate and report to the House.[4]

McMains knew it would be a while before the committee made its recommendations, and sometime in February he decided he could afford to wait no longer. His health had not improved, so he went back to Stonewall. Everyone noticed a decided change for the worse, although he insisted he would recover.[5] His eyes brightened when he learned that on March 19 the legislature adopted a report recommending that settlers having government papers be compensated by Congress and urging that Colorado senators and representatives seek such relief.[6] If it had happened it would have been a minor achievement for all his years of dedicated work. But, like so many other promising starts, the intent was never realized.

Tinges of spring were in the Stonewall country when death came. Oscar P. McMains expired peacefully shortly after midnight on April 15, 1899. Mary and some old friends were with him. He had been unconscious for some time when he opened his eyes and called, "Mary." Then, giving his hand to each of his friends, he said, "Goodbye, goodbye, I can do no more."[7] That was the last time he opened his eyes.

Two days later the Reverend F. B. Lawler, Baptist minister from Trinidad, preached the funeral sermon. Many settlers came to pay last respects to their Agent, who had tried to do so much for them. They knew his failure was not the rightful measure of the man, and they respected him for having continued the struggle long after most of them had given up. With the lowering of his casket into the muslin-lined grave, near Richard D. Russell's in the cemetery overlooking the Stonewall and Purgatoire valleys, the older ones knew that an era had ended.[8]

F. B. Chaplin, McMains' friend and anti-grant colleague, wrote that McMains had long fought against "crime and corruption, ever pleading for the right in defense of the poor," and "sacrificing all that is worldly for the good of others," a clear message for most readers.[9] And someone wrote in the Trinidad *Chronicle-News* that "it was an affecting scene when crowds of Mexicans came to shed tears over him who was their great friend and benefactor."[10] Yet others who had fought McMains doubtless felt that the *Raton Range* said it all with its brusque and only observation — "O. P. McMains, the agitator, is dead."[11]

Chapter 27

Retrospect

AN INDOMITABLE WILL and dedication to the cause kept Oscar P. McMains active against the Maxwell Grant almost to the moment of his death. Undoubtedly the strength of his religious faith was transferred to the anti-grant struggle. Of course, other traits were present — some more benign than others. Whatever his self-denial during twenty years of anti-grantism, McMains was not a meek person. His independence of mind was evident in Colorado when he rejected some Methodist orthodoxies, and it showed again in New Mexico during his search for Tolby's murderer. But it also brought friction with people whom he should not have offended. Strained relations with the Reverend Thomas Harwood and Surveyor General Julian, for example, certainly did no good, and the alienation of J. H. Hunt was avoidable.

McMains' reluctance to share direction certainly discouraged some good men from stronger participation in the anti-grant movement, although the record discloses no alternative plans of action that contained real promise of success. His more extreme public utterances and actions may have prevented fuller support from the Knights of Labor and the Farmers' Alliance, yet there is no evidence that the leaders of those groups saw much that they held in common with the anti-granters.

In the balance, however, was McMains' great persuasiveness with Secretary Kirkwood, Commissioner Sparks, Attorney General Brewster, and Congressman Otis. No one can gainsay his positive impression in presenting the antigrant case to them, a success that transcended political party lines and rested on contentions of substance and merit.

Yet those qualities were not unusual, and it took more personal elements to bring it all together in McMains, the leader of men — an attractive panache, a necessary articulateness and alertness to broader implications, and a certain touch of class. Most of those traits, in varying mixtures, of course, were also found in Comp Reed and Clay Allison, and probably in Jacinto Santistevan and W. W. Boggs, thus providing an understanding and respect in their associations with McMains, whatever their differences in background. But McMains had something more, which was the foundation for everything else — an enduring rapport with ordinary men and women, clearly shown by the remarkable recurrence over twenty years of money raised by them to send him fifteen times to Washington to work for them against the Maxwell Grant, although the results of his labors were only occasionally encouraging.

The tendency of some writers to regard McMains as an eccentric crank, simply on the evidence of his more extreme reactions, ignores the pressures of immense frustration. How nerve-wracking for him must have been the dilatoriness of congressional committees, for example, and the ambiguities of men in the executive department. During the ineffective prosecution of the government's case against the grant company, courtroom sequences must have had for McMains the inexorableness of tragedy, when he saw the obvious flaws in Judge Brewer's handling of the allegations of fraud, covered by the blanket of the Tameling decision and perpetuated by the Supreme Court.

However trite the expressions, the Agent for the Settlers was a crusader and a champion of the underdog, but those characteristics, along with his unshakable convictions and compelling charisma, were in the end defeated by another person — the corporate *person* of the Maxwell Land Grant Company, a legal concept created by the same judicial system through which McMains and the Justice Department sought to overcome the company. In a sense, his failure to break the Maxwell patent was like his inability to alter Methodist Episcopal dogma. In neither instance was he able to buck the system.

Oscar P. McMains was a man of the hour, to stretch the term a bit. His personality and beliefs were as close to the ideal combination needed to confront the Maxwell Land Grant Company as could reasonably be expected. His own foibles did not keep him from destroying the Maxwell patent. Rather it was his and the settlers' misfortune to be pitted against men of considerable business and professional acumen, who represented a corporation, that economic entity so often uncritically accepted in the late nineteenth century. One may suggest that today or in Andrew Jackson's time McMains' might have·succeeded, but in the Gilded Age the odds were heavily against him. More realistically, the political and economic climate of New Mexico in the 1880s, the critical period, was not hospitable to reformers like McMains, and his own experiences showed that the national scene was scarcely more receptive.

In 1976 there was a reminder of the Maxwell Company's triumph. The CF&I Steel Corporation, successor to the Colorado Fuel and Iron Corporation (which bought the so-called Colorado Portion of the Maxwell Grant in 1900) named a new coal mine after Lucien B. Maxwell, who severed his connection with the property in 1870 and died in 1875. There is significant evidence that Maxwell never really believed that he owned land on the drainage of the Purgatoire River in Colorado. But the Maxwell patent of 1879 and Judge Brewer in 1886 said that he did, despite what O. P. McMains and other reputable men contended about the size of the grant in relation to Mexican law and Secretary Cox's application of it.

The Maxwell Land Grant Company still exists, holding reserved oil, coal, and certain mineral rights on the property. A few descendants of anti-granters are living on places their forebears reluctantly bought from the grant company. But the leading participants and dramatic events in the long, bitter conflict over the Maxwell Land Grant in the late nineteenth century remain only in a few dim and uncertain memories.

Appendix:
People on the Grant

⟲⟳

Only an approximation of the number of settlers, let alone anti-granters, at the height of the trouble is possible. In March 1887 Harry Whigham thought there were about 500 heads of families, with a few single men "baching" on some of the places. The *Raton Range*'s statement in August 1887 that McMains had several hundred followers is open to interpretation — either adult males or inclusive of family members. The latter is more likely since the paper seemed to refer to activists in support of the Agent for the Settlers. And a contemporary Vermejo resident gave a total figure of 1,600 for all settlers.[1]

Although their numbers increased importantly in the 1880s, coal miners were not thought of as settlers in terms of anti-grantism. Most of them were employees of companies that had mineral rights from the grant company. Occasionally they supported the anti-grant settlers in political association or when it suited their purpose in the course of a strike.[2] Some gold prospecting and mining consisted of individual enterprises in defiance of the grant company, and those men provided some of the earliest resistance to the Maxwell.

The majority of anti-granters were farmers and ranchers of various backgrounds and fortunes. Most of the time their

[281]

common opposition to the grant was binding enough to sub-
due ethnic frictions, but every now and then the so-called
Anglos and the Mexicans acted independently. Especially in
the 1890s the latter people occasionally operated within *Las
Gorras Blancas*, the White Caps, an organization that spread
northward from San Miguel County, where it was very ener-
getic in another land grant controversy. There is little evidence that social segregation was broken down.

Expressions of defiance against the Maxwell Grant had
a wide range — amusing, wantonly destructive, sophisticated,
petty, dangerous, and very determined. Some examples,
derived mainly from personal interviews, are given here in
the hope of recreating a little of the atmosphere of the time,
the places, and the people.

Whenever rancher Andrew McKee went to Raton, from
his place south of town, he passed the former McMains home,
where the settlers had stood off the sheriff and his deputy in
1882. The grant company had recovered the ranch after
McMains left it and for a while leased it to the Reverend
J. McGaughey, Presbyterian. If the minister were outside, the
anti-granter would call out: "Good morning, Mr. McGaughey,
and I'm not for the grant either!"[3]

In the foothills where the Vermejo had cut its cañon was
the L S horse ranch, owned by L. S. Shotwell, of Chicago.
Another Chicagoan lived in the vicinity; Bill Harness, a bank-
er's son, had heard of the Maxwell troubles and came out to
help Shotwell and others "iron out" their differences with the
company. An eccentric fellow with a long beard and graying
hair, no shoes, and a fine collection of guns, his notion of dealing with the company left little room for negotiation. He

frankly told Comp Reed, "Why, God A'mighty, Comp, there is nothing that would please me more than to sit here on a point and shoot at that outfit!"

The tale was many times told that one day Harness was sitting on a promontory above the Vermejo, when he saw a man driving a buckboard up the cañon. Since he did not recognize the rig, he assumed the driver was a Maxwell man. He shot before and behind the buckboard, greatly agitating the horses. The man jumped out and commenced praying (it being later learned that he was a priest). After the marksman had his fun the padre quickly climbed onto the vehicle and whipped his team, galloping them down the cañon.[4]

On the plains along the east line of the grant the posts of the boundary fence occasionally furnished wood for cook-fires. One chuck-wagon cook told his helper to bring in several posts from the Maxwell fence nearby; if the boy could not pull up the posts he should chop them off close to the ground.

Shooting of Maxwell cattle was not uncommon. Comp Reed's son, Ollie, expressed little surprise at finding the carcasses of twenty to thirty fat ones, some shot singly and others in small groups near a waterhole. Frequently a steer was butchered and the meat carried away, and some bolder settlers displayed Long H hides on their fences or in other conspicuous places. When the Maxwell venture in cattle later failed, some people believed that the importation of less hardy breeds and the killing of company cattle had wrecked it. Many settlers, although anti-granters, disapproved of such destruction; it offended their sense of right and they realized it harmed their cause. R. D. Russell and Comp Reed managed to dissuade one bitter settler from burning the timber on the place he had recently sold to the company.[5]

Along the swift-flowing Vermejo lived some of the most determined anti-granters on the New Mexico portion. Most of them could be seen sooner or later around the large, two-storied, adobe building that housed the Elkins Post Office. A general store was on one side of the ground floor and the post office on the other. Six-foot-seven-inch Andy Cameron presided over the combined establishment; he was very much against the grant and was famous for the big dance he gave every year. For that affair he furnished hams, chickens, butter, eggs, and the like, while the ladies of the area brought pies, cakes, and salads.

McMains' good friend, Comp Reed, had a ranch on the Vermejo above the post office. The road was on the left bank, so to get to the Reeds' hewed-log house it was necessary to ford the Vermejo; son Ollie always kept a strong horse pastured near the crossing for use when the river was swollen.[6]

Comp Reed's ranch (he had a small cow camp on Red River also) was an average spread, with a hundred acres under ditch for the cultivation of wheat, corn, and oats. The usual "one-sixty" was fenced with two miles of good fence. He had eight horses on the place and ran 105 head of cattle, which, of course, grazed on the grant.[7]

Farther up the cañon, but on the same side as the road, was the long log house in which lived A. J. Young, his wife, six daughters, and several sons. (Mrs. Young was Comp Reed's cousin.) Financially the Youngs were in better shape than many of their neighbors. Their house was one room wide, unusually long, with a room built at one end at right angles. As with others, it was Young's intention to build an adobe house but never did because of the continuing threat of ejectment.

Several of the men on the Vermejo were ex-Confederates, who had come from Missouri in the mid-seventies. The Youngs, the Reeds, the Shys, and the Gillums were of that background. A closely-knit group, they were strongly anti-grant.[8]

One of the toughest of the Maxwell enemies was Jacinto Santistevan, on the Middle Vermejo about three miles above Salyer's Cañon since December 1873, who refused to release information about his crops, livestock, or improvements and rode far and wide urging others to tell nothing. Indirect information said Santistevan had about eighty acres under ditch and eighty more being farmed. He also had 160 acres fenced and ran twenty cattle, 950 sheep, goats, and burros. Two houses — one log and the other adobe — and a log corral were on his place.[9]

Quite a few settlers had more sheep than cattle; C. B. Ladd had 8,000. He and his wife differed on the grant question: Mrs. Ladd was tired of trouble and violence and at one time tried to buy their land from Pels.[10]

Adding to the variety were the Manby brothers, Arthur, Jocelyn, and Alfred, at Castle Rock. They were Englishmen whose holdings were greater than those of most of the settlers. Their place was like a hamlet with its four hewed-log houses, four round-log ones, and a big corral. With 200 acres fenced (twenty under cultivation) they had 1,432 head of cattle and twenty-three horses. At one time twenty of their countrymen were there, all valiantly trying to become cowboys. The Manbys were opposed to the grant, but they disliked McMains.[11]

Nearly everyone on the Maxwell knew the small man on the willow-tailed horse. His saddle with sidepockets was a source of amusement to the cowmen. Few people realized when they stopped to talk that just a moment before he had unpinned the tails of his Prince Albert coat and let them fall in place, only to pin them up again when he was out of sight, because he did not want his coat tails wrinkled. The Agent for the Settlers was never one to be sloppy about his personal appearance. Once he told Mrs. Comp Reed in fun that he thought it advisable to disguise the advances of age by giving more attention to one's dress.

McMains was a welcome guest in many homes. In some he was more than a symbol; he was a personal friend. The Reed ranch on the Vermejo was one of his favorite stopping places from the time of the Tolby murder. Many a move against the Maxwell Grant was planned in the living room of the comfortable log house, McMains often pacing back and forth as he warmed to a subject. And then, occasionally, he let despondence show as when he said, "Comp, now I know what our Father went through. They have done everything but nail me to the cross, but I guess I can take it." [12]

Reed had a steadying influence on McMains and certainly was not an unquestioning follower. He was member of the special settlers' committee that reached the compromise with Whigham, and in anti-grant resistance he worked closely with the Manbys, who were against McMains. As the major anti-grant figure on the New Mexico portion of the Maxwell, Reed showed nothing of what was expected of an ex-Quantrill raider, which persistent rumor said he was. His daughter denied the report to the writer. His importance as a leader is suggested by the allegation that Maxwell officials offered him $50,000 for his two places. [13]

On the other side of the fence, so to speak, most of the active pro-Maxwell men did not live on the grant — the chief exception being Harry Whigham, long-time company official in many capacities. Another was an Englishman, Francis Clutton, who was the son-in-law of M. P. Pels, the grant company manager. Clutton ran his own spread, the well-known Urraca Hereford Ranch south of Cimarron, and he was in charge of the Maxwell Land Grant Company's cattle for some years, having been hired for that job in 1887.[14] As Maxwell cattle manager, of course, he had many contacts with anti-grant settlers.

Probably better known, and certainly more feared, was a grant company henchman by the name of Garnett Lee. A burly 250-pounder, he was known as an excellent horseman and an unscrupulous hired gun.[15] There are few details about him. An interesting entry in the Maxwell Company records notes that he was paid $30.00 for services rendered during a so-called riot on the Vermejo, and M. P. Pels felt obligated enough to him to try to arrange a loan. Later Lee bungled a couple of jobs, and the grant company let him go.[16]

There were pro-grant settlers, to be sure — men who believed in the correctness of the Maxwell patent or men who accepted it as a fait accompli. It is notable that active support was given by men such as "Uncle Dick" Wootton and Tom Boggs, who had known Lucien Maxwell in the old fur-trapping and Indian-trading days. But for the most part they were everyday people who believed that the forces of law and order would sustain the Maxwell title.

ABBREVIATIONS IN NOTES

MLG

Maxwell Land Grant Company Records, Zimmerman Library, University of New Mexico, Albuquerque.

Reed-Wills

Reed-Wills Manuscript, in the possession of D. G. MacHendrie, Englewood, Colorado.

Taylor Collection

Morris F. Taylor Collection, Trinidad, Colorado.

Springer Affidavit

Affidavit of Frank Springer in the Frank Angel Warner Report, copy in the State Records Center and Archives, Santa Fe, New Mexico.

Transcript of Record

Transcript of Record, *The United States* v. *The Maxwell Land Grant Company et al.*; Records of the United States Supreme Court, Record Group 267, National Archives, Washington, D.C.

Notes to the Chapters

CHAPTER 1

1. LeRoy R. Hafen, ed., *Colorado and Its People: A Narrative and Topical History of the Centennial State* (New York: Lewis Historical Publishing Co., 1948), 1:290–91; Martin Rist, "History of Religion in Colorado," ibid., 2:204.

2. Hafen, 1:301, 312–13.

3. Louis H. Everts, *History of Clermont County, Ohio* (Philadelphia: J. B. Lippincott and Co., 1880), pp. 460, 473.

4. *Liberty Hall*, October 11, 1809; March 7, 1810; January 11, 1811.

5. *Seventh Census of the United States: Clermont County, Ohio, Miami Township* (1850), Record Group No. 29, National Archives, Washington, D.C.; Byron Williams, *History of Clermont and Brown Counties, Ohio* (Milford, Ohio: Hobart Publishing Company, 1913), 1:375.

6. Everts, p. 480.

7. Mabel Fisher to the writer, June 22, 1949; obituary of McMains by F. B. Chaplin, Taylor Collection; *Seventh Census*; Everts, pp. 474–5.

8. Mabel Fisher to the writer, June 22, 1949, Mrs. C. D. Herron to the writer, March 3, 1949; *Seventh Census*.

9. Mabel Fisher to Mrs. C. D. Herron, March 21, 1949; Mabel Fisher to the writer, June 22, 1949.

10. Jacob Piatt Dunn, ed., *Memorial Record of Distinguished Men of Indianapolis and Indiana* (Chicago: Lewis Publishing Co.,

1912), pp. 379–84; Cottman Scrapbook, 2:70–72, and Indiana Biography Series Scrapbook, 4:44, both in the William Henry Smith Memorial Library, Indiana Historical Society, Indianapolis.

11. Obituary of O. P. McMains, Taylor Collection.

12. Minutes of the Twenty-sixth Session of the Annual Illinois Conference, Methodist Episcopal Church, 1859, Library of Congress, Washington, D.C., pp. 6, 44; Minutes of the Twelfth Annual Colorado Conference, Methodist Episcopal Church, 1873, Colorado Methodist Historical Society, Iliff School of Theology, University of Denver.

13. Minutes of the Twelfth Annual Colorado Conference, 1873.

14. Percy Stanley Fritz, *Colorado, The Centennial State*, (New York: Prentice Hall, 1941), p. 301; LeRoy R. Hafen and Carl Coke Rister, *Western America*, 2nd ed. (Englewood Cliffs, N. J.: Prentice Hall, 1950), pp. 409–10.

15. Isaac Haight Beardsley, *Echoes from Peak and Plain; or, Tales of Life, War, Travel, and Colorado Methodism* (Cincinnati: Curts & Jennings, 1898), p. 274.

16. Ibid., p. 275.

17. Colin B. Goodykoontz, "Colorado As Seen by a Home Missionary, 1863–1868," *The Colorado Magazine*, 12 (March 1935): 61; *The Rocky Mountain Directory and Colorado Gazetteer for 1871* (Denver: S. S. Wallihan & Company), p. 136; *Daily Mining Journal*, October 29, 1864.

18. *Daily Mining Journal*, January 5, 1865, and March 11, 1865.

19. Ibid., April 17, 1865.

20. Beardsley, pp. 296, 558.

21. Leon H. Sweetland, *History of the First Methodist Church of Loveland, Colorado* (By the author, 1941), p. 5.

22. Beardsley, pp. 278, 451.

23. *Daily Rocky Mountain News*, January 2, 1867.

24. Ibid., December 20, 1866.

25. Beardsley, pp. 279–80.

26. Jerome C. Smiley, ed., *Semi-Centennial History of the State of Colorado* (Chicago: Lewis Publishing Company, 1913), 1:267, 368–69; Hafen, 1:182; Beardsley, pp. 279–80.

27. Beardsley, p. 280; *Daily Miner's Register*, June 28, 1867.

28. Mabel Fisher to the writer, June 22, 1949; Martin Rist to the writer, August 3, 1949.

29. *Daily Rocky Mountain News*, February 13, 1868; Hafen, 1:318–19.

30. Martin Rist to the writer, August 1 and 3, 1949; Beardsley, p. 282; *Daily Rocky Mountain News,* June 23, 1868.

31. *Daily Rocky Mountain News,* July 9, 1868.

CHAPTER 2

1. *Colorado Chieftain,* July 2, 1868.

2. Milo Lee Whittaker, *Pathbreakers and Pioneers of the Pueblo Region* (n.p.: Franklin Press, 1917), pp. 70–71; *Colorado Chieftain,* June 1, 1868.

3. *Daily Rocky Mountain News,* June 29, 1869; Isaac Haight Beardsley, *Echoes from Peak and Plain; or, Tales of Life, War, Travel, and Colorado Methodism* (Cincinnati: Curts & Jennings, 1898), p. 291.

4. *Colorado Chieftain,* December 16, 1869, and January 13, 1870.

5. *Daily Rocky Mountain News,* January 25, 1870; *Colorado Chieftain, passim,* 1870–72.

6. *Daily Rocky Mountain News,* March 18, 1870.

7. Beardsley, p. 320; *Colorado Chieftain,* June 30, 1870; Martin Rist, "Methodist Beginnings in New Mexico," *The 1966 Brand Book of the Denver Westerners,* ed. William D. Powell (Boulder, Colo.: Johnson Publishing Co., 1967), pp. 86–87.

8. Rist, "Methodist Beginnings," pp. 86–87; Elial J. Rice, "Pioneering in Southern Colorado," *The Colorado Magazine* 14 (May 1937):108–15.

9. Beardsley, pp. 320–21.

10. *Colorado Chieftain,* November 17, 1870.

11. Ibid., April 20, 1871.

12. *Daily Rocky Mountain News,* July 21, 1871; Martin Rist to the writer, August 1, 1949.

13. *Colorado Chieftain,* September 14, 1871.

14. Ibid., February 1, 1872.

15. Ibid, May 23, 1873.

16. Ibid., May 15, 1873, and May 29, 1873.

17. *Daily Chieftain,* April 28, 1972. On this date the *Chieftain* became a daily. Hereafter any citations of the weekly edition will be referred to as the *Colorado Chieftain.*

18. *Daily Chieftain,* May 5, 1872, and May 7, 1872; Martin Rist, "History of Religion in Colorado," in Leroy R. Hafen, *Colorado*

and Its People: A Narrative and Topical History of the Centennial State (New York: Lewis Historical Publishing Co., 1948), 2:212.

19. *Daily Chieftain*, June 20, 1872, and June 22, 1872; Joseph Thomas, ed., *Universal Pronouncing Dictionary of Biography and Mythology*, 5th ed. (Philadelphia: J. B. Lippincott Company, 1930, p. 1560; Herbert O. Brayer, *William Blackmore* (Denver: Bradford-Robinson, 1949), 2:149; *Daily Chieftain*, July 3, 1872.

20. *Daily Chieftain*, August 16, 1872; August 18, 1872; January 1, 1873.

21. *Daily Chieftain*, October 1, 1872, and October 8, 1872.

22. Ibid., March 6, 1873.

23. Ibid., April 13, 1873.

24. *Daily Chieftain*, December 14, 1872.

25. *Colorado Chieftain*, May 15, 1873.

26. *Daily Chieftain*, May 23, 1873.

27. *Daily Rocky Mountain News*, May 25, 1873.

28. *Las Animas, Col., Leader*, June 6, 1873.

29. Ibid., June 6, 1873 and June 13, 1873; Charles W. Bowman, "History of Bent County," in *History of the Arkansas Valley, Colorado* (Chicago: O. L. Baskin & Company, 1881), p. 846.

30. *Las Animas, Colo., Leader*, June 6, 1873.

31. Ibid.

32. Ibid., November 1, 1873, and November 15, 1873.

33. Ibid., October 11, 1873; June 12, 1874; July 31, 1874.

34. Ibid., June 19, 1874.

35. Ibid., September 18, 1874; *Daily Chieftain*, September 22, 1874; *The People*, September 26, 1874; *Trinidad Enterprise*, November 7, 1874; *Colorado Business Directory and Annual Register for 1875* (Denver: J. A. Blake, 1875), pp. 102–03.

36. Martin Rist to the writer, August 1, 1949.

37. *Las Animas, Col., Leader*, October 16, 1874; October 23, 1874; November 27, 1874; *The People*, November 14, 1874.

CHAPTER 3

1. *Las Animas, Col., Leader*, June 12, 1875.

2. Thomas Harwood, *History of the New Mexico Spanish and English Missions of the Methodist Episcopal Church from 1850 to 1910* (Albuquerque: El Abogado Press, 1908), 1:204; Martin Rist to the writer (undated), containing excerpts from a church record and scrapbook, now apparently lost.

3. W. R. Morley to John Collinson, February 8, 1873, Letter Book 1872–1877, pp. 69–70, Maxwell Land Grant Company Records, Zimmerman Library, University of New Mexico, Albuquerque (hereafter cited as MLG); Norman Cleaveland, *The Morleys: Young Upstarts on the Southwest Frontier* (Albuquerque, N. M.: Calvin Horn, 1971), p. 84.

4. *Colorado Chieftain,* July 22, 1875.

5. U.S., *Statutes at Large,* 12:71–72.

6. *Transcript of Title of the Maxwell Land Grant Situated in New Mexico and Colorado* (Chicago: Rand McNally and Co., 1881), pp. 6–64; W. R. Morley to John Collinson, January 16, 1873, Letter Book 1872–1877, pp. 26–27, MLG; Van Lint Manuscript, MLG.

7. Norman Cleaveland, pp. 40–59; W. A. Bell to W. J. Palmer, May 11, 1870, William Jackson Palmer Collection, Documentary Resources Department, State Historical Society of Colorado, Denver; *Transcript of Title,* p. 85; Minutes, Maxwell Land Grant and Railway Company Stockholders' Meeting, August 23, 1870, MLG.

8. Norman Cleaveland, p. 63; Minutes, Maxwell Land Grant and Railway Company Board of Directors, March 29, 1872, and July 2, 1872, MLG; Agreement, Folder 1872, MLG; Henry M. Porter, *Pencilings of an Early Western Pioneer* (Denver: World Press, 1929), pp. 18–19.

9. W. R. Morley to John Collinson, February 8, 1873, and to T. B. Catron, February 11, 1874, Letter Book 1872–1877, pp. 69–70, 75–77, MLG; Norman Cleaveland, pp. 72–73.

10. Agreement, November 11, 1872, Folder 1872, MLG; Minutes, Maxwell Land Grant and Railway Company Board of Directors, October 10, 1873, and November 3, 1873, MLG; W. R. Morley to T. B. Catron, February 11, 1873, Letter Book 1872–1877, pp. 75–77, MLG: Norman Cleaveland, p. 73; Philip J. Rasch, "The People of the Territory of New Mexico vs. the Santa Fe Ring," *New Mexico Historical Review,* 47 (April 1972):185–202; Victor Westphall, *Thomas Benton Catron and His Era* (Tucson: University of Arizona Press, 1973), pp. 185–86.

11. U.S., Department of the Interior, *Annual Report of the Commissioner of Indian Affairs, 1870* (Washington: Government Printing Office, 1870), pp. 158–59; Colfax County (New Mexico) Deed Book, pp. 12–15; Hubert Howe Bancroft, *History of New Mexico and Arizona* (San Francisco: The History Company, 1889), p. 782n; *Daily New Mexican,* September 18, 1875; Norman Cleaveland, p. 87.

12. *Cimarron News and Press*, August 7, 1875.

13. Affidavit of Frank Springer in the Frank Warner Angel Report and Testimony in the Matter of Charges against Samuel B. Axtell, Governor of New Mexico, Record Group 48, National Archives, Washington (copy in the New Mexico State Records Center and Archives, Santa Fe; cited hereafter as Springer Affidavit); *Colorado Chieftain*, May 25, 1876; Agnes Morley Cleveland, *Satan's Paradise, from Lucien Maxwell to Fred Lambert* (Boston: Houghton Mifflin and Company, 1952), pp. 73–74; Norman Cleaveland, p. 87, and *Colfax County's Chronic Murder Mystery* (Santa Fe: The Rydal Press, 1977), pp. 1–2.

14. *Colorado Chieftain*, May 25, 1876.

15. *Daily New Mexican*, September 18, 1875, and May 1, 1876; Martin Rist to the writer (undated); Springer Affidavit.

16. *Daily New Mexican*, September 18, 1875. Mrs. Tolby's name was found in the Colfax County Deed Book, pp. 23–24.

17. Harwood, 2:390; Delbert Littrell Hughes and Leonore Harris Hughes, *Give Me Room!* (El Paso, Texas: Hughes Publishing Company, 1971), p. 67.

18. Harwood, 1:266–67, 299, 390.

19. *Indianapolis Journal*, November 17, 1885.

20. *Daily New Mexican*, September 18, 1875, and November 15, 1875; *Weekly New Mexican*, September 4, 1877; Harwood, 2:268–69.

21. *Colorado Chieftain*, May 26, 1876; Rasch, p. 191.

22. Springer Affidavit; *Weekly New Mexican*, September 4, 1877.

23. *Weekly New Mexican*, September 4, 1877.

24. Ibid.

25. Ibid.

26. *Colorado Chieftain*, November 4, 1875; *Daily New Mexican*, November 15, 1875; Norman Cleaveland, p. 100.

27. *Colorado Chieftain*, November 4, 1875, supported by the *Daily New Mexican*, November 5, 1875.

28. *Daily New Mexican*, November 15, 1875; Norman Cleaveland, pp. 101–3.

29. *Daily New Mexican*, November 9, 15, 1875; *Colorado Chieftain*, May 26, 1876; George B. Anderson, *History of New Mexico: Its Resources and People* (Los Angeles: Pacific States Publishing Co., 1907), 2:682; Norman Cleaveland, pp. 101–2.

30. *Daily New Mexican*, November 15, 17, 1875; *Colorado Chieftain*, November 18, 1875; Anderson, 2:686; Calvin Horn, *New*

Mexico's Troubled Years, The Story of the Early Territorial Governors (Albuquerque: Horn and Wallace, 1963), pp. 176–77.

31. *Daily New Mexican*, November 9, 15, 1875, May 1, 1876; *Colorado Chieftain*, November 18, 1875, May 26, 1876; Springer Affidavit; Norman Cleaveland, pp. 103–06.

32. Harwood, 1:267, 301.

33. Springer Affidavit; Norman Cleaveland, pp. 109–10.

34. Norman Cleaveland, pp. 110–13; Ralph Emerson Twitchell, *The Leading Facts of New Mexican History* (Cedar Rapids, Ia.: Torch Press, 1911), 2:397–98; Arie W. Poldervaart, *Black-Robed Justice: A History of the Administration of Justice in New Mexico from the American Occupation in 1846 until Statehood in 1912* (n.p.: Historical Society of New Mexico, 1948), p. 89.

35. Dale T. Schoenberger, *The Gunfighters* (Caldwell, Idaho: Caxton Printers), pp. 1–5; Harry E. Kelsey, Jr., "Clay Allison: Western Gunman," *1957 Brand Book of the Denver Westerners*, ed. Numa James (Boulder, Colo.: Johnson Publishing Co., 1958), pp. 385–87; interview with Mrs. Lucy Reed Wills, September 3, 1948.

36. Schoenberger, p. 2.

37. Ibid., pp. 7–8.

38. Norman Cleaveland, "Clay Allison's Cimarron," *New Mexico* 52 (March-April 1974): 14, 42.

CHAPTER 4

1. *Colorado Chieftain*, January 27, 1876; Norman Cleaveland, *The Morleys: Young Upstarts on the Southwest Frontier* (Albuquerque, N. M.: Calvin Horn, 1971), pp. 114–15; Lawrence R. Murphy, *Philmont: A History of New Mexico's Cimarron Country* (Albuquerque: University of New Mexico Press, 1972), pp. 121–22.

2. *Raton Range*, July 22, 1887. This version was published at the time of Allison's death. See also Norman Cleaveland, pp. 114–15; Murphy, pp. 121–22; Westphall, *Thomas Benton Catron and His Era* (Tucson: University of Arizona Press, 1973), p. 117. Murphy doubts that Allison was responsible.

3. Norman Cleaveland, p. 115; *Colorado Chieftain*, January 27, 1876.

4. Norman Cleaveland, pp. 113–14; Springer Affidavit.

5. Springer Affidavit; Ralph Emerson Twitchell, *The Leading Facts of New Mexican History* (Cedar Rapids, Ia.: Torch Press, 1911), 2:484–86; Philip J. Rasch, "The People of the Territory of New Mexico vs. the Santa Fe Ring," *New Mexico Historical Review* 47 (April, 1972): 186.

6. *Daily New Mexican*, May 1, 1876; *Colorado Chieftain*, May 25, 1876; Norman Cleaveland, pp. 123–24.

7. Thomas Harwood, *History of the New Mexico Spanish and English Missions of the Methodist Episcopal Church from 1850 to 1910* (Albuquerque: El Abogado Press, 1908), 1:299.

8. *Daily New Mexican*, May 15, 1876; Norman Cleaveland, p. 124.

9. *Daily New Mexican*, May 15, 1876; May 25, 1876; May 26, 1876; Norman Cleaveland, pp. 124, 126.

10. *Colorado Chieftain*, May 25, 1876; *Las Animas, Col., Leader*, May 26, 1876.

11. Harwood, 1:302.

12. Agnes Morley Cleaveland, *Satan's Paradise, from Lucien Maxwell to Fred Lambert* (Boston: Houghton Mifflin and Company, 1925), p. 75; interviews with Mrs. Lucy Reed Wills, September 3, 1948, October 4, 1948; Reed-Wills.

13. Norman Cleaveland, pp. 124–26, 129–32.

14. Joseph Piatt Dunn, ed., *Memorial Record of Distinguished Men of Indianapolis and Indiana* (Chicago: Lewis Publishing Company, 1912), pp. 379–84. *Indianapolis Journal*, November 17, 1885.

15. *Daily New Mexican*, April 2, 1877.

16. Ibid.

17. Ibid., June 20, 1876; April 28, 1877; May 12, 1877; June 12, 1877; Indictment, *Territory of New Mexico* v. *O. P. McMains*, April 4, 1877; Springer Affidavit.

18. *Daily New Mexican*, June 12, 1877; *Indianapolis Journal*, November 17, 1885; Harwood, 1:295.

19. *Daily New Mexican*, August 27, 1877; *Weekly New Mexican*, September 4, 1877; *Colorado Chieftain*, September 6, 1877, quoting the *Cimarron News and Press*.

20. *Colorado Chieftain*, September 6, 1877; William A. Keleher, *Maxwell Land Grant: A New Mexico Item* rev. ed. (New York: Argosy Antiquarian, 1964), p. 77.

21. *Colorado Chieftain*, September 6, 1877.

22. *Las Vegas Daily Gazette*, April 6, 1878; Keleher, p. 77; Arie W. Poldervaart, *Black-Robed Justice: A History of the Administration of Justice in New Mexico from the American Occupation in*

1846 until Statehood in 1912 (n.p.: Historical Society of New Mexico, 1948), pp. 97–98.

23. Harwood, 1:302–3.

24. Ibid., pp. 299–303; Harris Elwood Starr, "Matthew Simpson," *Dictionary of American Biography* ed. Dumas Malone (New York: Charles Scribner's Sons, 1935), 17:182.

25. O. P. McMains to Robert Fisher, December 18, 1877; interview with Mrs. Lucy Reed Wills, September 4, 1948.

26. Harwood, 1:303; excerpt from church record, Martin Rist to the writer (undated); Mary B. McMains to Robert Fisher, January 18, 1900.

27. Interview with Wilbur Davis, August 13, 1957.

28. Ibid.; interview with Mrs. Lucy Reed Wills, September 14, 1948.

CHAPTER 5

1. *Transcript of Title of the Maxwell Land Grant Situated in New Mexico and Colorado* (Chicago: Rand McNally and Co., 1881), pp. 5–19, 25–38, 107–9; Thomas Donaldson, ed., *The Public Domain: Its History* (Washington: Government Printing Office, 1884), pp. 126–34, 394–98; U.S., *Statutes at Large*, 12:71–72.

2. U.S., Department of the Interior, *Annual Report of the Commissioner of the General Land Office, 1885* (Washington: Government Printing Office, 1885), pp. 126–29; *Transcript of Title*, pp. 11, 20–21, 31–52; Frank Springer to R. V. Martinsen, March 11, 1891, Folder 1888 [*sic*], MLG.

3. *Transcript of Title*, pp. 60–66, 69–73, 88–91; Charles E. Gast to the Committee of Share and Bondholders, September 1, 1877, Folder 1877, MLG; Jim Berry Pearson, *The Maxwell Land Grant* (Norman: University of Oklahoma Press, 1961), pp. 61–62; Minutes of Board of Directors Meeting, Maxwell Land Grant and Railway Company, May 20, 1870, MLG.

4. Minutes of Board of Directors Meeting, Maxwell Land Grant and Railway Company, August 23, 1870, MLG; *Daily Citizen*, September 5, 1888 (Thomas Martin to the editor); W. R. Morley to John Collinson, January 1 and 16, 1873, Letter Book 1872–77, pp. 5–6, 26–27, MLG.

5. C. Delano to Messrs. Barlow, Laroque and McFarland, July 27, 1871, Records of the Office of the Secretary of the Interior, Record Group 48, National Archives, Washington, D.C.; W. R. Morley to Robert Dillon, February 4, 1873, Letter Book 1872–77, pp. 52–53, MLG; *Transcript of Title*, p. 67; Pearson, p. 62; W. R.

Morley to John Collinson, January 1, 16, 21, 23, 1873, Letter Book 1872–1877, pp. 5–6, 26–27, 32–33, 41–42, MLG; Van Lint Manuscript, MLG; *Annual Report of the Commissioner of the General Land Office, 1885*, p. 129.

6. *Tameling* v. *United States Freehold Land and Emigration Company,* 2 Colorado Reports 411 (1874); *John G. Tameling* v. *The United States Freehold Land and Emigration Company,* 23 U.S. 998 (1877).

7. *Transcript of Title,* pp. 25–26; Harold H. Dunham, "Some Crucial Years of the General Land Office, 1875–1890," *Agricultural History* 2 (April 1937):126; U.S., Department of the Interior, *Annual Report of the Commissioner of the General Land Office, 1877* (Washington: Government Printing Office, 1877), p. 53, and *1885*, pp. 129–131.

8. *Annual Report of the Commissioner of the General Land Office,* 1885, pp. 129, 132–33.

9. 2 Colorado Reports, 411 (1874); 23 U.S. 998 (1877); *Raton Comet,* October 3, 1884; contract from Transcript of Record, *The United States* v. *The Maxwell Land Grant Company, et al,* Records of the United States Supreme Court, Record Group 267, National Archives, Washington, D.C. (hereafter cited as Transcript of Record).

10. Transcript of Record; *The United States* v. *Maxwell Land Grant Company: Records and Briefs, 1882–1889* (privately printed) p. 760; *The United States* v. *the Maxwell Land Grant Company et al; Suit in Equity to Cancel Patent: Pleading, Testimony and Exhibits* (privately printed), p. 237.

11. Transcript of Record; *Annual Report of the Commissioner of the General Land Office, 1885,* p. 126; *Transcript of Title,* pp. 18–19, 107–23: Dunham, p. 126.

12. *Las Vegas Daily Optic,* June 22, 1880.

13. *Cimarron News and Press,* November 20, 1879, and November 25, 1880; Transcript of Record; Morris F. Taylor, "The Uña de Gato Grant in Colfax County," *New Mexico Historical Review,* 51 (April 1976):121–43.

14. Jay T. Conway, *A Brief Community History of Raton, New Mexico, 1880–1930 Commemorating Her Fiftieth Birthday* (Raton, N. M.: Gazette Printing, 1930), pp. 5–6; interview with Frank Stubblefield, November 8, 1948; Record of Settlers, March 1887, MLG.

15. Several settlers' letters are in the Transcript of Record.

16. *Las Vegas Daily Optic*, February 4, 1881; *Cimarron News and Press*, March 31, 1881; *Trinidad Daily Times*, May 14, 1881; Norman Cleaveland, *The Morleys, Young Upstarts on the Southwest Frontier* (Albuquerque, N. M.: Calvin Horn, 1971), pp. 206–7.

17. Norman Cleaveland, pp. 206–7.

18. *Transcript of Title*, pp. 183–206; Van Lint Manuscript, MLG; *Cimarron News and Press*, May 26, 1881; Pearson, *passim*.

19. Frank R. Sherwin to W. F. Ziegelaar, September 6, 1881, Letter Book July 15–October 12, 1881, pp. 216–31, MLG.

20. *Trinidad Daily Times*, May 14, 1881; Norman Cleaveland, p. 207.

21. *Trinidad Daily Times*, May 27, 1881.

22. *Trinidad Daily Times*, May 15, 1881; June 2, 1881; June 24, 1881; *Las Vegas Daily Optic*, June 6, 1881; *Trinidad Democrat*, August 1, 1882; *Raton Guard*, December 9, 1881; Frank R. Sherwin to W. F. Ziegelaar, September 6, 1881, Letter Book July 15–October 12, 1881, pp. 216–31, MLG.

CHAPTER 6

1. *Trinidad Daily Times*, July 8, 1881.

2. U.S. Department of the Interior, *Annual Report of the Commissioner of the General Land Office, 1885* (Washington: Government Printing Office, 1885), pp. 133–34; undated pamphlet by Frank Springer, MLG.

3. *Annual Report of the Commissioner of the General Land Office, 1885*, pp. 133–34.

4. *Trinidad Daily Times*, August 30, 1881.

5. Frank R. Sherwin to J. Edwards Clark, September 5, 1881, Letter Book July 15–October 12, 1881, pp. 232–42, MLG.

6. Springer pamphlet, MLG; John V. Fuller, "Isaac Wayne MacVeagh," *Dictionary of American Biography*, ed. Dumas Malone (New York: Charles Scribner's Sons, 1933), 12:170–71.

7. *Trinidad Daily Times*, November 8, 1881.

8. Springer pamphlet, MLG; *Trinidad Daily Times*, December 9, 1881; Transcript of Record.

9. Springer pamphlet, MLG.

10. *Raton Guard*, December 16, 1881; December 30, 1881; January 6, 1882; *Raton News and Press*, December 24, 1881; U.S., Department of the Interior, *Annual Report of the Commissioner of*

the General Land Office, 1877 (Washington: Government Printing Office, 1877), p. 53; N. C. McFarland to the Register and Receiver of the Pueblo Land Office, January 17, 1882, Maxwell Land Grant Company Letters 1882, MLG.

11. *Raton Guard*, December 30, 1881.

12. Ibid., December 9, 1881, and December 16, 1881.

13. Ibid., January 6, 1882.

14. Ibid., January 13, 1882, quoting the *Trinidad Daily News.*

15. *Raton Guard*, January 13, 1882.

16. Ibid.

17. Ibid., February 17, 1882; *William T. Thornton and E. Platt Stratton, Receivers,* v. *O. P. McMains*, District Court Record of Judgements (Colfax County, New Mexico), No. 137 Book A, pp. 8–9, 10–11, and Record, Civil and Criminal, Colfax County, pp. 158, 167.

18. *Raton News and Press*, November 19, 1881; December 24, 1881; January 28, 1882.

19. *Trinidad Daily Times*, March 1, 1882.

CHAPTER 7

1. *Trinidad Daily Times*, March 1, 1882; *Raton Guard*, March 10, 1882, and March 17, 1882.

2. *Raton Guard*, March 2, 1882, and March 10, 1882.

3. *Trinidad Daily Times*, March 2, 1882, and March 5, 1882; *Trinidad Weekly Times*, March 4, 1882.

4. *Raton Guard*, March 17, 1882.

5. *Las Animas, Col., Leader*, March 17, 1882.

6. *Raton Guard*, March 17, 1882.

7. Ibid., March 17, 1882, and March 24, 1882.

8. Ibid., March 24, 1882.

9. Ibid.

10. Ibid.

11. *Raton News and Press*, March 25, 1882; *Raton Guard*, March 31, 1882.

12. *Raton Guard*, March 31, 1882; April 7, 1882; April 14, 1882; *Daily Optic*, April 21, 1882; *William T. Thornton and E. Platt Stratton* v. *O. P. McMains, Ejectment*, No. 137, District Court Record of Judgements (Colfax County, New Mexico) Book A, pp. 8–9.

13. *Raton Guard*, March 31, 1882; District Court Record of Judgements, Book A, pp. 8–9.

14. U.S., *Statutes at Large*, 16:646; U.S., Department of the Interior, *Annual Report of the Commissioner of the General Land Office, 1885* (Washington: Government Printing Office, 1885), pp. 123–24; Morris F. Taylor, "The Two Land Grants of Gervacio Nolán," *New Mexico Historical Review*, 47 (April 1972):151–84; *Raton News and Press*, January 28, 1882; *Daily Chieftain*, January 1, 1873.

15. *Raton Guard*, April 7, 1882.

16. Ibid.

17. Ibid., April 14, 1882.

18. Ibid., April 21, 1882.

19. Ibid.

20. Ibid.

21. Interview with Frank Stubblefield, September 8, 1948; see also *Raton Guard*, April 21, 1882; "History of the Maxwell Grant" in a communication from M. P. Pels to Chief Justice Smith, 1894, Case A, File 17, No. 44, MLG.

22. "History of the Maxwell Grant," MLG.

23. *Raton Guard*, June 16, 1882.

24. Ibid., March 17, 1882; June 16, 1882; June 23, 1882.

25. Ibid., June 23, 1882; letter of introduction, Letter Book July 15–October 12, 1881, pp. 251–53, MLG.

26. Victor Westphall, *Thomas Benton Catron and His Era* (Tucson: University of Arizona Press, 1973), pp. 184–85.

27. *Raton Guard*, June 23, 1882.

CHAPTER 8

1. *Raton Comet*, July 14, 1882.

2. Ibid. See U.S., *Statutes at Large*, 16:646.

3. *Raton Comet*, July 14, 1882. See also Victor Westphall, *The Public Domain in New Mexico, 1854–1891* (Albuquerque: University of New Mexico Press, 1965).

4. *Raton Comet*, July 14, 1882, and July 21, 1882.

5. Ibid., July 28, 1882.

6. Ibid.; Transcript of Record.

7. *Las Vegas Daily Gazette*, August 22, 1882.

8. *Las Vegas Daily Optic*, November 18, 1882; George B. Anderson, *History of New Mexico, Its Resources and People* (Los Angeles: Pacific States Publishing Company, 1907), 2:709.

9. *Trinidad Democrat*, October 3, 1882.

10. Ibid.

11. *Albuquerque Morning Journal*, October 8, 1882.

12. *Raton Comet*, November 10, 1882; *Las Vegas Daily Optic*, November 1, 1882. This account is an unadorned composite from the two newspapers, which agree in general but vary in detail. Contemporary issues of the *Raton News and Press* are not available.

13. *Raton Comet*, November 10, 1882.

14. *Las Vegas Daily Optic*, November 3, 1882.

15. *Las Vegas Daily Optic*, November 18, 1882.

16. Ibid., November 1, 1882; November 14, 1882; November 20, 1882; *Raton Comet*, November 10, 1882; Transcript of Record.

17. *Raton Comet*, March 16, 1883.

18. Ibid.

19. *Raton Comet*, May 4, 1883.

20. Oscar P. McMains to Robert Fisher, March 22, 1883.

21. *Raton Comet*, April 6, 1883.

22. Oscar P. McMains to Robert Fisher, March 22, 1883.

23. Mabel Fisher to the writer, May 1, 1949.

24. *Raton Comet*, May 11, 1883; May 18, 1883; June 8, 1883; June 29, 1883; July 20, 1883; August 10, 1883.

25. Ibid., August 3, 1883.

26. McMains testimony, Transcript of Record; Morris F. Taylor, *Trinidad, Colorado Territory* (Trinidad, Col.: Trinidad State College, 1966), pp. 8–13.

27. Archibald and Jones testimonies, Transcript of Record; "Notes of A. W. Archibald Concerning Fisher's Peak and the Maxwell Grant," Samuel W. Debusk Collection (Trinidad State Junior College Library); *Weekly Advertiser*, November 5, 1883.

28. Jaramillo testimony, Transcript of Record.

29. 23 U.S. 998 (1877); *Raton Comet*, October 3, 1884, and October 24, 1884.

30. W. A. Keleher, "Law of the New Mexico Land Grant," *Texas Law Quarterly* (October 1929), pp. 154–169; *United States* v. *Maxwell Land Grant Company and Others*, 21 Fed. Rep. 19 (1884); *Raton Comet*, October 24, 1884, and November 7, 1884.

CHAPTER 9

1. *House Journal of the Twenty-sixth Legislative Assembly* (New Mexico Territory), pp. 5–10, 10–16, 35–36; *Council Journal of the Twenty-sixth Legislative Assembly* (New Mexico Territory), pp. 11–14; 16; Ralph Emerson Twitchell, *The Leading Facts*

of New Mexican History (Cedar Rapids, Ia.: Torch Press, 1911),
2:493; *Las Vegas Daily Optic*, February 25, 1884; *Las Vegas Daily
Gazette*, February 28, 1884; *Santa Fe New Mexican Review*, February 29, 1884.

2. *House Journal*, p. 137; *Las Vegas Daily Optic*, March 27,
1884; Twitchell, 2:493–94.

3. *Las Vegas Daily Optic*, March 17, 1884; McMains Resolution,
C 302, Box 10, University of New Mexico Special Collections,
Albuquerque, N.M.; Victor Westphall, *Thomas Benton Catron
and His Era* (Tucson: University of Arizona Press, 1973), p. 193;
Las Vegas Daily Gazette, March 16, 1884.

4. *House Journal*, pp. 106, 152; *Weekly Advertiser*, April 7,
1884.

5. *Las Vegas Daily Gazette*, March 28, 1884.

6. *Santa Fe New Mexican Review*, April 7, 1884.

7. Ibid., April 5, 1884; *New York Times*, March 30, 1884.

8. *Las Vegas Daily Optic*, April 16, 1884.

9. Ibid., March 20, 1884, and April 25, 1884; *Weekly Advertiser*, May 26, 1884.

10. 20 Fed. Rep. v (1884).

11. *Las Vegas Daily Optic*, June 20, 1884, and July 26, 1884;
Frank Springer to S. F. Philips, August 28, 1884, General Records
of the Department of Justice, Record Group 60, National Archives,
Washington, D.C.

12. *Las Vegas Daily Optic*, June 20, 1884 and July 26, 1884;
Frank Springer to S. F. Philips, August 28, 1884; Harry Whigham
to Hume Webster, Hoare and Company, May 16, 1883, Maxwell
Cattle Company Letters, February 1883–October 1884, pp. 101–3,
MLG.

13. *Maxwell Land Grant Company* v. *Oscar P. McMains*, No.
558, Records of the District Court B (Colfax County, New Mexico),
No. 558 (1884); Docket of the District Court (Colfax County,
New Mexico), 1:155.

14. *Las Vegas Daily Optic*, July 21, 1884.

15. *United States* v. *Maxwell Land Grant Company and Others*,
21 Fed. Rep. 19 (1884).

16. Ibid.

17. Ibid.

18. *Raton News and Press*, April 28, 1881; *O. P. McMains* v.
I. C. Showerman, No. 631, Records of the District Court B (Colfax
County, New Mexico).

19. *Raton Comet*, October 24, 1884.

20. *Raton Comet*, October 24, 1884; S. F. Philips to the Maxwell Land Grant Company, August 19, 1884, Maxwell Land Grant Company Letters 1884, 1885, & 1886 (Harry Whigham, Receiver), MLG.

21. Frank Springer to S. F. Philips, August 28, 1884, General Records of the Department of Justice, Record Group 60, National Archives, Washington, D.C.

22. O. P. McMains to Henry M. Teller, August 27, 1884, Records of the Office of the Secretary of the Interior, Lands and Railroads Division, Miscellaneous Letters Received, Record Group 48, National Archives, Washington, D.C.

23. O. P. McMains to M. L. Joslyn, August 30, 1884, and N. C. McFarland to M. L. Joslyn, September 4, 1884, ibid.

24. O. P. McMains, *Conspiracy to Defraud!* (undated pamphlet), p. 8, Taylor Collection; U.S., Department of the Interior, *Annual Report of the Commissioner of the General Land Office, 1885* (Washington: Government Printing Office, 1885), p. 124.

25. U.S., *Statutes at Large*, 16:646.

26. McMains, pp. 10–16; *Annual Report of the Commissioner of the General Land Office, 1885*, p. 124.

27. *Raton Comet*, September 12, 1884.

28. O. P. McMains, *Conspiracy to Defraud!*.

29. *Raton Comet*, September 12, 1884, and September 19, 1884.

30. Ibid.

31. William A. Keleher, *Maxwell Land Grant: A New Mexico Item*, rev. ed. (New York: Argosy-Antiquarian, 1964), p. 227.

32. *Raton Comet*, November 14, 1884.

33. *Maxwell Land Grant Company v. Oscar P. McMains*, No. 558, Docket of the District Court (Colfax County, N.M.), 1:155.

34. *Raton Comet*, September 19, 1884.

35. Ibid., September 26, 1884.

36. *Raton Comet*, October 10, 1884, and October 24, 1885.

37. Ibid., September 5, 1884, and November 7, 1884.

38. Ibid., November 14, 1884.

39. Ibid.

CHAPTER 10

1. *Raton Comet*, July 10, 1885.

2. Haywood J. Pearce, Jr., "Lucius Quintus Cincinnatus Lamar," *Dictionary of American Biography*, ed. Dumas Malone (New York: Charles Scribner's Sons, 1933), 10:552; O. P. McMains

to President Cleveland, August 19, 1887, published in the *St. Louis Globe-Democrat*, August 23, 1887; U.S., Department of the Interior, *Annual Report of the Commissioner of the General Land Office, 1885* (Washington: Government Printing Office, 1885), p. 125; *Raton Comet*, July 10, 1885.

3. Harold H. Dunham, "William Andrew Jackson Sparks," *Dictionary of American Biography*, ed. Dumas Malone (New York: Charles Scribner's Sons, 1935), 17:434–35.

4. *Raton Comet*, June 19, 1885, *Annual Report of the Commissioner of the General Land Office, 1885*, pp. 121–25.

5. *Annual Report of the Commissioner of the General Land Office, 1885*, pp. 125–35; *Colorado and New Mexico Cattlemen's Advertiser*, June 18, 1885.

6. *Annual Report of the Commissioner of the General Land Office, 1885*, pp. 134–35.

7. *Raton Comet*, June 19, 1885.

8. Bela M. Hughes to Charles J. Canda, May 25, 1885, and Charles J. Canda to Bela M. Hughes, June 15, 1885, Folder 1885, MLG.

9. Harry Whigham to Baron de Constant Rebecque, June 17, 1885, Maxwell Land Grant Company Letters 3, MLG.

10. Transcript of Record.

11. *Raton Comet*, June 26, 1885; *Las Vegas Daily Optic*, June 20, 1885.

12. *Daily Optic*, June 20, 1885.

13. *Raton Comet*, July 10, 1885.

14. Ibid.

15. Ibid.

16. S. B. Elkins to Commissioner of the General Land Office, June 22, 1885, Records of the Bureau of Land Management, Miscellaneous Letters Received, Record Group 49, National Archives, Washington, D.C.

17. Minutes of the Maxwell Land Grant and Railway Company Annual Meeting, July 8, 1871; Stockholders Meetings, November 9, 1872 and October 10, 1873, MLG; Charles E. Gast to Committee of the Share and Bondholders, September 1, 1877, MLG.

18. *The Maxwell Land Grant: Opinions as to Title by Noah Davies, Wm. M. Everts, J. F. Bayard, George T. Curtis, and J. P. Benjamin* (privately printed; copy in the writer's possession); *Indianapolis News*, July 4, 1885.

19. *Raton Comet*, July 10, 1885.

20. Interview with Thomas Brannin, April 10, 1948.

21. *Raton Comet,* July 17, 1885.

22. Ibid.; Paul L. Haworth, "George Washington Julian," *Dictionary of American Biography,* ed. Dumas Malone (New York: Charles Scribner's Sons, 1933), 10:245–46.

23. *Raton Comet,* July 17, 1885, and August 7, 1885.

24. *O. P. McMains* v. *I. C. Showerman,* No. 631, Docket of the District Court (Colfax County, New Mexico), 1:228, and Record of the District Court B, p. 283.

25. O. P. McMains to George W. Julian, August 6, 1885, MLG.

CHAPTER 11

1. *Maxwell Land Grant Company* v. *George Hixenbaugh,* No. 578, Records of the District Court (Colfax County, New Mexico).

2. William A. Vincent to President Cleveland, November 5, 1885, *Indianapolis Journal,* November 16, 1885; *New York Tribune,* October 17, 1885.

3. *Indianapolis Journal,* November 16, 1885; *Daily New Mexican,* October 16, 1885.

4. *New York Tribune,* October 17, 1885.

5. *Las Vegas Daily Optic,* October 19, 1885; *Colorado and New Mexico Cattlemen's Advertiser,* October 22, 1885.

6. *Las Vegas Daily Optic,* October 22, 1885; *Colorado and New Mexico Cattlemen's Advertiser,* October 22, 1885.

7. *Indianapolis Journal,* November 16, 1885.

8. *New York Tribune,* October 17, 1885.

9. *Las Vegas Daily Optic,* November 2, 1885.

10. *Indianapolis Journal,* November 16, 1885. The paper published the Vincent-Cleveland telegrams and letters.

11. *Indianapolis Journal,* November 17, 1885.

CHAPTER 12

1. *Las Vegas Daily Optic,* December 5, 1885.

2. *Las Vegas Daily Optic,* January 18, 1886; U.S. Department of the Interior, *Decisions of the Department of the Interior and General Land Office in Cases Relating to the Public Lands from July, 1885, to June, 1886* (Washington: Government Printing Office, 1886), 4:311–14; Morris F. Taylor, "The Two Land Grants of Gervacio Nolán," *New Mexico Historical Review,* 47 (April 1972):170–75.

3. Harry Whigham to M. P. Pels, June 25, 1885, Maxwell Land Grant Company Letters 3, pp. 150–53, MLG.

4. *United States* v. *Maxwell Land Grant Company and Others.* 26 Fed. Rep. 118 (1886) and 21 Fed. Rep. 19 (1884).

5. 26 Fed. Rep. 118 (1886).

6. *Raton Comet,* January 29, 1886.

7. Ibid.

8. *Cattlemen's Advertiser,* February 11, 1886, and February 18, 1886.

9. *Raton Comet,* March 12, 1886.

10. Ibid.

11. Ibid., March 26, 1886.

12. Ibid.

13. Bushnell and Whigham to Prowers and Hough, May 21, 1875, Letter Book 1872–1877, MLG; interview with Mrs. Lucy Reed Wills, October 7, 1948; Victor Westphall, *Thomas Benton Catron and His Era* (Tucson: University of Arizona Press, 1973), p. 110.

14. *Raton Comet,* April 2, 1886.

15. Ibid., April 9, 1886, and April 23, 1886; Harry Whigham to Bela M. Hughes, April 5, 1886, Maxwell Land Grant Company Letters 3, pp. 296–98, MLG.

16. *Raton Comet,* April 9, 1886; *Las Vegas Daily Optic,* April 29, 1886; Harry Whigham to J. P. George, April 17, 1886, Maxwell Land Grant Company Letters 3, pp. 303–4, MLG.

17. O. P. McMains to President Cleveland, August 19, 1887, published in the *St. Louis Globe-Democrat,* August 23, 1887.

18. Ibid.

19. *Raton Comet,* April 23, 1886, and April 30, 1886; *Cattlemen's Advertiser,* April 15, 1886.

20. *Raton Comet,* April 23, 1886.

21. Ibid., April 30, 1886; O. P. McMains, *Conspiracy to Defraud!* (broadside dated April 24, 1886, using the same title as his pamphlet of 1884), Taylor Collection.

22. McMains, *Conspiracy to Defraud!.*

23. *Raton Comet,* April 30, 1886.

24. Ibid.

25. Ibid., May 7, 1886.

26. *Raton Comet,* May 28, 1886.

27. O. P. McMains to President Cleveland, August 19, 1887; *Raton Range,* August 26, 1887.

28. U.S., *Congressional Record*, 49th Cong., 1st sess., April 5, 1886, 17, pt. 3: 3124; and May 17, 1886, 17, pt. 4: 4594.
29. *Raton Comet*, June 4, 1886.
30. Ibid., May 14, 1886.
31. Ibid., May 28, 1886.
32. Ibid., June 4, 1886.
33. Ibid., May 28, 1886, and June 4, 1886.
34. Ibid., June 4, 1886, and July 2, 1886.
35. Ibid., July 9, 1886; *Colfax County Stockman*, July 17, 1886.

CHAPTER 13

1. Van Lint Manuscript, MLG; extract from Maxwell Land Grant Company Directors' Meeting, February 2, 1885, Folder 1885, MLG; Pels Appointment, Folder 1885, MLG.
2. Obituary of M. P. Pels, *Denver Republican*, February 9, 1906.
3. Charles J. Canda to Bela M. Hughes, May 19, 1885, and Charles Fairchild to M. P. Pels, May 20, 1885, Folder 1885, MLG.
4. B. M. Hughes to Charles J. Canda, May 25, 1885, Folder 1885, MLG.
5. *Raton Weekly Independent*, undated supplement, October 1886.
6. Ibid.; *Cattlemen's Advertiser*, October 7, 1886.
7. *Raton Weekly Independent*, undated supplement, October 1886.
8. *Raton Daily Independent*, October 11, 1886, quoting *La Flecha*.
9. M. P. Pels to the Maxwell Land Grant Committee, March 3, 1887, and M. P. Pels to Frank Springer, October 17, 1887, Letters March 3–November 7, 1887, pp. 1–5, 443–45, MLG.
10. D. F. Wilkins to Harry Whigham, January 31, 1887, Letters 14, 1887, MLG.
11. Ibid., February 2, 1887; Harry Whigham to M. P. Pels, March 2, 1887, Letters 5, pp. 8–15, MLG; D. F. Wilkins to Harry Whigham, March 4, 1887, Letters 14, 1887, MLG; Maxwell Land Grant Record of Settlers, March 1887, MLG; M. P. Pels to Frank Springer, March 22, 29, 1887, pp. 32, 37–38, and to the Maxwell Land Grant Committee, April 5, 1887, Letters March 3–November 7, 1887, MLG.

12. *The United States* v. *The Maxwell Land Grant Company et al,* 121 U.S. 325 (1887); William A. Keleher, *Maxwell Land Grant: A New Mexico Item,* rev. ed. (New York: Argosy-Antiquarian, Ltd., 1964), p. 110.

13. *Raton Range,* April 22, 1887.

14. Ibid., May 20, 1887.

15. S. M. Stockslager to L. Q. C. Lamar, 1887; L. Q. C. Lamar to A. H. Garland, May 10, 1887, Transcript of Record; *Raton Range,* May 13, 1887.

16. A. H. Garland to the Supreme Court, and Motion for a Rehearing, Transcript of Record; Keleher, p. 111; *Raton Range,* May 13, 1887.

17. M. P. Pels to the Maxwell Land Grant Committee, May 19, 1887, Letters March 3–November 7, 1887, pp. 124–34, MLG.

18. Ibid.

19. Ibid.

20. M. P. Pels to the Maxwell Land Grant Committee, April 29, 1887, ibid., pp. 75–79.

21. Ibid., undated pamphlet by Frank Springer, MLG; *The United States* v. *The Maxwell Land Grant Company, et al.: Opinion of the Court* (n.p.: New Mexican Printing Company, n.d.), MLG.

22. O. P. McMains to President Cleveland, August 19, 1887, published in the *St. Louis Globe-Democrat,* August 23, 1887.

CHAPTER 14

1. *Raton Range,* May 20, 1887.

2. M. P. Pels to the Maxwell Land Grant Committee, May 19, 1887, Letters March 3–November 7, 1887, pp. 124–34, MLG.

3. *Raton Range,* May 20, 1887.

4. Ibid., May 27, 1887.

5. *Las Vegas Daily Optic,* May 19, 1887.

6. *Raton Range,* May 27, 1887.

7. *United States* v. *Maxwell Land Grant Company et al.,* 122 U.S. 365 (1887); William A. Keleher, *Maxwell Land Grant: A New Mexico Item,* rev. ed. (New York: Argosy-Antiquarian, Ltd.), p. 111.

8. M. P. Pels to C. J. Canda, May 28, 1887, Letters March 3–November 7, 1887, p. 155, MLG.

9. M. P. Pels to C. J. Canda, May 30, 1887, ibid., p. 156.

10. M. P. Pels to C. J. Canda, June 1, 1887, ibid., p. 159.

11. M. P. Pels to C. J. Canda, June 17, 1887, ibid., p. 214.

12. *Raton Range,* June 17, and July 1, 1887.

13. M. P. Pels to Henry L. Waldo, June 20, 1887, Letters March 3–November 7, 1887, p. 210, MLG; Uña de Gato, Report 94, File 167, Reel 22, Frame 414, Microfilm of Papers Relating to New Mexico Land Grants, New Mexico State Records Center and Archives, Santa Fe..

14. *Raton Range,* July 8, 1887; interview with Mrs. Lucy Reed Wills, September 3, 1948.

15. *Raton Range,* July 8, 1887.

16. Ibid., July 25, 1887. Co-editor and publisher of the *Raton Range* was A. Clauson. Ibid., February 25, 1887.

17. *Raton Range,* July 22, 1887.

18. M. P. Pels to the Maxwell Land Grant Committee, July 16, 1887, Letters March 3–November 7, 1887, pp. 231–246, MLG.

19. Ibid.; M. P. Pels to the Maxwell Land Grant Committee, May 19, 1887, ibid., pp. 124–34; and July 16, 1887, ibid., pp. 231–46, MLG.

20. M. P. Pels to the Maxwell Land Grant Committee, July 16, 1887, ibid., pp. 231–46, MLG.

21. Las Animas County (Colorado) Deed Record, Book 4, pp. 71–72; *Marion Russell et al. v. the Maxwell Land Grant Company* 158 U.S. 971 (1894); Mrs. Hal Russell, ed., "Memoirs of Marion Russell," *The Colorado Magazine,* 20 (November 1943):235; Albert W. Thompson, *They Were Open Range Days: Annals of a Western Frontier* (Denver: World Press, 1946), pp. 49–54.

22. M. P. Pels to the Maxwell Land Grant Committee, July 16, 1887, Letters March 3–November 7, 1887, pp. 231–46, MLG.

23. Ibid.; interview with Wilbur Davis, August 13, 1957.

24. M. P. Pels to F. B. Chaplin, July 4, 1887, Letters 14 1887, MLG.

25. M. P. Pels to the Maxwell Land Grant Committee, July 16, 1887, Letters March 3–November 7, 1887, MLG.

26. *Raton Range,* July 8, 1887; Keleher, p. 153; M. P. Pels to the Maxwell Land Grant Committee, July 16, 1887, Letters March 3–November 7, 1887, pp. 321–246, MLG.

27. *Raton Range,* July 22, 1887; August 5, 1887; August 12, 1887.

28. M. P. Pels to the Maxwell Land Grant Committee, August 9, 1887, Letters March 3–November 7, 1887, p. 330, MLG.

29. M. P. Pels to Shryock & Holdsworth, July .30 and August 8, 1887, ibid., pp. 289–90, 323–24.

30. George W. Julian, "Land Stealing in New Mexico," *North American Review*, 145 (July 1887):17–31.

31. *Raton Range*, August 5, 1887.

CHAPTER 15

1. O. P. McMains to President Cleveland, August 19, 1887.

2. Ibid. McMains may have written more than one letter to Cleveland. M. P. Pels to Maxwell Land Grant Committee, September 3, 1887, Maxwell, March 3, 1887–November 7, 1887, pp. 379–80, MLG.

3. M. P. Pels to President Cleveland, August 31, 1887, March 3, 1887–November 7, 1887, pp. 358–63, 371, MLG.

4. Ibid.

5. Ibid.; M. P. Pels to C. J. Canda, September 1, 1887, ibid., p. 366.

6. *M. P. Pels* v. *W. J. McClure et al*, No. 900 Docket of the District Court 2 (Colfax County, New Mexico); Harry Whigham to M. P. Pels, September 7, 1887, Letter Book 4, pp. 68–73, MLG.

7. Harry Whigham to M. P. Pels, September 7, 1887, Letter Book 4, pp. 68–73, MLG; J. M. John to Harry Whigham, September 13, 1887, Letters 14, 1887, MLG; *Raton Range*, September 19, 1887.

8. M. P. Pels to Frank Springer, September 27, 1887, Letters March 3–November 7, 1887, pp. 425–29, MLG.

9. Ibid.; *M. P. Pels* v. *W. J. McClure et al*, No. 900, Docket of the District Court 2 (Colfax County, New Mexico).

10. M. P. Pels to Frank Springer, September 27, 1887, Letters March 3–November 7, 1887, pp. 425–29, MLG; *Raton Range*, September 30, 1887.

11. *Raton Range*, September 23, 1887.

12. Ibid., October 7, 1887; Wilfred I. McPheron, "A History of the Maxwell Land Grant" (Master's thesis, Colorado State College of Education, 1936), pp. 77–78.

13. M. P. Pels to C. J. Canda, October 8, 1887, Letter Book 4, pp. 456–57, MLG; *Raton Range*, October 8, 1887.

14. *Raton Range*, October 14, 1887.

15. Ibid.

16. R. B. Holdsworth to Harry Whigham, October 15, 1887, Letters 14, 1887, and M. P. Pels to C. J. Canda, October 8, 1887, Letter Book 4, pp. 456–57, MLG.

17. *Raton Range*, October 14, 1887.

18. *Daily Citizen*, November 9, 1887.

CHAPTER 16

1. *Raton Range*, October 21, 1887.
2. *Raton Range*, November 4, 1887; interview with Thomas Brannin, April 10, 1948; Harry Whigham to M. P. Pels, November 4, 1887, Letter Book 4, pp. 200–2, MLG.
3. *Raton Range*, November 25, 1887.
4. Ibid., September 23, 1887.
5. Helen Sumner Woodbury, "Terence Vincent Powderly," *Dictionary of American Biography*, ed. Dumas Malone (New York: Charles Scribners Sons, 1933), 15:142–43; Louis M. Hacker and Benjamin B. Kendrick, *The United States Since 1865* (New York: F. S. Crofts and Company, 1938), pp. 224, 227.
6. Robert W. Larson, "The White Caps of New Mexico: A Study of Ethnic Militancy in the Southwest," *Pacific Historical Review*, 44 (May 1975):178, 180.
7. *Raton Range*, September 30, 1887.
8. Helen Sumner Woodbury, "Johann Joseph Most," *Dictionary of American Biography*, ed. Dumas Malone (New York: Charles Scribner's Sons, 1934), 13:282.
9. *Raton Range*, November 18, 1887.
10. *Raton Weekly Independent*, December 3, 1887.
11. *Raton Range*, April 6, 1888; *Raton Weekly Independent*, April 7, 1888.
12. *Raton Range*, April 6, 1888.
13. Ibid.; *Raton Weekly Independent*, April 7, 1888.
14. *Raton Weekly Independent*, April 7, 1888.
15. *Daily Citizen*, April 13, 1888.
16. *Raton Weekly Independent*, April 14, 1888.
17. M. P. Pels to C. J. Canda, November 26, 1887, Letters November 7, 1887–February 20, 1888, p. 49, MLG.
18. Harold H. Dunham, "William Andrew Jackson Sparks," *Dictionary of American Biography*, ed. Dumas Malone (New York: Charles Scribner's Sons, 1935), 17:434–35.
19. *Raton Weekly Independent*, December 3, 1887.
20. Ibid.
21. Ibid., December 10, 1887, quoting the Trinidad *Citizen*.

CHAPTER 17

1. Thomas Boggs to Harry Whigham, December 19, 1887, Letters 14, 1887, MLG.

2. Harry Whigham to Thomas Boggs, November 29, 1887, Letter Book 4, p. 287, MLG; Boggs to Whigham, December 19, 1887, Letters 14, 1887, MLG; T. A. Schomburg to M. P. Pels, December 25, 1887, Letter Book 4, pp. 352–54, MLG; interview with Mrs. Lucy Reed Wills, September 14, 1948.

3. M. P. Pels to the Maxwell Land Grant Committee, December 19, 1887, Letters November 7, 1887–February 20, 1888, pp. 83–87, MLG; *Maxwell Land Grant Company* v. *Jose Luis Torres* [no number], Records of the District Court, Las Animas County Colorado.

4. *Maxwell Land Grant Company* v. *Louis Torres* [no number], and *Maxwell Land Grant Company* v. *R. D. Russell*, No. 1246, and *Maxwell Land Grant Company* v. *F. B. Chaplin*, No. 1247, Records of the District Court (Las Animas County, Colorado); interview with Wilbur Davis, August 13, 1957; *Daily Advertiser*, December 23, 1887.

5. *Raton Weekly Independent*, December 31, 1887, and January 21, 1888.

6. Ibid., January 28, 1888, and February 11, 1888; *Raton Range*, January 27, 1888.

7. Harry Whigham to M. P. Pels, February 10, 1888, Letters 5, pp. 235–37, MLG.

8. *Raton Weekly Independent*, February 11, 1888; M. P. Pels to R. V. Martinsen, January 19, 1888, Letters November 7, 1887–February 20, 1888, pp. 181–84, MLG.

9. M. P. Pels to R. B. Holdsworth, December 17, 1887, p. 78, and M. P. Pels to J. M. John, December 29, 1887, Letters November 7, 1887–February 20, 1888, p. 127, MLG; letter from M. P. Pels to Harry Whigham, February 28, 1888, Letters 700, pp. 17–19, MLG; *Daily Citizen*, September 8, 1888.

10. M. P. Pels to Thomas O. Boggs, December 22, 1887, Letters November 7, 1887–February 20, 1888, pp. 105–10, MLG; *Raton Range*, December 23, 1887.

11. *Raton Weekly Independent*, January 21, 1888, and February 4, 1888; *Raton Daily Independent*, July 27, 1888; *Raton Range*, February 17, 1888; U.S., *Congressional Record*, 50th Cong., 1st sess., February 14 and February 27, 1888, 19, pt. 2:1176, 1513; William A. Robinson, "Henry William Blair," *Dictionary of American Biography*, ed. Allen Johnson (New York: Charles Scribner's Sons, 1957), 2:334–35; William A. Robinson, "William Steele Holman," *Dictionary of American Biography*, ed. Dumas Malone (New York: Charles Scribner's Sons, 1932), 9:158–59.

12. *Raton Weekly Independent*, March 17, 1888.

13. *Raton Weekly Independent*, March 31, 1888.

14. Ibid.; *Oscar P. McMains et al.* v. *Russell Marcy et al*, No. 1043, Records of the District Court (Colfax County, New Mexico).

15. *Raton Weekly Independent*, March 31, 1888.

16. *Daily Citizen*, March 22, 1888, and March 23, 1888; J. M. John to M. P. Pels and Harry Whigham, March, 1888, Letters January 1, 1888–January 20, 1889, MLG.

17. M. P. Pels to Francis Clutton, April 25, 1888, and M. P. Pels to R. V. Martinsen, May 29, 1888, Letters 700, February 20–October 16, 1888, pp. 193–94, 322–27, MLG; Lawrence R. Murphy, *Philmont: A History of New Mexico's Cimarron Country* (Albuquerque: University of New Mexico Press, 1972), p. 137; M. P. Pels to R. V. Martinsen, May 29, 1888, Letters 700, February 20–October 16, 1888, pp. 322–27, MLG.

18. *Raton Range*, May 4, 1888; *Daily Advertiser*, June 3, 1888; T. A. Schomburg to Shryock & Holdsworth, Letters 6, pp. 34–35, MLG.

19. Harry Whigham to Frank Springer, April 21, 1888, Transfer 4, MLG.

20. R. B. Holdsworth to M. P. Pels, April 23, 1888, Folder 1888, MLG.

21. *Raton Range*, May 4, 1888.

22. Ibid., May 18, 1888.

23. M. P. Pels to Frank Springer, May 16, 1888, Letters 700, February 20–October 16, 1888, pp. 232–34, MLG; Harry Whigham to M. P. Pels, May 24, 1888, Transfer 4, MLG.

24. M. P. Pels to R. V. Martinsen, May 29, 1888, and M. P. Pels to Frank Springer, June 1 and June 11, 1888, Letters 700, February 20–October 16, 1888, pp. 322–27, 344–48, 425–26, MLG.

25. M. P. Pels to Frank Springer, June 1, 1888, Letters 700, February 20–October 16, 1888, pp. 344–48, MLG.

26. R. B. Holdsworth to M. P. Pels, May 19, 1888, and June 3, 1888, Folder 1888, MLG.

27. M. P. Pels to the Maxwell Land Grant Committee, January 27, 1888, Letters November 7, 1888–February 20, 1888, pp. 201–4, MLG; R. B. Holdsworth to M. P. Pels, February 7, 1888, and August 8, 1888, Letters January 1, 1888–January 20, 1889; MLG; *Daily Advertiser*, February 19, 1888; June 20, 1888; June 30, 1888.

28. R. B. Holdsworth to M. P. Pels, May 19, 1888, Folder 1888, MLG; J. M. John to M. P. Pels, May 21, 1888, Letters January 1, 1888–January 20, 1889, MLG.

29. R. B. Holdsworth to M. P. Pels, July 13, 1888, Folder 1888, MLG.

30. M. P. Pels to R. B. Holdsworth, July 16, 1888, Letters 700, February 20–October 16, 1888, pp. 506–7, MLG.

31. *Raton Range*, July 13, 1888; *Raton Daily Independent*, July 23, 1888.

32. *Daily Citizen*, July 13, 1888.

CHAPTER 18

1. John D. Hicks, *The Populist Revolt: A History of the Farmers' Alliance and the People's Party* (Lincoln: University of Nebraska Press, 1961), pp. 104–9; Solon J. Buck, *The Agrarian Crusade: A Chronicle of the Farmer in Politics* (New Haven: Yale University Press, 1920), pp. 111–16; Robert W. Larson, *New Mexico Populism: A Study of Radical Protest in a Western Territory* (Boulder: Colorado Associated University Press, 1974), pp. 21–23; Howard Roberts Lamar, *The Far Southwest, 1846–1912: A Territorial History* (New Haven: Yale University Press, 1966), p. 196.

2. *Raton Range*, July 13, 1888; *Raton Daily Independent*, July 23, 1888; Larson, pp. 21–22.

3. *Raton Daily Independent*, July 23, 1888.

4. Ibid.

5. M. P. Pels to the Board of Trustees, July 28, 1888, Letters 700, February 20–October 16, 1888, pp. 542–44, MLG.

6. *Daily Citizen*, July 24, 1888; M. P. Pels to Frank Springer, August 1, 1888, Letters July 5–September 14, 1888, pp. 144–45, MLG.

7. M. P. Pels to Frank Springer, August 1, 1888, Letters July 5–September 14, 1888, pp. 141–45, MLG; *Raton Daily Independent*, July 23, 1888.

8. Ibid.; interview with Thomas Brannin, April 10, 1948, and George W. Moore, May 22, 1948.

9. *Daily Citizen*, July 24, 1888.

10. M. P. Pels to Frank Springer, August 1, 1888, Letters July 5–September 14, 1888, pp. 141–45, MLG.

11. Harry Whigham to M. P. Pels, July 23, 1888, ibid., p. 78; M. P. Pels to R. V. Martinsen, July 26, 1888, Letters 700, February 20–October 16, 1888, pp. 532–33, MLG; *Raton Daily Independent*, July 23, 1888, and July 27, 1888.

12. M. P. Pels to M. W. Mills, June 26, 1888, Letters 700, February 20–October 16, 1888, p. 524, MLG.

13. M. P. Pels to R. V. Martinsen, July 26, 1888, ibid., pp. 532–33.

14. Ibid.

15. Ibid.; M. P. Pels to Frank Springer, August 1, 1888, Letters July 5–September 14, 1888, pp. 141–45, MLG.

16. M. P. Pels to Frank Springer, August 1, 1888, Letters July 5–September 14, 1888, pp. 141–45, MLG.

17. Ibid.

18. M. P. Pels to the Board of Trustees, August 2, 1888, Letters 700, February 20–October 16, 1888, MLG.

19. R. B. Holdsworth to M. P. Pels, July 24, 1888, Letters 15, January 1–August 7, 1888, MLG.

20. *Raton Range,* July 27, 1888.

21. R. B. Holdsworth to M. P. Pels, July 25, 1888, Letters January 1–August 7, 1888, MLG; *Daily Citizen,* August 7, 1888.

22. R. B. Holdsworth to M. P. Pels, July 31, 1888, Letters January 1–August 7, 1888, MLG.

23. *The United States* v. *O. P. McMains,* No. 754, U.S. District Court (Colorado); *Daily Citizen,* August 16, 1888.

24. *Daily Citizen,* August 7, 1888.

25. Ibid., August 28, 1888.

26. Ibid., August 29, 1888; U.S., *Congressional Record,* 50th Cong., 1st sess., August 27, 1888, 19, pt. 8:7998–99.

CHAPTER 19

1. Maxwell Land Grant Company Record of Settlers, March 1887, p. 8, MLG; Report of T. J. O'Neil to James McParland, August 27, 1888, Case A, File 17, MLG; *Daily Advertiser,* August 1, 1886, and February 19, 1888; M. P. Pels to Governor Alva Adams (telegram), August 25, 1888, Letters 700 Maxwell, February 20, 1888–October 16, 1888, p. 626, MLG.

2. Affidavit of I. P. George, August 20, 1888, Case A, File 17, MLG; M. P. Pels to M. W. Mills, August 20, 1888, Letters 700, February 20–October 16, 1888, pp. 602–3, MLG.

3. M. P. Pels to R. V. Martinsen, August 21, 1888, Letters 700, February 20–October 16, 1888, p. 605, MLG.

4. M. W. Mills to M. P. Pels, August 22, 1888, Letters January 1, 1888–January 20, 1889, MLG.

5. Ibid.

6. *Daily Citizen*, August 23, 1888; M. P. Pels to R. V. Martinsen, September 11, 1888, Letters July 5–September 14, 1888, p. 451, MLG.

7. M. P. Pels to the Board of Trustees, August 24, 1888, Letters 700, February 20–October 16, 1888, p. 608, MLG; *Daily Citizen*, August 23, 1888, p. 1; affidavit of T. J. O'Neil, August 28, 1888, Case A, File 17, MLG; M. P. Pels to R. V. Martinsen, September 11, 1888, Letters July 5–September 14, 1888, p. 451, MLG.

8. *Daily Citizen*, August 24, 1888.

9. *Daily Citizen*, August 24, 1888; R. B. Holdsworth to M. P. Pels, August 24, 1888, Van Lint Scrapbook, MLG; Mrs. Randolph's testimony, *The People* v. *O. P. McMains, Martin Kephart, et al.*, No. 1618, Records of the District Court (Las Animas County, Colorado).

10. *Daily Citizen*, August 25, 1888.

11. *Daily Citizen*, September 13, 1888; *Daily News*, November 2, 1888; Report of T. J. O'Neil, MLG; James McParland to M. P. Pels, August 27, 1888, MLG.

12. *Daily Advertiser*, October 9, 1889; interview with George Moore, May 22, 1948; Reed-Wills; interview with Mrs. Lucy Reed Wills, September 2, 1948; Reed-Wills.

13. Report of T. J. O'Neil, MLG.

14. Affidavit of T. J. O'Neil, MLG.

15. Ibid.; testimony of John Moss (125), testimony of John Selles (125 or more), *The People* v. *O. P. McMains et al*; affidavit of T. J. O'Neil, MLG (150–200); *Daily Citizen*, August 25, 1888 (some 200); telegram from R. B. Holdsworth to M. P. Pels, August 25, 1888 (200–300), Letters January 1, 1888–January 20, 1889, MLG; Reed-Wills (about 400 — probably a total figure, including many who did not arrive until after the fight).

16. Testimonies of John Selles, Frank Lewis, William Hunn, and Ed Brown, *The People* v. *O. P. McMains et al.*; affidavit of T. J. O'Neil, MLG; *Daily Advertiser*, October 5, 1889.

17. Affidavit of T. J. O'Neil, MLG; Reed-Wills; interview with George W. Moore, May 22, 1948; testimonies of deputies, and instructions to the jury, *The People* v. *O. P. McMains et al.*; *Daily Citizen*, September 12, 1888, and September 13, 1888; *Daily News*, November 2, 1888.

18. Affidavit of T. J. O'Neil, MLG; testimonies of Frank Lewis and William Hunn, *The People* v. *O. P. McMains et al.*

19. Reed-Wills; interview with George W. Moore, May 22, 1948; letter from O. P. McMains, *Daily Citizen*, September 13,

1888; *Daily Advertiser,* October 5, 1889; affidavit of T. J. O'Neil, MLG.

20. *Daily Citizen,* August 28, 1888; interview with George W. Moore, May 22, 1948; affidavit of T. J. O'Neil, MLG; interview with Hal Russell, August 14, 1954; *Daily News,* November 2, 1888, quoting F. B. Chaplin.

21. *Daily Citizen,* August 31, 1888; Reed-Wills; interview with George W. Moore, May 22, 1948; *Daily Advertiser,* October 5, 1889.

22. Affidavit of T. J. O'Neil, MLG.

23. *Daily Citizen,* September 13, 1888.

24. Undated interview with Mrs. Marion Duling; Reed-Wills.

25. Testimony of William Hunn, *The People* v. *O. P. McMains et al.;* Reed-Wills; interview with George W. Moore, May 22, 1948.

26. Reed-Wills; *The People* v. *O. P. McMains et al.;* affidavit of T. J. O'Neil, MLG; M. P. Pels to R. V. Martinsen, September 11, 1888, Letters July 5–September 14, 1888, p. 451, MLG; *Daily Citizen,* August 28, 1888.

27. *Daily Citizen,* August 25, 1888.

28. Ibid.

29. Ibid.

30. Colonel Benjamin F. Klee to Governor Alva Adams, August 28, 1888, Records of the Office of Governor Alva Adams, Division of State Archives and Public Records, Denver, Colorado (cited hereafter as Colorado State Archives).

31. Reed-Wills; interview with George W. Moore, May 22, 1948; M. P. Pels to R. V. Martinsen, September 11, 1888, Letters July 5–September 14, 1888, pp. 452–61, MLG; Colonel Klee to Governor Adams, August 28, 1888, Colorado State Archives, Denver.

32. Reed-Wills.

33. Ibid.; Colonel Klee to Governor Adams, August 28, 1888, Colorado State Archives, Denver; M. P. Pels to R. V. Martinsen, September 11, 1888, Letters July 5–September 14, 1888, pp. 452–61, MLG; Francis Clutton to M. P. Pels, Transfer 4, MLG; *Daily Citizen,* August 28, 1888.

34. *Daily Citizen,* August 31, 1888. Russell's widow set down a very brief account of the Stonewall War and his death. See Mrs. Hal Russell, ed., "Memoirs of Marion Russell," *The Colorado Magazine* 21 (May 1944):108–9.

35. *Daily Citizen,* August 31, 1888.

36. Ibid.

37. Ibid.; M. P. Pels to R. V. Martinsen, September 11, 1888, Letters July 5–September 14, 1888, pp. 452–61, MLG; testimony of John Moss, *The People* v. *O. P. McMains et al.*

38. M. P. Pels to S. L. Parrish, August 29, 1888, Letters 700, February 20–October 16, 1888, pp. 643–45, MLG; *Daily Citizen,* August 31, 1888.

39. *Daily Citizen,* August 31, 1888.

CHAPTER 20

1. M. P. Pels to the Board of Trustees, August 28, 1888, Letters 700, February 20–October 16, 1888, pp. 638–39, MLG; telegram from R. B. Holdsworth to M. P. Pels, September 1, 1888, ibid., p. 658; *Daily Citizen,* September 11, 1888.

2. M. P. Pels to R. V. Martinsen, August 31, 1888, Letters 700, February 20–October 16, 1888, pp. 651–4.

3. M. P. Pels to M. H. Judd, September 3, 1888, ibid., p. 660.

4. *Daily Citizen,* August 29, 1888; U.S., *Congressional Record,* 50th Cong., 1st sess., August 27, 1888, 19, pt. 8:7998–99; R. V. Martinsen to M. P. Pels, August 31, 1888, Letters May 19, 1888–June 4, 1890, pp. 20–21, MLG.

5. *Daily Citizen,* September 3, 1888.

6. Ibid.

7. M. P. Pels to J. M. John, September 3, 1888, Letters 700, February 20–October 16, 1888, p. 661, MLG; Harry Whigham to M. P. Pels, July 5–September 14, 1888, pp. 349–51, MLG.

8. *Daily Citizen,* August 31, 1888; M. P. Pels to R. B. Holdsworth, September 3, 1888, Letters 700, February 20–October 16, 1888, p. 663, MLG.

9. Interview with Mrs. Lucy Reed Wills, November 26, 1948; L. S. Preston to M. P. Pels, September 5, 1888, Folder 1888, MLG.

10. L. S. Preston to M. P. Pels, September 5, 1888, Folder 1888, MLG; affidavit of L. S. Preston, Case A, File 17, MLG.

11. Affidavit of L. S. Preston, MLG.

12. M. P. Pels to Harry Whigham, October 15, 1888, Letters 700, February 20–October 16, 1888, pp. 699–700, MLG.

13. M. P. Pels to R. B. Holdsworth, September 3, 1888, Letters 700, February 20–October 16, 1888, p. 663, MLG.

14. M. P. Pels to R. V. Martinsen, September 11, 1888, Letters July 5–September 14, 1888, pp. 452–61, MLG.

15. M. P. Pels to Marshal Hill, September 7, 1888, Letters January 1, 1888–January 20, 1889, MLG.

16. M. P. Pels to R. V. Martinsen, September 11, 1888, Letters July 5–September 14, 1888, pp. 452–61, MLG.

17. *Daily Citizen*, September 13, 1888. F. B. Chaplin said essentially the same thing in a letter published in the *Trinidad Daily News*, November 2, 1888.

18. *Daily Citizen*, September 21, 1888.

19. Ibid.

20. Ibid.; John D. Hicks, *The Populist Revolt: A History of the Farmers' Alliance and the People's Party* (Lincoln: University of Nebraska Press, 1961), pp. 107–10.

21. Frank Springer to M. P. Pels, September 29, 1888, Letters January 1, 1888–January 20, 1889, MLG; telegram from M. P. Pels to R. V. Martinsen, September 27, 1888, ibid., MLG.

22. Harry Whigham to M. P. Pels, September 30, 1888, Letters September 14–November 25, 1888, pp. 96–97, MLG.

23. *Daily Citizen*, September 26, 1888.

24. M. P. Pels to R. B. Holdsworth, October 2, 1888, Letters September 14–November 25, 1888, p. 112, MLG.

25. Original in the Pamphlet and Tract Collection, University of Colorado Library, Boulder.

26. R. B. Holdsworth to M. P. Pels, October 3, 1888, Van Lint's Scrapbook, MLG; *Daily Citizen*, October 1, 1888; indictment, *The People* v. *O. P. McMains et al.*

27. *Raton Weekly Independent*, October 28, 1888.

CHAPTER 21

1. *Raton Weekly Independent*, October 6, 1888.

2. J. M. John to M. P. Pels, October 26, 1888, Letters January 1, 1888–January 20, 1889, MLG; Harry Whigham to R. B. Holdsworth, November 8, 1888, Letters September 14–November 25, 1888, p. 326, MLG; Harry Whigham to M. P. Pels, November 2, 1888, ibid., pp. 296–300; Jacob Piatt Dunn, ed., *Memorial Record of Distinguished Men of Indianapolis and Indiana* (Chicago: Lewis Publishing Co., 1912), p. 381; *Raton Range*, October 19, 1888, and September 28, 1888; *Daily Citizen*, November 13, 1888.

3. Harry Whigham to M. P. Pels, November 8, 1888, Letters September 14–November 25, 1888, p. 326, MLG.

4. Affidavit of L. S. Preston, MLG; *Daily Citizen*, December 11, 1888; M. P. Pels to R. B. Holdsworth, December 11, 1888, Letters September 14–November 25, 1888, p. 493, MLG.

5. *Daily Citizen*, December 12, 1888, and December 18, 1888.

6. Harry Whigham to M. P. Pels, December 26, 1888, Transfer 4, MLG; Harry Whigham to Frank Springer, January 3, 1889, ibid., MLG.

7. *Daily Citizen*, December 25, 1888.

8. R. B. Holdsworth to M. P. Pels, December 31, 1888, Letters January 1–January 20, 1888, MLG.

9. Miss E. Russell to the *Daily Citizen*, January 9, 1889, Russell Collection.

10. Harry Whigham to Frank Springer, January 3, 1889, Transfer 4, MLG.

11. *Daily Citizen*, October 10, 1888, and January 19, 1889; *Kansas City Times*, March 12, 1889; *Interstate Land Company* v. *Maxwell Land Grant Company et al.*, 41 Fed. Rep. 275 (1889).

12. *Daily Citizen*, January 19, 1889.

13. Ibid., February 2, 1889.

14. *Kansas City Times*, March 12, 1889.

15. 41 Fed. Rep. 275 (1889).

16. *Interstate Land Company* v. *Maxwell Land Grant Company et al.*, 139 U.S. 569 (1891).

17. *Daily Citizen*, January 19, 1889.

CHAPTER 22

1. *Daily Advertiser*, February 3, 1889.

2. Ibid.

3. *Daily Citizen*, February 3, 1889.

4. Ibid.; *Daily News*, February 5, 1889.

5. *Raton Range*, February 4, 1889; *Daily Citizen*, February 15, 1889.

6. *William Pinkerton* v. *Epifanio Ledoux* 129 U.S. 346 (1888); Morris F. Taylor, "The Two Land Grants of Gervacio Nolán," *New Mexico Historical Review*, 47 (April 1972):172–73.

7. Undated clipping in Taylor Collection; original broadside given to the writer by Bernie Beshoar Joerger.

8. *Daily Advertiser*, March 21, 1889; Indictments, *The People* v. *O. P. McMains et al.*, No. 1618, Records of the District Court, Las Animas County, Colorado (1889).

9. *Daily Citizen,* March 20, 1889.

10. Bonds, *The People* v. *O. P. McMains et al.*

11. Charles E. Gast to M. P. Pels, April 16, 1889, Letters January 20, 1889–, MLG.

12. M. P. Pels to Francis Clutton, March 30, 1889, Letters February 28–April 29, 1889, pp. 268–69, MLG.

13. Letter from Harry Whigham to Frank Springer, April 1, 1889, ibid., pp. 299–300.

14. *Colfax County Stockman,* April 6, 1889.

CHAPTER 23

1. Petition to President Harrison, April 13, 1889, Taylor Collection; letter from Charles W. Russell to President Harrison, April 22, 1889, ibid.

2. *Daily Citizen,* June 1, 1889.

3. Harry Whigham to M. P. Pels, June 12, 1889, Letters April 29–July 2, 1889, pp. 363–68, MLG.

4. *Raton Range,* June 21, 1889.

5. Ibid.

6. R. B. Holdsworth to M. P. Pels, June 24, 1889, Folder 1889, MLG; *Raton Range,* July 26, 1889.

7. Frank Springer to R. V. Martinsen, April 2, 1889, General Letters New York, 1889 & 1890, MLG: Harry Whigham to M. P. Pels, June 8, 1889, Letters April 4–July 2, 1889, pp. 340–42, MLG.

8. R. B. Holdsworth to M. P. Pels, June 24, 1889, Folder 1889, MLG.

9. Ibid.; M. P. Pels to Harry Whigham, September 6, 1889, Letters 21, August 1–November 1, 1889, MLG; J. M. John to M. P. Pels, August 7, 1889, ibid.

10. M. P. Pels to J. M. John, June 25, 1889, Letters 11, April 4–July 2, 1889, pp. 442–43, MLG.

11. *Daily Citizen,* Augst 14,1889.

12. Ibid., September 18, 1889, and September 21, 1889; M. P. Pels to R. B. Holdsworth, September 19, 1889, Letters 13, September 16–November 6, 1889, p. 59, MLG.

13. *Daily News,* October 3, 1889; *Daily Citizen,* October 4, 1889; *Daily Advertiser,* October 4, 1889.

14. *Daily Advertiser,* October 8, 1889, and October 9, 1889; *Daily Citizen,* October 8, 1889; deposition of S. C. Snyder, *The*

People v. *O. P. McMains et al.*, No. 1618, Records of the District Court, Las Animas County; Colorado (1889).

15. *Daily Advertiser*, October 9, 1889; *Daily Citizen*, October 8, 1889; October 9, 1889; October 11, 1889; and October 12, 1889.

16. *Daily Advertiser*, October 13, 1889; *Daily News*, October 12, 1889.

17. *Daily Citizen*, October 15, 1889.

18. Complaint, *United States* v. *O. P. McMains*, No. 94, U.S. District Court, Colorado (1890).

19. *Daily Citizen*, October 13, 1889; *Daily News*, October 14, 18, 1889; *Daily Advertiser*, October 18, 1889; M. P. Pels to James L. De Fremery, October 15, 17, 1889, Letters 13, September 16–November 6, 1889, pp. 266, 300, MLG.

20. *Daily Citizen*, October 17, 1889; *Daily Advertiser*, October 19, 1889.

21. Frank Springer to Harry Whigham, October 21, 1889, Letters 21, August 1–November 1, 1889, MLG; M. P. Pels to Frank Springer, October 25, 1889, Letters 13, September 16–November 16, 1889, pp. 322–23, MLG.

22. M. P. Pels to James L. De Fremery, November 2, 1889, Letters 13, September 16–November 16, 1889, pp. 416–17, MLG.

23. Harry Whigham to M. P. Pels, November 16, 1889, Transfer 4, MLG; T. A. Schomburg to M. P. Pels, December 21, 1889, Letters 14, November 6, 1889–January 18, 1890, pp. 323–24, MLG; Harry Whigham to M. P. Pels, December 25, 1889, Transfer 4, MLG; telegrams from Whigham to Pels, December 24, 25, 1889, ibid.

24. Harry Whigham to M. P. Pels, December 25, 1889, Transfer 4, MLG; M. P. Pels to Harry Whigham, December 26, 1889, Letters 22, November 1, 1889–January 1, 1890, MLG.

25. M. P. Pels to R. B. Holdsworth, December 21, 1889, Letters 14, November 6, 1889–January 18, 1890, back of p. 326, MLG; *Interstate Land Company* v. *Maxwell Land Grant Company et al.*, 41 Fed. Rep. 275 (1889).

26. *Daily Citizen*, December 19, 1889.

27. Indictment, *United States* v. *O. P. McMains*.

28. Ibid.; Plea to Second Count of Indictment, *United States* v. *O. P. McMains*.

29. Indictment, *United States* v. *O. P. McMains*; *Daily Citizen*, January 9, 1890; *Daily Advertiser*, January 8, 1890.

30. *The National Anti Land Grant Monthly* 1 (June 1890):8–9.

31. Harry Whigham to M. P. Pels, March 22, 1890, Letters 15, January 18–April 30, 1890, p. 318, MLG.

32. M. P. Pels to John D. Fleming, March 24, 1890, ibid., inserted at p. 321.

33. *Daily Advertiser*, March 29, 1890.

34. Letter from Harry Whigham to M. P. Pels, April 14, 1890, Letters 15, January 18–April 30, 1890, pp. 414–15, MLG; letters from Harry Whigham to M. P. Pels, April 15, 1890, and April 19, 1890, ibid., pp. 426–30, 449–50.

35. *Daily Advertiser*, May 6, 1890.

36. Ibid.

37. *The National Anti Land Grant Monthly*, 1 (June 1890):57. This appears to be the only issue published.

38. *Daily Advertiser*, July 11, 1890.

39. Harry Whigham to M. C. Reed, July 31, 1890, Letters 17, July 23, 1890–September 30, 1890, pp. 51–54, MLG; M. P. Pels to Frank Springer, August 1, 1890, ibid., pp. 76–77; M. P. Pels to F. E. Bissell, August 4, 1890, ibid., pp. 101–2; M. P. Pels to James L. De Fremery, August 7, 1890, ibid., pp. 145–48; M. P. Pels to O. L. Reed, August 10, 1890, ibid., p. 226; Harry Whigham to M. P. Pels, Transfer 4, MLG; William Bond Skerten to M. P. Pels, July 23, 1890, Letters No. 2, pp. 121–23, MLG.

40. *Daily Advertiser*, August 27, 1890.

41. M. P. Pels to James M. John, September 5, 1890, Letters 17, July 23–September 5, 1890, p. 355, MLG.

42. Harry Whigham to Marcy, Geer & McCarn, September 18, 1890, ibid., p. 420; Report to the Board of Trustees, October 10, 1890, Records A, MLG; Charles E. Gast to M. P. Pels, September 15, 1890, Letters 25, June 16–September 30, 1890, p. 25, MLG; Report of the Legal Department, 1890, Letters A, pp. 183–201, MLG.

43. M. P. Pels to James M. John, September 5, 1890, Letters 17, July 23–September 30, 1890, p. 355, MLG; M. P. Pels to John D. Fleming, March 24, 1890, Letters 15, January 18–April 30, 1890, inserted at p. 321, MLG.

44. *Daily News*, September 30, 1890; *Colorado Chieftain*, October 9, 1890.

45. J. M. John to M. P. Pels, October 16, 1890, Letters 26, October 1–November 20, 1890, MLG.

46. Ibid.; Report of M. P. Pels to the Board of Trustees, November 13, 1890, Letters A, pp. 89–101, MLG.

CHAPTER 24

1. *Daily Advertiser*, April 19, 1891; sentence and mittimus, *United States* v. *O. P. McMains*, No. 94, U.S. District Court, Colorado (1891).

2. M. P. Pels to J. M. John, October 19, 1891, Letters 1891, October 10–December 9, p. 69, MLG; *Colorado Chieftain*, October 22, 1891; undated clipping from Taylor Collection.

3. *Daily Advertiser*, August 26, 1892; Otis obituary, *Topeka Capital*, February 23, 1916; U.S., *Congressional Record*, 52nd Cong., 1st sess., March 5, 1892, 23, pt. 4:1765.

4. U.S., *Statutes at Large*, 26:854–62; Richard Wells Bradfute, *The Court of Private Land Claims* (Albuquerque: University of New Mexico Press, 1975), pp. 23, 235; U.S., *Congressional Record*, 52nd Cong., 1st sess., April 13, 1892, 23, pt. 4: p. 3272, and April 29, 1892, pp. 3797–98; U.S., Congress, *House Reports*, 52nd Cong., 1st sess., 1891–92, no. 1253, vol. 4, pp. 1–8 (Serial 3045), and no. 1824, vol. 7, pp. 3–5 (Serial 3048).

5. Frank Springer to R. V. Martinsen, March 11, 1891, Folder 1891, MLG.

6. U.S., Congress, *House Reports*, 52nd Cong., 1st sess., 1891–92, no. 1253, vol. 4, pp. 1–8 (Serial 3045), and no. 1824, vol. 7, pp. 3–5 (Serial 3048); U.S., *Congressional Record*, 52nd Cong., 1st sess., June 13, 1892, 23, pt. 6:5248, and July 9, 1892, p. 5950; *Daily Advertiser*, August 26, 1892; *Daily News*, August 26, 1892.

7. M. P. Pels to Frank Springer, September 6, and September 24, 1892, and M. P. Pels to J. M. John, September 26, 1892, Letters 28, August 22–November 14, 1892, pp. 92–93, 187–88, 131–32, MLG; Minutes, Board of Trustees, February 1–2, 1892, pp. 81–83, MLG; *Biographical Dictionary of the American Congress, 1774–1961* (Washington: Government Printing Office, 1961), p. 1413.

8. *Trinidad Daily Populist*, August 25, 1894; Louis M. Hacker and Benjamin B. Kendrick, *The United States Since 1865* (New York: F. S. Crofts and Company, 1938), p. 306; *Daily Advertiser*, August 24, 1892; *Evening Chronicle*, August 24, 1892; James Edward Wright, *The Politics of Populism: Dissent in Colorado* (New Haven, Conn.: Yale University Press, 1974), p. 149.

9. Solon T. Buck, *The Agararian Crusade: A Chronicle of the Farmer in Politics* (New Haven: Yale University Press, 1920), pp. 149–51; LeRoy R. Hafen, ed., *Colorado and Its People: A Narrative and Topical History of the Centennial State* (New York:

Lewis Historical Publishing Company, 1948), 1:465; Abstract of Votes Cast in Las Animas County, Book 1, pp. 137–38, Records of the Las Animas County Clerk and Recorder, Trinidad, Colorado.

10. Mary McMains to Robert Fisher, January 18, 1900.

11. *Daily Advertiser*, April 5, 1893, and May 1, 1893.

CHAPTER 25

1. *Daily Advertiser*, September 29, 1893.

2. Ibid., October 4, 1893.

3. Ibid., November 5, 1893.

4. Abstract of Votes Cast in Las Animas County, Book 1, p. 156, Records of the Las Animas County Clerk and Recorder, Trinidad, Colorado.

5. *Daily Advertiser*, December 29, 1893.

6. *Trinidad Daily Populist*, August 25, 1894; *Daily News*, August 14, 18, 1894.

7. *Daily Advertiser*, October 4, 1894.

8. Ibid., October 3, 1894.

9. Ibid., July 11, 1893; Morris F. Taylor, ed., "Early Days in Trinidad," *The Colorado Magazine* 40 (October 1963):279–80.

10. *Daily Advertiser*, October 11, 1894.

11. *Weekly Advertiser*, October 13, 11, 1894.

12. *Daily Advertiser*, October 11, 1894; *Daily News*, October 11, 1894.

13. *Daily Advertiser*, November 7, 1894; Percy Stanley Fritz, *Colorado, The Centennial State* (New York: Prentice Hall, 1941), p. 356; Abstract of Votes Cast in Las Animas County, Book 1, p. 164; James Edward Wright, *The Politics of Populism: Dissent in Colorado* (New Haven, Conn.: Yale University Press, 1974), p. 195.

14. Abstract of Votes Cast, Book 1, p. 164; *Daily News*, October 22, 1894.

15. *Daily Advertiser*, September 2, 1894.

16. Minutes, Board of Trustees Executive Committee, December 8, 1894, pp. 270–72, MLG; deed, Board of Trustees, Maxwell Land Grant Company to Marion Russell, October 13, 1899, Las Animas County (Colorado), Deed Record, Book 98, p. 574.

17. 158 U.S. 971 (1895); Las Animas County Deed Record, Book 98, p. 574; Wilfred I. McPheron, "A History of the Maxwell Land Grant" (Master's thesis, Colorado State College of Educa-

tion, 1936), p. 87; Harold H. Dunham, "Coloradans and the Maxwell Grant," *The Colorado Magazine*, 33 (April 1955):131–145.

18. *Daily Advertiser*, October 13, 1895.

19. *Weekly Advertiser*, January 9, 1896; Fritz, p. 495; Louis B. Hacker and Benjamin B. Kendrick, *The United States Since 1865* (New York: F. S. Crofts and Company, 1938), p. 308.

20. O. P. McMains to Speaker Thomas B. Reed, February 10, 1896, Taylor Collection.

21. U.S., *Congressional Record*, 54th Cong., 1st sess., February 18, 1896, 28, pt. 2:1908, and February 25, 1896, 28, pt. 3:2146.

CHAPTER 26

1. Mary McMains to Robert Fisher, July 1899.

2. Ibid.

3. Ibid.

4. *Denver Republican*, September 25, 1899; *House Journal of the General Assembly of the State of Colorado, Twelfth Session*, pp. 291–92.

5. Mary McMains to Robert Fisher, July 1899.

6. *House Journal, Twelfth Session*, pp. 1484–93.

7. Mary McMains to Robert Fisher, July 1899.

8. Ibid.; F. B. Chaplin obituary of McMains, Taylor Collection.

9. Ibid.

10. *Chronicle-News*, undated clipping in the writer's possession.

11. *Raton Range*, April 20, 1899.

APPENDIX

1. Harry Whigham to M. P. Pels, March 2, 1887, Letters 5, pp. 8–15, MLG; interview with Mrs. Lucy Reed Wills, February 12, 1948. The figure given was from her father, M. C. (Comp) Reed. Pearson, *The Maxwell Land Grant* (Norman: University of Oklahoma Press, 1961), p. 112, gives the estimate of 600 settlers.

2. E. C. Savage to Harry Whigham, November 20, 1886, Harry Whigham Receiver: Letters 1884, 1885, 1886, MLG.

3. Harry Whigham to Hans Mattson, April 25, 1885, Letters 3, pp. 99–100, MLG; interview with Mr. and Mrs. Hugh McKee, April 9, 1948.

4. Interview with Mrs. Lucy Reed Wills, October 7, 1948.

5. Ibid.; interview with Mr. and Mrs. Hugh McKee, April 9, 1948; Morris F. Taylor, "The Maxwell Cattle Company, 1881–1888," *New Mexico Historical Review*, 49 (October 1974):289–324.

6. Interview with Mrs. Lucy Reed Wills, November 26, 1948.

7. Maxwell Land Grant Record of Settlers, March 1887, p. 13, MLG.

8. Interviews with Mrs. Lucy Reed Wills, October 4, 1948 and November 26, 1948; M. P. Pels to C. J. Canda, August 8, 1887, Letters March 3–November 7, 1887, pp. 326–27, MLG.

9. Maxwell Land Grant Record of Settlers, March 1887, p. 15, MLG; *Maxwell Land Grant Company* v. *Jacinto Santistevan*, Records of the District Court, Colfax County, New Mexico, No. 974 (1888).

10. Mrs. C. B. Ladd to M. P. Pels, June 24, 1887, Letters 14, 1887, MLG.

11. Maxwell Land Grant Company Record of Settlers, March 1887, p. 12, MLG; Myra Ellen Jenkins, "Arthur Rockford Manby," *The 1966 Brandbook of the Denver Westerners*, pp. 241–55; interview with Mrs. Lucy Reed Wills, October 7, 1948; Arthur Manby to Judge Lee, September 9, 1888, E. V. Long Papers.

12. Interview with Mrs. Lucy Reed Wills, September 20, 1948.

13. Ibid., February 12, 1948.

14. Murphy, pp. 137–39; M. P. Pels to Frank Springer, October 17, 1887; March 3, 1887–November 7, 1887, pp. 443–45, MLG.

15. Interview with Mrs. Lucy Reed Wills, September 14, 1948; interview with Frank Stubblefield, November 8, 1948.

16. Accounts submitted to the Maxwell Land Grant Committee; Letters, March 3, 1887–November 7, 1887, pp. 462–64, MLG; M. P. Pels to Maxwell Land Grant Committee, December 19, 1887, ibid., pp. 83–87, MLG; interview with Mrs. Lucy Reed Wills, September 14, 1948.

Bibliography

MANUSCRIPT COLLECTIONS

E. V. Long Papers. New Mexico State Records Center and Archives, Santa Fe.

Maxwell Land Grant Company Records. Zimmerman Library, University of New Mexico, Albuquerque.

Michael Beshoar Papers. Western History Department, Denver Public Library, Denver, Colorado.

Morris F. Taylor Collection. Trinidad, Colorado.

Records of the Surveyor General of New Mexico; Records of the Court of Private Land Claims. New Mexico State Records Center and Archives, Santa Fe.

Reed-Wills Manuscripts. D. G. MacHendrie, Englewood, Colorado.

Samuel W. DeBusk Collection. Trinidad State Junior College Library, Trinidad, Colorado.

William Jackson Palmer Collection. Documentary Resources Department, State Historical Society of Colorado Library, Denver.

William G. Ritch Collection. Henry E. Huntington Library, San Marino, California.

OTHER UNPUBLISHED MATERIALS

"Cottman Scrapbook," vol. 2. William Henry Smith Memorial Library, Indiana Historical Society, Indianapolis.

"Indiana Biography Series Scrapbook," vol. 4. William Henry Smith Memorial Library, Indiana Historical Society, Indianapolis.

McPheron, Wilfred I. "A History of the Maxwell Land Grant." Master's thesis, Colorado State College of Education, 1936.

"Minutes of the Twelfth Annual [Colorado] Conference of the Methodist Episcopal Church, 1873." Library of the Colorado Methodist Historical Society, Iliff School of Theology, University of Denver.

"Minutes of the Twenty-Sixth Session of the Annual Illinois Conference, Methodist Episcopal Church, 1859." Library of Congress, Washington, D.C.

GOVERNMENT DOCUMENTS AND PUBLICATIONS

United States

Biographical Dictionary of the American Congress, 1774–1961. Washington: Government Printing Office, 1961.

Bureau of the Census, *Seventh Census of the United States* (Clermont County, Ohio, Miami Township). Record Group 29, National Archives, Washington, D.C.

Congress, *Congressional Globe,* 29th Cong., 2nd sess., 1847.

Congress, *Congressional Record,* 49th Cong., 1st sess., 1886, 17; 50th Cong., 1st sess., 1888, 19; 52nd Cong., 1st sess., 1892, 23; 54th Cong., 1st sess., 1896, 28.

Congress, *House Reports, 1st Session, 52nd Congress, 1891–92.* No. 1253, vol. 4 (Serial 3045).

Congress, Senate, *Letter from the Secretary of the Interior Transmitting Copies of Reports upon the Subject of Fraudulent Acquisition of Titles to Lands in New Mexico,* Ex. Doc. 106, 48th Cong., 2nd sess. (Serial 2263).

Congress, *Statutes at Large,* vols. 12, 16, 26.

Department of the Interior. *Annual Report of the Commissioner of Indian Affairs, 1870.* Washington: Government Printing Office, 1870.

Department of the Interior. *Annual Report of the Commissioner of the General Land Office, 1877.* Washington: Government Printing Office, 1877.

Department of the Interior. *Annual Report of the Commissioner of the General Land Office, 1885.* Washington: Government Printing Office, 1885.

Department of the Interior. *Decisions of the Department of the Interior and General Land Office in Cases Relating to the Public Lands from July, 1885, to June, 1886.* Washington: Government Printing Office, 1886.

Department of the Interior. *Report and Testimony in the Matter of Charges against Samuel B. Axtell, Governor of New Mexico, Submitted by Frank Warner Angel.* Microcopy 750, National Archives Microfilm Publications, copy in State Records Center and Archives, Santa Fe, New Mexico.

Donaldson, Thomas, ed. *The Public Domain: Its History.* Washington: Government Printing Office, 1884.

Colorado

General Assembly. *House Journal of the General Assembly of the State of Colorado, Twelfth Session* (1899).

Las Animas County, Abstract of Votes Cast, Book 1.

Las Animas County. Deed Records (1871–1901).

Office of the Governor. Records of the Office of Governor Alva Adams. Colorado State Archives, Denver.

New Mexico

Colfax County. Deed Records (1875–1880).

Legislative Assembly. *Council Journal of the Twenty-Sixth Legislative Assembly* (1884).

Legislative Assembly. *House Journal of the Twenty-Sixth Legislative Assembly* (1884).

Legislative Assembly. *Laws of New Mexico, 1884.*

LITIGATIONS

Federal Courts

Interstate Land Company v. *Maxwell Land Grant Company et al.* 41 Fed. Rep. 275 (1890), and 139 U.S. 569 (1891).

John G. Tameling v. *The United States Freehold Land and Emigration Company.* 23 U.S. 998 (1877).

Marion Russell et al. v. *The Maxwell Land Grant Company.* 158 U.S. 971 (1894).

Maxwell Land Grant Company v. *Vicente Pretica et al.* 41 Fed. Rep. 275 (1890), and 139 U.S. 569 (1891).

Transcript of Record. *The United States* v. *The Maxwell Land Grant Company et al.* Records of the United States Supreme Court, Record Group 267, National Archives, Washington, D.C.

United States v. *Maxwell Land Grant Company et al.* 21 Fed. Rep. 19 (1884), and 26 Fed. Rep. 118 (1886).

United States v. *O. P. McMains,* Records of the United States District Court (Colorado), No. 754 (1889).

William Pinkerton v. *Epifanio Ledoux.* 129 U.S. 346 (1888).

State and Territorial Courts

Maxwell Land Grant Company v. *F. B. Chaplin.* No. 1247, Records of the District Court, Las Animas County (1887).

Maxwell Land Grant Company v. *George Hixenbaugh.* No. 578, Records of the District Court, Colfax County, New Mexico (1885).

Maxwell Land Grant Company v. *Jacinto Santistevan.* No. 974, Records of the District Court, Colfax County, New Mexico (1888).

Maxwell Land Grant Company v. *Luis Torres.* [no number], Records of the District Court, Las Animas County, Colorado (1887).

Maxwell Land Grant Company v. *Oscar P. McMains.* No. 558, Records of the District Court, Colfax County, New Mexico (1884).

Maxwell Land Grant Company v. *R. D. Russell.* No. 1246, Records of the District Court, Las Animas County, Colorado (1887).

M. P. Pels v. *W. J. McClure et al.* No. 900, Records of the District Court, Colfax County, New Mexico (1887).

O. P. McMains v. *I. C. Showerman.* No. 631, Records of the District Court, Colfax County, New Mexico (1885).

Oscar P. McMains et al. v. *Russell Marcy et al.* No. 1043, Records of the District Court, Colfax County, New Mexico (1888).

The People v. *O. P. McMains, Martin Kephart et al.* Nos. 1618, 1619, 1625, Records of the District Court, Las Animas County, Colorado (1889).

Tameling v. *United States Freehold Land and Emigration Company.* 2 Colorado Reports 411 (1874).

Territory of New Mexico v. *O. P. McMains.* No. 353, Records of the District Court, Colfax County, New Mexico (1877).

William T. Thornton and E. Platt Stratton, Receivers v. *O. P. McMains.* No. 137, Records of the District Court, Colfax County, New Mexico (1881).

INTERVIEWS

Thomas Brannin (early settler in Colfax County), April 10, 1948.
Wilbur Davis (grand-nephew of F. B. Chaplin), August 13, 1957.
Marion Duling (daughter of Marion and Richard D. Russell), undated.
George W. Moore (early settler on Poñil Creek), May 22, 1948.
Hal Russell (son of Marion and Richard D. Russell), August 14, 1954.
Frank Stubblefield (early settler on Red River), November 8, 1948.
Nicholas Vigil (born 1869 near Trinidad), November 30, 1954.
Lucy Reed Wills (daughter of Julia and M. C. [Comp] Reed), September 3 and 14, October 4 and 7, and November 26, 1948.

CORRESPONDENCE

Berry, Paul L. (chief, Serials Division, Library of Congress), to the writer, September 9, 1955.
Fisher, Mabel (niece of McMains), to Mrs. C. D. Herron (grand-niece of McMains), March 21, 1949.
Fisher, Mabel, to the writer, June 22, 1949.
Herron, Mrs. C. D., to the writer, March 3, 1949.
McMains, Oscar P., to his brother, Robert Fisher, December 18, 1877, March 22, 1883, and May 11, 1883. (courtesy of Mabel Fisher.)
McMains, Mary B., to Robert Fischer, July 1899, August 11, 1899, September 18, 1899, and January 18, 1900. (courtesy of Mabel Fisher.)
Rist, Martin (president-librarian, Colorado Methodist Historical Society), to the writer August 1, 3, and 18, 1949, and undated letter [October 1949].
Thaxter, Paul L. (acting chief, Serials Division, Library of Congress), to the writer, September 9, 1955.
Van Lint, Victor J. (manager, Maxwell Land Grant Company), to the writer, February 28, 1950.

NEWSPAPERS

Albuquerque Morning Journal (New Mexico), 1882.
Cattlemen's Advertiser (Trinidad, Colorado), 1886–1887.
Cimarron News and Press (New Mexico), 1875–1881.
Colfax County Stockman (Springer, New Mexico), 1886–1889.
Colorado and New Mexico Cattlemen's Advertiser (Trinidad, Colorado), 1885–1886.
Colorado Chieftain (Pueblo), 1868–1872.
Daily Advertiser (Trinidad, Colorado), 1881–1897.
Daily Chieftain (Pueblo, Colorado), 1872–1900.
Daily Citizen (Trinidad, Colorado), 1886–1890.
Daily Miners' Register (Central City, Colorado), 1867.
Daily Mining Journal (Blackhawk, Colorado), 1864–1865.
Daily New Mexican (Santa Fe), 1875–1885.
Daily Reporter (Trinidad, Colorado), 1883.
Daily Rocky Mountain News (Denver, Colorado), 1864–1875.
Denver Republican (Colorado), 1899, 1906.
Evening Chronicle (Trinidad, Colorado, 1892–1899).
Indianapolis Journal (Indiana), 1885.
Indianapolis News (Indiana), 1885.
Indianapolis Sentinel (Indiana), 1884.
Kansas City Times (Missouri), 1889.
Las Animas, Col., Leader (Colorado), 1874–1875.
Las Vegas Daily Gazette (New Mexico), 1882–1884.
Las Vegas Daily Optic (New Mexico), 1879–1887.
Liberty Hall (Cincinnati, Ohio), 1809–1811.
Morning Light (Trinidad, Colorado), 1936.
New Mexico Stock Grower (Las Vegas), 1885.
New York Times, 1884–1890.
New York Tribune, 1885–1887.
The People (Pueblo, Colorado), 1872–1874.
Raton Comet (New Mexico), 1882–1886.
Raton Daily and *Weekly Independent* (New Mexico), 1886–1889.
Raton Guard (New Mexico), 1881–1882.
Raton News and Press (New Mexico), 1881–1882.
Raton Range (New Mexico), 1887–1973.
Raton Reporter (New Mexico), 1899.
St. Louis Globe-Democrat (Missouri), 1887.
Santa Fe New Mexican Review (New Mexico), 1884.
Topeka Capital (Kansas), 1916.
Trinidad Daily News (Colorado), 1883–1894.

Trinidad Daily Populist (Colorado), 1894.
Trinidad Daily Times (Colorado), 1881–1882.
Trinidad Democrat (Colorado), 1882.
Trinidad Enterprise (Colorado), 1874.
Trinidad Weekly Times (Colorado), 1882.
Washington Post, 1888.
Washington Star, 1888.
Weekly Advertiser (Trinidad, Colorado), 1883–1891.
Weekly New Mexican (Santa Fe), 1875–1877.

BOOKS AND PAMPHLETS

Anderson, George B. *History of New Mexico, Its Resources and People*. 2 vols. Los Angeles: Pacific States Publishing Company, 1907.
Bancroft, Hubert Howe. *History of Arizona and New Mexico, 1530–1888*. 1889. Reprint. Albuquerque: Horn and Wallace, 1962.
————. *History of Nevada, Colorado and Wyoming*. San Francisco: History Publishing Company, 1890.
Beardsley, Isaac Haight. *Echoes from Peak and Plain; or, Tales of Life, War, Travel, and Colorado Methodism*. Cincinnati: Curts and Jennings, 1898.
Bradfute, Richard Wells. *The Court of Private Land Claims: The Adjudication of Spanish and Mexican Land Grant Titles, 1891–1904*. Albuquerque: University of New Mexico Press, 1975.
Brayer, Herbert O. *William Blackmore*. 2 vols. Denver: Bradford-Robinson, 1949.
Buck, Solon J. *The Agrarian Crusade: A Chronicle of the Farmer in Politics*. Chronicle of America Series, edited by Allen Johnson, vol. 45. New Haven, Conn.: Yale University Press, 1920.
Cleaveland, Agnes Morley. *No Life for a Lady*. Boston: Houghton Mifflin Company, 1941.
————. *Satan's Paradise, from Lucien Maxwell to Fred Lambert*. Boston: Houghton Mifflin Company, 1952.
Cleaveland, Norman. *Colfax County's Chronic Murder Mystery*. Santa Fe: Rydal Press, 1977.
————. *The Morleys: Young Upstarts on the Southwest Frontier*. Albuquerque: Calvin Horn, 1971.

Colorado Business Directory and Annual Register for 1875. Denver: J. A. Blake, 1875.

Conway, Jay T. *A Brief Community History of Raton, New Mexico, 1880–1930. Commemorating Her Fiftieth Birthday.* Raton, N.M.: Gazette Printing, 1930.

Dunham, Harold H. *Government Handout: A Study in the Administration of Public Lands.* Ann Arbor, Mich.: Edwards Brothers, 1941.

Dunn, Joseph Piatt, ed. *Memorial Record of Distinguished Men of Indianapolis and Indiana.* Chicago: Lewis Publishing Company, 1912.

Eitzen, D. Stanley. *David J. Brewer, 1837–1910: A Kansan on the United States Supreme Court.* Emporia State Research Studies, vol. 12. Emporia: Kansas State Teachers College, 1964.

Everts, Louis H. *History of Clermont County, Ohio.* Philadelphia: J. B. Lippincott and Company, 1880.

Frink, Maurice; Jackson, W. Turrentine; Spring, Agnes Wright. *When Grass Was King: Contributions of the Western Range Cattle Industry Study.* Boulder: University of Colorado Press, 1956.

Fritz, Percy Stanley. *Colorado, The Centennial State.* New York: Prentice-Hall, 1941.

Guide to the Maxwell Grant: 1¾ Million Acres in Colorado and New Mexico. Chicago: Rand McNally and Company, n.d.

Hacker, Louis M. and Kendrick, Benjamin B. *The United States Since 1865.* New York: F. S. Crofts and Company, 1938.

Hafen, LeRoy R., ed. *Colorado and Its People: A Narrative and Topical History of the Centennial State.* 4 vols. New York: Lewis Historical Publishing Company, 1948.

———— and Carl Coke Rister. *Western America.* 2nd ed. Englewood Cliffs, N. J.: Prentice-Hall, 1950.

Haley, J. Evetts. *Charles Goodnight: Cowman and Plainsman.* Norman: University of Oklahoma Press, 1949.

Harwood, Thomas. *History of the New Mexico Spanish and English Missions of the Methodist Episcopal Church from 1850 to 1910.* 2 vols. Albuquerque: El Abogado Press, 1908.

Hening, H. B., ed. *George Curry, 1861–1947: An Autobiography.* Albuquerque: University of New Mexico Press, 1958.

Hicks, John D. *The Populist Revolt: A History of the Farmers' Alliance and the People's Party.* 1931. Reprint. Lincoln: University of Nebraska Press, 1961.

History of the Arkansas Valley, Colorado. Chicago: O. L. Baskin and Company, 1881.

Hoig, Stan. *The Sand Creek Massacre.* Norman: University of Oklahoma Press, 1961.

Horn, Calvin. *New Mexico's Troubled Years: The Story of the Early Territorial Governors.* Albuquerque: N. M.: Horn and Wallace, 1963.

Hughes, Delbert Littrell, and Leonore Harris Hughes. *Give Me Room!* El Paso, Texas: Hughes Publishing Company, 1971.

Keleher, William A. *Maxwell Land Grant: A New Mexico Item.* Rev. ed. New York: Argosy-Antiquarian, Ltd., 1964.

Kemper, Willis Miller. *Genealogy of the Fishback Family in America.* New York: Thomas Madison Taylor, 1914.

Lamar, Howard Roberts. *The Far Southwest, 1846–1912: A Territorial History.* New Haven: Yale University Press, 1966.

Larson, Robert W. *New Mexico Populism: A Study of Radical Protest in a Western Territory.* Boulder: Colorado Associated University Press, 1974.

—————. *New Mexico's Quest for Statehood, 1846–1912.* Albuquerque: University of New Mexico Press, 1968.

Lavender, David. *Bent's Fort.* Garden City, N. Y.: Doubleday and Company, 1954.

The Maxwell Land Grant: Opinions as to Title by Noah Davies, Wm. M. Evarts, J. F. Bayard, George T. Curtis, and J. P. Benjamin. N.p.: Maxwell Land Grant Company, n.d.

Riley, James Whitcomb. *Complete Works.* 10 vols. Indianapolis: Bobbs-Merrill and Company, 1916.

Murphy, Lawrence R. *Philmont: A History of New Mexico's Cimarron Country.* Albuquerque: University of New Mexico Press, 1972.

Myers, Gustavus. *History of the Supreme Court of the United States.* Chicago: Charles H. Kerr and Company, 1912.

Opinion: Brewer, C. J. [D. J.] in the Circuit Court of the United States, District of Colorado. The Interstate Land Company vs. the Maxwell Land Grant Company. Also, the Maxwell Land Grant Company vs. Vicente Preteca et al. Santa Fe: New Mexican Printing Company, 1890.

Pearce, Thomas Matthews, ed. *New Mexico Place Names: A Geographical Dictionary.* Albuquerque: University of New Mexico Press, 1965.

Pearson, Jim Berry. *The Maxwell Land Grant.* Norman: University of Oklahoma Press, 1961.

Peters, Steve. *Incident on Red River and Other True Stories of New Mexico.* Santa Fe: By the author, 1971.

Poldervaart, Arie W. *Black-Robed Justice: A History of the Administration of Justice in New Mexico from the American Occupation in 1846 until Statehood in 1912.* N.p.: Historical Society of New Mexico, 1948.

Porter, Henry M. *Pencilings of an Early Western Pioneer.* Denver: World Press, 1929.

The Rocky Mountain Directory and Colorado Gazetteer for 1871. Denver: S. S. Wallihan and Company.

Schoenberger, Dale T. *The Gunfighters.* Caldwell, Idaho: The Caxton Printers, 1971.

Smiley, Jerome C., ed. *Semi-Centennial History of the State of Colorado.* 2 vols. Chicago: Lewis Publishing Company, 1913.

Sweetland, Leon H. *History of the First Methodist Church of Loveland, Colorado.* N.p.: By the author, 1941.

Taylor, Morris F. *First Mail West: Stage Lines on the Santa Fe Trail.* Albuquerque: University of New Mexico Press, 1971.

————. *Trinidad, Colorado Territory.* Trinidad: Trinidad State Junior College, 1966.

Thomas, Joseph, ed. *Universal Pronouncing Dictionary of Biography and Mythology.* 5th ed. Philadelphia: J. B. Lippincott and Company, 1930.

Thompson, Albert W. *They Were Open Range Days: Annals of a Western Frontier.* Denver: World Press, 1946.

Torres, Joe V. *Life History of Jose Luis Torres.* La Junta, Col.: La Junta Printing Company, n.d.

Transcript of Title of the Maxwell Land Grant Situated in New Mexico and Colorado. Chicago: Rand McNally and Company, 1881.

Twitchell, Ralph Emerson. *The Leading Facts of New Mexican History.* 2 vols. Cedar Rapids, Iowa: Torch Press, 1912.

The United States vs. Maxwell Land Grant Company: Records and Briefs. N.p.: Privately printed, n.d.

The United States vs. The Maxwell Land Grant Company et al.: Opinion of the Court. N.p.: New Mexican Printing Company, n.d.

The United States vs. the Maxwell Land Grant Company et al., Suit in Equity to Cancel Land Patent: Pleading Testimony and Exhibits. N.p.: Privately printed, n.d.

Waters, L. L. *Steel Trails to Santa Fe.* Lawrence: University of Kansas Press, 1950.

Westphall, Victor. *The Public Domain in New Mexico, 1854–1891.* Albuquerque: University of New Mexico Press, 1965.

————. *Thomas Benton Catron and His Era.* Tucson: University of Arizona Press, 1973.

White, William Allen. *The Autobiography of William Allen White.* New York: Macmillan Company, 1946.

Whitford, William Clarke. *Colorado Volunteers in the Civil War: The New Mexico Campaign in 1862.* Denver: State Historical and Natural History Society, 1906.

Whittaker, Milo Lee. *Pathbreakers and Pioneers of the Pueblo Region.* N.p.: Franklin Press, 1917.

Williams, Byron. *History of Clermont and Brown Counties, Ohio.* 2 vols. Milford, Ohio: Hobart Publishing Company, 1913.

Wright, James Edward. *The Politics of Populism: Dissent in Colorado.* New Haven, Conn.: Yale University Press, 1974.

ARTICLES

Bowman, Charles W. "History of Bent County." In *History of the Arkansas Valley, Colorado.* Chicago: O. L. Baskin and Company, 1881, pp. 825–89.

Cleaveland, Norman. "Clay Allison's Cimarron." *New Mexico,* 52 (March–April 1974):11–14, 38–48.

Cushman, Robert E. "David Josiah Brewer." *Dictionary of American Biography,* vol. 3, edited by Allen Johnson. New York: Charles Scribner's Sons, 1957.

Dorsey, Stephen W. "Land Stealing in New Mexico, A Rejoinder." *North American Review,* 145 (October 1887):396–409.

Dunham, Harold. "New Mexican Land Grants with Special Reference to the Title Papers of the Maxwell Grant." *New Mexico Historical Review,* 30 (January 1955):1–22.

————. "William Andrew Jackson Sparks." *Dictionary of American Biography,* vol. 17, edited by Dumas Malone. New York: Charles Scribner's Sons, 1935.

Fuller, John V. "Isaac Wayne MacVeagh." *Dictionary of American Biography,* vol. 12, edited by Dumas Malone. New York: Charles Scribner's Sons, 1933.

Goodykoontz, Colin B. "Colorado as Seen By a Home Missionary, 1863–1868." *The Colorado Magazine,* 12 (March 1935):60–69.

Haworth, Paul L. "George Washington Julian." *Dictionary of American Biography*, vol. 10, edited by Dumas Malone. New York: Charles Scribner's Sons, 1933.

Jenkins, Myra Ellen. "Arthur Rockfor[d] Manby." *The 1966 Brandbook of the Denver Westerners*. Edited by William D. Powell. Boulder, Col.: Johnson Publishing Company, 1967.

Julian, George W. "Land Stealing in New Mexico." *North American Review*, 145 (July 1887):17–31.

Keleher, W. A. "Law of the New Mexico Land Grant." *Texas Law Quarterly Review* 4 (October 1929):154–69.

Kelsey, Harry E., Jr. "Clay Allison: Western Gunman." *1957 Brand Book of the Denver Westerners*. Edited by Numa L. James. Boulder, Col.: Johnson Publishing Company, 1958.

Lamar, Howard R. "Edmund G. Ross as Governor of New Mexico Territory: A Reappraisal." *New Mexico Historical Review*, 36 (July 1961):177–209.

Larson, Robert W. "The White Caps of New Mexico: A Study of Ethnic Militancy in the Southwest." *Pacific Historical Review*, 44 (May 1975):171–85.

Newman, Simeon H., III. "The Santa Fe Ring: A Letter to the *New York Sun*." *Arizona and the West*, 12 (Autumn 1970): 269–88.

Noel, Leon. "The Largest Estate in the World." *Overland Monthly*, 12 (November 1888):480–94.

Pearce, Haywood, J., Jr. "Lucius Quintus Cincinnatus Lamar." *Dictionary of American Biography*, vol. 10, edited by Dumas Malone. New York: Charles Scribner's Sons, 1933.

Rasch, Philip J. "The People of the Territory of New Mexico vs. the Santa Fe Ring." *New Mexico Historical Review*, 47 (April 1972):185–202.

Reeve, Frank D. "The Federal Indian Policy in New Mexico, 1858–1880." *New Mexico Historical Review*, 13 (April 1938): 146–91.

Rice, Elial J. "Pioneering in Southern Colorado." *The Colorado Magazine*, 14 (May 1937):108–15.

Rist, Martin. "History of Religion in Colorado." *Colorado and Its People: A Narrative and Topical History of the Centennial State*, vol. 2, edited by LeRoy R. Hafen. New York: Lewis Historical Publishing Company, 1948.

————. "Methodist Beginnings in New Mexico." *The 1966 Brand Book of the Denver Westerners*. Edited by William D. Powell. Boulder, Col.: Johnson Publishing Company, 1967.

Robinson, William A. "Henry William Blair." *Dictionary of American Biography*, vol. 2, edited by Allen Johnson. New York: Charles Scribner's Sons, 1957.

————. "William Steele Holman." *Dictionary of American Biography*, vol. 9, edited by Dumas Malone. New York: Charles Scribner's Sons, 1932.

Russell, Mrs. Hal. "Memoirs of Marion Russell." *The Colorado Magazine*, 21 (March and May 1944):62–74, 101–112.

Starr, Harris Elwood. "Matthew Simpson." *Dictionary of American Biography*, vol. 17, edited by Dumas Malone. New York: Charles Scribner's Sons, 1935.

Stevenson, R. M. "History of Pueblo County." *History of the Arkansas Valley, Colorado*. Chicago: O. L. Baskin and Company, 1881.

Taylor, Morris F. "Capt. William Craig and the Vigil and St. Vrain Grant, 1855–1870." *The Colorado Magazine*, 45 (Fall 1968): 301–321.

————. "Early Days in Trinidad." *The Colorado Magazine*, 40 (October 1963):278–93.

————. "Stephen W. Dorsey, Speculator-Cattleman." *New Mexico Historical Review*, 49 (January 1974):27–48.

————. "The Two Land Grants of Gervacio Nolán." *New Mexico Historical Review*, 48 (April 1972):151–84.

————. "The Maxwell Cattle Company, 1881–1888." *New Mexico Historical Review*, 49 (October 1974):289–324.

————. "The Uña de Gato Grant in Colfax County." *New Mexico Historical Review* 51 (April 1976):121–43.

Theisen, Lee Scott, ed. "Frank Warner Angel's Notes on New Mexico Territory, 1878." *Arizona and the West*, 18 (Winter 1976):333–37.

Van Lint, Victor J. "Notes on the History and Development of the Maxwell Land Grant." *New Mexico Professional Engineer and Contractor* 2 (February 1950):5–6, 24–25.

Westphall, Victor. "Fraud and the Implications of Fraud in the Land Grants of New Mexico." *New Mexico Historical Review*, 49 (July 1974):189–218.

Woodbury, Helen Sumner. "Johann Joseph Most." *Dictionary of American Biography*, vol. 13, edited by Dumas Malone. New York: Charles Scribner's Sons, 1934.

————. "Terence Vincent Powderly." *Dictionary of American Biography*, vol. 15, edited by Dumas Malone. New York: Charles Scribner's Sons, 1935.

Acknowledgments

⊙⚞☙⊙

Over the years from the mid-1940s, when I began delving into the struggle of the settlers against the Maxwell Land Grant, many people have given me invaluable help. Some of those people have since died, but I shall make no distinction on that basis in expressing my gratitude.

If one person deserves special mention, I am sure it is Mrs. Lucy Reed Wills, daughter of pioneer settlers in Vermejo Park, whose intimate recollections of O. P. McMains and many others, both pro- and anti-grant, have given personal touches and substantial insights that I could not have found elsewhere. Mabel A. Fisher and Mrs. Charles D. Herron, McMains' niece and grandniece respectively, not only imparted family information but also generously made letters and pictures available to me. But I would not have known of those ladies but for the assistance of Caroline Dunn, librarian of the William Henry Smith Memorial Library of the Indiana Historical Society. My work was made much easier by the enthusiastic services of Marie Dickoré, professional genealogist and researcher (of Cincinnati, Ohio), who secured data on McMains' early life in Ohio and Illinois. In recounting McMains' life as a Methodist minister in Colorado, I had great help from Martin Rist, then librarian-historian of the Colorado Methodist Historical Society at the Iliff School of Theology, Denver.

When I began work ca. 1945 in the voluminous records of the Maxwell Land Grant Company, now at the Zimmerman Library of the University of New Mexico, those papers were in the company office at Raton, New Mexico. It was through the kind permission of Victor J. Van Lint, company manager, and George W. Robertson, company attorney, that I was given access to the collection. Much of that material, of course, is at the core of my work.

A. R. Mitchell, western artist and historian of Trinidad, Colorado, recognized the potential of the McMains story and encouraged my investigation of it. Lawrence R. Murphy, professor of history at Western Illinois University, kindly loaned me his microfilm of the Transcript of Record in the government's case against the Maxwell Land Grant Company before the Supreme Court.

Significant help came from Maxine Benson and her staff of the Documentary Resources Department, State Historical Society of Colorado; Alys Freeze and Eleanor Gehres, directors of the Western History Department, Denver Public Library, and Pam Rose, of their staff; Harry Kelsey, formerly Colorado state historian and now chief curator of history at the Los Angeles County Museum of Natural History; J. Vivian Hedgcock, librarian of New Mexico Highlands University; Robert Svenningsen, director of the Federal Records Center, Denver; John Brennan, curator of the Western History Collections, University of Colorado Library; Frances Samaniego and Ena Sroat, Trinidad State Junior College librarians; Edna Atwood and Lois Gorman, of the Carnegie Public Library, Trinidad, Colorado; Betty Lloyd, librarian of the Arthur Johnson Memorial Library, Raton, New Mexico; and Charles W. Hurd, southern Colorado historian. Others who have helped are acknowledged in footnotes and picture credits.

Numerous county clerks, court clerks, and law librarians, as well as newspaper publishers and editors have aided me, as have the professional staffs of the Henry E. Huntington Library, San Marino, California; the National Archives in

Washington; the Zimmerman Library, University of New Mexico; the Library of Congress; and the New Mexico State Records Center and Archives, whose chief of historical services, Myra Ellen Jenkins, has made the important contribution of foreword to this book. My wife, Betty, has understood the demands of research for over thirty years, and I thank her for help in preparing the index.

In finally bringing this work to publication, I have benefitted greatly from the expert advice of Marshall Townsend, director of the University of Arizona Press, and from the criticism and recommendations of John M. Spaulding, assistant editor, with whom I have worked closely and pleasantly.

M. F. T.

Index

Gutierrez, Juan, 71 n

Hadden, William, 234
Hagen, George, 234
Hagen, John L., 234
Hagen, Joseph, 234
Hallett, Moses, 229, 258, 259
Hannon, John, 214
Happy Jack, 221
Harness, Bill, 234, 251, 252,
    282–83
Harrison, Benjamin, 235, 236,
    241, 242, 246
Harrison, L., 116
Harwood, Thomas, 34, 38–39,
    45, 49–50, 54, 55, 56, 276;
    takes charge of N.M.
    missions, M. E. Church, 24
Hayes, Rutherford B., 52, 53 n,
    57; signs quitclaim to
    Maxwell Grant, 67
Hendricks, Thomas A., 136
Higbee & Smith's Ranch, Colo.,
    28
Hill, Zeph T., 229, 230
Hixenbaugh, George, 132
Hixenbaugh, John, 118–19
Hobbs, Frank D., 136 n
Hodding, Henry, 156 n
Holdsworth, Richard B., 197,
    198, 199, 200, 208, 212, 226,
    232, 236 n, 243, 246,
    247, 250
Holland. *See* Netherlands,
    Kingdom of the
Holly, Charles F., 60
Holman, William S., 194, 207
Holmes, John C., 107, 143 n, 182
Honey, William, 198 n
House Committee on
    Territories. *See* Committee
    on Territories (House)

House Private Land Claims
    Committee. *See* Committee
    on Private Land Claims
    (House)
Howard, George, 214
Hubbard, Edward J., 100
Huerfano County, Colo., 26, 30
Hughes, Bela M., 123, 152
Hundred Days Men, 10, 16 n
Hunn, William, 214, 218, 219,
    220, 222, 228, 242
Hunt, A. Cameron, 18
Hunt, Charles, 143 n, 146
Hunt, J. H., 84, 87, 88, 100 n,
    117, 119, 146, 149, 167, 168,
    178, 276

Illinois Conference,
    M. E. Church, 13
Indianapolis, Ind., 52
Indianapolis Journal, 52, 135
Indianapolis News, 127
Indianapolis Sentinel, 109 n
Indians. *See* Tribal names
Interstate Commerce Commis-
    sion Act, 90, 173
Interstate Land Company,
    238, 239, 242, 252
Interstate Land Company v.
    *Maxwell Land Grant
    Company*, 238, 240, 252,
    266; Supreme Court rules
    in favor of Maxwell
    Co., 240
"Iron Horse Is Coming, The"
    (McMains' poem), 18

Jacksonville Circuit, Ill., Con-
    ference, M. E. Church, 13
Jaffa Opera House, Trinidad,
    Colo., 269
Jaramillo, Faustin, 102